Trajectories of Impressions Management and Image Formation

Ebtihaj Al A'ali
https://orcid.org/0009-0003-1208-618X
University of Bahrain, Bahrain

Khairi Mohamed Ali
Applied Science University, Bahrain

Gardenia Jassim AlSaffar
Royal Bahrain Hospital, Bahrain

Mohammed Abdulla AlMannaei
Independent Researcher, Bahrain

IGI Global
Scientific Publishing
Publishing Tomorrow's Research Today

Vice President of Editorial	Melissa Wagner
Director of Acquisitions	Mikaela Felty
Director of Book Development	Jocelynn Hessler
Production Manager	Mike Brehm
Cover Design	Jose Rosado

Published in the United States of America by
IGI Global Scientific Publishing
701 East Chocolate Avenue
Hershey, PA, 17033, USA
Tel: 717-533-8845 | Fax: 717-533-7115
Website: https://www.igi-global.com E-mail: cust@igi-global.com

Library of Congress Cataloging-in-Publication Data

LCCN: 2025034241 (CIP Data Pending)
ISBN13: 9798337355191
Isbn13Softcover: 9798337355207
EISBN13: 9798337355214
British Cataloguing in Publication Data
A Cataloguing in Publication record for this book is available from the British Library.

To those who left their fingerprints on our souls

Editorial Advisory Board

Table of Contents

Detailed Table of Contents

strategies that balance self-presentation with authenticity to promote well-being and trust in diverse, hybrid environments.

The hospitality industry is increasingly shaped by the complex interplay between food security governance, policy imperatives, and the strategic presentation of culinary experiences. This paper explores how hospitality stakeholders—hotels, resorts, and tourism establishments—engage in impression management to align with food security goals while enhancing their culinary image. By examining the transition "from policy to plate," the study analyzes how regulations related to sustainable sourcing, food safety, nutrition, and local procurement are translated into visible practices that influence guest perception and satisfaction. Drawing upon theories of symbolic interactionism and institutional isomorphism, the paper argues that food-related policies are not only operational frameworks but also tools for image-building and competitive positioning in the global hospitality market.

Cultural diversity has a profound influence on organizational behavior, yet empirical evidence from the public sector in the Arab Gulf remains limited. This chapter investigates how nationality, religion, and other diversity factors influence cultural values and impression management within Bahrain's Works Affairs Institution. Using Hofstede's Values Survey Module 2013 (VSM13) and SPSS-based quantitative analysis, the study examines fifteen diversity variables, nine of which showed statistically significant—though mostly moderate—associations with Hofstede's cultural dimensions. Nationality and religion emerged as the strongest predictors of cultural orientation, while generational cohort had a negligible impact, countering the popular narrative of generational determinism. The findings reveal an organizational culture marked by extreme collectivism, low power distance, and high indulgence, reflecting both traditional norms and evolving modernization patterns.

This chapter examines the role of Family and Consumer Sciences (FCS) education in the shaping and management of personal image across personal, professional, and digital contexts. At its core, FCS (also known to many as "home economics") is an interdisciplinary field that prepares individuals to lead effective lives through knowledge of personal and family skills, housing, clothing, nutrition, human development, and interpersonal communication. However, its role in impression management and image formation, while implicit in many of its subdisciplines, is often under-theorized in mainstream academic discourse. This chapter seeks to bring this to the forefront of scholarship by making a case for FCS as a vital contributor to the intellectual understanding of personal image management.

Social media has normalized narcissistic forms of self-presentation, where users emulate celebrity-like practices such as exaggerated self-display and the flaunting of excessive wealth. However, public outrage arose when a young social media user displayed luxury goods believed to be beyond the means of his father, a government employee. This case triggered a wave of crowdsourced surveillance and digital vigilantism, as users searched for and exposed other officials and their family members who similarly showcased their wealth. Using corpus-assisted discourse studies (CADS) on 44,445 comments from 575 YouTube videos, this study maps users' reactions to understand their sentiments, perceptions, and expectations regarding corruption and law enforcement. The findings reveal the power of collective online investigations in uncovering perceived corruption and compelling moral compliance and institutional responses, as well as generating public shaming toward those who commit moral transgressions.

In social interaction, including the organisational environment, individuals use impression management (IM) to create the image they want others to see of themselves to obtain endorsement, which can translate to organisational rewards. This image is defined by the behaviours, communication, and other attributes that the individual presents using IM. Impression management has been presented as a multidimensional construct with many dimensions. Past studies have tried to capture the benefits and shortcomings of IM. However, the review of the past studies in this book chapter identified four areas that need to be emphasised by future IM studies to understand the construct adequately. The four areas are: the effectiveness of IM dimensions over time, the establishment of an accurate dimensionality of IM, how impression management can be made effective in virtual interactions, and how to understand the double-edged nature of IM. The book chapter made some suggestions on how these areas can be included in future studies on IM.

This chapter explores how generative AI (GenAI) technologies are transforming the landscape of digital impression management by reconfiguring how individuals construct, perform, and optimize their online identities. Using an interdisciplinary framework grounded in Goffman's dramaturgical theory, affordance theory, social identity theory, and emotional labor theory, the chapter introduces the ABCDE model, Appearance, Behavior, Communication, Digital Presence, and Emotional Balance, to analyze the socio-technical dimensions of AI-mediated self-presentation. Drawing on an empirical audit of 1,200 GenAI-generated professional profiles, the study reveals how algorithmic systems both enable and constrain identity expression, often reinforcing cultural, gendered, and occupational biases. The findings underscore the dual role of GenAI as both a democratizing tool and a vector of standardization, raising urgent ethical, psychological, and design challenges for equitable digital selfhood.

Preface

The subject of impression management and image formation is utmost important for individuals and organizations alike. Impressions and images developed assist to convey ethics and values of the individuals and organizations concerned. Individuals in all walks of life benefit from their positive and appreciated impressions by the public . This enables them to achieve their personal and professional targets. The desirable images sought by organizations can capture the loyalty of customers during the era of accountability and social responsibility. This book contains twelve chapters out of many proposals submitted . The book attempts to provide various perspectives about the subject of impression management and image formation. It can enhance knowledge of students, different practitioners, leaders and politicians in relation to the issues of impression and image formation. Real case studies and theoretical chapters included in this book revolve around the following themes:

The definitions of image and impressions management and their contemporary literature

The benefits of image and impressions management to enhance the work of leaders.

The role of image and impressions management in political arena

Individuals in different walks of life and their perceptions and the use of image and impressions management

Gender differences in relation to understanding and promoting image and impressions

Cultural Impacts on image and impressions management

Religious impacts on image and impressions management

Image and impressions management effects on individuals' behaviors, appearance, communication, digital presence and emotional balance

The first chapter examines gender differences and impression management in relation to leaders in the context of private organizations in the kingdom of Bahrain. The chapter exhibits that self promotion, ingratiation, intimidation are males' strategies. Women mainly followed supplication strategy.

The second chapter then claims that impression management is a context based phenomenon. It can lead to positive self and organizational consequences but it has own limitations as well.

Chapter 3 asserts that the role of impression management is to convey ethics related to transparency, sustainability and authenticity to stakeholders in hospitality industry. This is to sustain corporate governance.

Chapter 5 exhibits that managing cultural values is a necessity to reflect positive impressions in public sector .

Chapter 5 then scrutinizes the role of family and consumer sciences in shaping images for individuals and firms in different walks of life.

Chapter 6 illustrates that digital vigilantism is a tool to question individuals' wealth affluence as reflections of narcissism. This is to subject those individuals to online public shaming if wealth is believed to be illicit .

Chapter 7 claims that self regulatory variables should be included in impression management research in the future. Such variables act as moderators of the relationships between impression management and the perception of others of such impressions.

The last chapter then exhibits that generative artificial intelligence risks identity diversity and heightening the gender and cultural hierarchies. The chapter argues for a system to maintain the authenticity and equitability of gender identity.

Ebtihaj Al A'Ali
Khairi Mohamed Ali
Gardenia AlSaffar
Mohammed Abdulla Al Mannaei

Chapter 1
Gender and Impression Management:
Impressions Management and Leadership – Gender Differences

Ebtihaj Ahmed Al-Aali
https://orcid.org/0009-0003-1208-618X
University of Bahrain, Bahrain

Khairi Mohamed Omar
Applied Sciences University, Bahrain

Mohammed Al Mannai
Independent Researcher, Bahrain

ABSTRACT

Women in leadership in Bahrain has been strengthened by the efforts of the government and the private sectors equally. However women are still perceived differently. This is illustrated in the posts that women seek at one side and on the positions which women are assigned at on the other side. This may be attributed to various reasons. Some of such reasons are cultural values, social stereotypes and impressions management strategies employed by women in leadership positions. The research presented in this chapter seeks to understand gender differences in terms of the most five discussed impressions management strategies . The five most identified strategies in the literature are self- presentation, ingratiation, exemplification, supplication and intimidation. These strategies can be grouped into two major categories. The first is named self enhancement and the second is other enhancement. This research employs qualitative methodology. Interview is the research method to collect information.

DOI: 10.4018/979-8-3373-5519-1.ch001

INTRODUCTION

The number of women leaders is still lagged behind in comparison to men leaders globally. Women encounter many different barriers to reach the top in organizations. The barriers are social, cultural, psychological and organizational. Men and women are brought up to be different . This leads to the development of the polarized thinking about feminism and masculinism. There is a few research about impression management and gender leadership globally. Similar research is scarce in the Middle East and especially in the Gulf Corporation Countries . This research examines the issue of impression management strategies in relation to gender leadership. The research presented in this chapter consists of seven sections. Section two examines the definition of impression management. Section three discusses the theories of impression management and gender differences. The fourth section elaborates on the impacts of impression management strategies on gender leadership. The fifth section expounds the methodology used in the research. Section sixth presents the analysis of information collected from participants to this research. Conclusion and future research are mentioned in the last section.

DEFINITION OF IMPRESSION MANAGEMENT

Individuals play different roles in their lives. This means that individuals promote various impressions (images) . These Impressions (images) shape the interactions and behaviours of individuals with the external environments . These images have impacts on others' perceptions of the same individuals as well (Vijayabanu, et al, 2019; and Kurt, 2022). Individuals employ impression management to achieve their goals based on their organizational contexts. This is illustrated in the arguments of Guadagno & Cialdini (2007). They explicate that individuals attempt to achieve different goals through their behaviours. The goals vary based on the situations. The self promotion as an impression strategy may be employed to exhibit competency or to be visible as a higher performer. Individuals therefore select the impression management strategy to achieve the desired goal (Sanaria, 2016). Guadagno & Cialdini (2007) clarify that impression management is different from social desirability and organizational citizenship behaviour construct. The social desirability assumes that Individuals exhibit situational behaviour which might not be accurate or realistic.

Impressions management however focuses on the behaviour leading to present the characteristics of the individuals. They (2007) add that impression management also is not similar to the organizational citizenship behaviour construct. The behaviour based on this later construct benefits the organizations but may not be beneficial for individuals. Impression management revolves around the desirable goals by individuals which may not be good for the organizations.

Impressions management can be viewed from two different perspectives. The fist is the universal focusing on the behaviour of an individual actor in a given culture. The second then is named multiple contextual perspective. This assumes that impression behaviours vary based on the situations and its related cultures and traditions (Nayyar & Raja, 2012). The strategies and tactics of impression management are used deliberately or not. The strategies employed are either to promote a positive image to the target audiences or to change the present one (Rister, 2016).

In conclusion impression management aims to reflect an image to the target audiences. The use of impression management strategies is to achieve personal targets. An individual has more than one image. The various situations entail individuals to promote different images. The process of image and impression management is conscious and deliberate.

THEORIES OF IMPRESSION MANAGEMENT AND GENDER DIFFERENCES

In this section Goffman 's impressions management theory related to face, face work and dramaturgy is briefly discussed based on Rister's work (2016) . The later states that Goffman was the first to operationalize the concept of face. Face is the public identity that is on continuous interactions with the external environment. This leads an individual to have multiple faces or identities (Vijayabanu, et al, 2019). The interactions may lead to create face threats. Such threats may be caused by self or by others. Individuals therefore use face work to maintain the desired self identities or to change the identities as needed. The tools employed to manage face work are preventive and corrective. The preventive refers to acts to avert identity loss . The corrective tools are called restorative. This helps individuals to restore their desired self identities. Tedeschi (1990) regroup strategies of impression management. Assertive is acquisitive and preventative is defensive . This is similar to corrective and protective. The assertive and defensive strategies are employed to protect or to change the present impressions (Bolino, Long and Turnley, 2016).

Rister (2016) mentions that the theory of face and face work have not been fully utilized to understand the conflict which women in power experience due to the their sex roles and performance roles. He adds that dramaturgy suggested by Goffman (1959) can shed light on the resolution of such conflict. Dramaturgy states that there are two stages for each face i.e. identity. The front stage and the back stage . The back stage enables women for example to prepare plan and decide which behaviours and acts to exhibit in front stage. The later stage refers to the audience in the contexts.

Rister (2016) illustrates that women and men are prescribed different social roles. The roles specify the expected behaviours for each gender (Larwood & wood, 1977). Rister (2016) shows as well that many pieces of research contend that gender roles' expectations are culturally based. The confirmation to the cultural based expectations can enhance self esteem. The violation however of the expectations can lead to the ostracization of the concerned gender. Harriman (1985) states that women are assumed to exhibit expertise related to feminism. Men are said to display capabilities reflecting masculinity traits. This segregation of feminism and masculinity are taught at the early lives of the two genders as explained by Hennig and Jardin (1977). The evolved gender stereotypes related to feminism and masculinity underpin social interactions. Each gender learns about the acceptable behaviour (Larwood & Wood, 1977). This may support the arguments of Marshall (1984) that men and women follow different life strategies. Men are said to follow agentic strategy . This strategy mirrors the traits of competitiveness, competency, assertiveness, confidence and doing attitude. These traits are compatible to the traits of organizational leaders. These traits as well justifies the dominant nature of men in the society. Women follow communion strategy which cares about wholeness. The communal strategy is said to interact with environment leading it to be in a state of continuous being. Marshall (1984) adds that women represent the muted group in the society. This group is characterised by passivity, submissiveness and conformity to their social expectations. Rister (2016) expounds that the organizational performance will be acceptable if it aligns with the expected social behaviour of each gender . He adds that if the performance is not in harmony with such expectations, the individual concerned will be outcasted. This is due to the rigid perspectives of social (gender) roles in relation to females and males. Al A'Ali (1991) and Bois (1978) clarify that such rigidity is the resultant of Aristotelian Structure of the language. This structure is based on three laws. The first law represents the "is" of identity. The second is the two value orientation. The last law is of the excluding middle. Leadership is masculine (is of identity) . Women are feminine (two value orientation). Women can not be leaders (excluding middle). This reinforces the polarised views about genders.

Gwal (2015) mentions that impression management strategies can be classified into two categories. The first is self enhancement aiming to improve individuals' images. The second is other enhancement which aspires to care for the target audiences' feeling . There are five most identified impression management strategies . These strategies are self promotion, ingratiation, exemplification, supplication; and intimidation (Jones and Pittman, 1982 ; Kurt, 2022; Gwal, 2015; Gupta & Sagadevan, 2024; Vijaybanu et al., 2019; Bolino et al., 2016; Guadagno & Cialdini, 2007; Edeh, et al, 2023; Debus, 2024).

These strategies were first developed by Jones and Pittman in 1982 . The first strategy is self promotion referring to the behaviors exhibiting competency, self confidence, capabilities and knowledge. This is to enhance the visibility of the individual (Kurt, 2022; Bolino et al. 2016; & Gwal, 2015). The second strategy is ingratiation . This is to suggest that individuals seek likenesses and acceptance of target audience. Individuals who accept the rules of the environment and the society can create positive impressions. The third strategy is exemplification meaning that the individuals set themselves as examples and role models for target audiences. This is achieved by creating an impression based on hard working, integrity, morals and ethics. The purpose of this is not to make sacrifices but to sustain the behaviours leading to the desirable impression. The supplication is the fourth strategy. This is to display disqualification in order to avoid responsibility and to seek support from others. The over use of this strategy may lead for the exclusion of the individuals presenting such strategy. The fifth and last strategy is intimidation. This is for the leaders to present themselves as menacing to employees. The later will implement the leadership' demands out of fear and to avoid being punished. Guadagno & Cialdini (2007) expounds that there are another two tactic used as well to reflect impressions. These are sandbagging and self- handicapping which both are employed by males. The first tactic is sandbagging . This tactic is recruited to exhibit claims affecting under performance expectation . The other tactic is self-handicapping which is directed to create obstacles to obstruct achievements. (Jones & Pittman, 1982; Guadagno & Cialdini, 2007).

Sing et al. (2002) show that male leaders use self promotion, ingratiation and networking strategies more than women. Women do not use self promotion strategy. McGowan & Sekaja (2022) mention that women according to Smith & Hinton (2013) do not engage in self promotion. This is for being conformists to their passive social roles. Besides they, according to Sing et al. (2002), focus on other enhancement strategies. This is due to their transformative leadership focusing on empowering employees. This may have negative impacts on women's advancement in the organizations. Women become less visible which shape their career path. Guadagno & Cialdini (2007) claim that men focus more on self enhancement strategies which increase their visibility in the organizations. Self promotion and intimidation is used frequently by men. Women employ supplication strategy more than men . This is because women are conformist . They (2007) demonstrate that women's impression management strategies show them as passive and submissive. This conforms to the social and cultural roles prescribed to women .

Bolino et al. (2016) and Guadagno & Cialdini (2007) state that women display impression management strategies which are compatible with their communal life strategy. This reflects traits of women's social roles of being submissive, passive, friendly, and useful and humility. Men however employ impression management strategies that reflect their masculinity; Competitiveness, self-confidence, assertiveness and competency. Men accordingly utilise more of self-promotion and intimidation. Women on the other hand depend mostly on ingratiation and supplication. It is argued that strategies of impression management are assumed to correspond to gender social roles (Bolino et al., 2016). There are factors to consider when discussing gender and strategies of impression management according to Bolino et al. (2016). The first factor is the composition of the work group. The dominant gender has impact on the use of impression management strategies of the other group. The second factor is the self images of women recruiting strategies of impression management. The third factor then is the age of the person engaging in impression management . Lastly is the gender of observers of the person employing impression management strategies. Al-Shatti, et al. (2022) describe the impacts of gender on impression management. They mention that men utilize intimidation strategy to forcing others to comply with orders, self promotion to project positive images and self-entitlement for setting themselves as examples. Women however employ supplication strategy by displaying their weak traits and ingratiation strategy. Women are more inclined to conform to the societal and cultural expectations . Therefore they are more subjected to criticism and more susceptible to fatigue in Kuwait. But no such gender differences exist in UK based on Al-Shatti, et al. (2022) . The above analysis of gender and impression management strategies can be based as well on gender differences in relation to the use of organizational sources power. Al A'Ali & Alazali (2018) expound that women resort to reward and referent power which may be linked to ingratiation strategy . They also use expert and legitimate power to groups that is dominated by females . This is similar to the findings of Bolino et al. (2016) arguing that the composition of the group affects the selection of strategies of impression management. However, The findings of Al A'Ali & Alazali exhibit that the coercive power is ranked at the last for women. The is because coercive power is not compatible to the social and gender roles of women. Men utilize expert power and legitimate power to show their superiority. The legitimate power allows men to use intimidation strategy to get the work done. Networking is a source for power for men however it is not available for females. Gwal (2015) mentions that women have no access to networking. This affects their organizational visibility and hence shapes their career advancement. Females engage in other enhancement strategies while men are focusing on self enhancement strategies. The exemplification impression strategy ranks number one according to Kurt (2022) for the two genders . This is due to the fact that the majority of participants in her research were men. Besides the variations between the two genders' views was not studied.

This section displays that gender influences the choice of impression management strategies. Feminism and masculinism reflect prescribed social and cultural roles for each gender. Men life strategy is characterised by doing and women life strategy is said to be of being. There are five impression management strategies. These are self-promotion, ingratiation exemplification, supplication and intimidation.

Strategies can be self enhancement which mainly used by males. Such strategies are self-promotion, exemplification and relying on network and intimidation. Men as well engage in sandbagging and self-handicapping tactics in order to affect the results of achievement and performance. Strategies as well can be classified as other enhancement. This according to the literature reviewed above is thought to be recruited by women. These strategies are ingratiation and supplication. The features of these strategies are compatible to women‘ s social roles.

MEN/WOMEN LEADERSHIP AND IMPRESSION MANAGEMENT

Rister (2016) explains that men reflect masculinity traits . These traits are of being competitive, competent, visionary, performance oriented and assertive . Women are believed to be tentative, responsive, empathy oriented and inclusive. Such traits for both genders affect their communications and hence their leadership styles. He (2016) elucidates that masculinity traits are assumed to be in harmony with the traits of leadership. Therefore women experience conflict in leadership posts. Rister suggests two approaches to deal with such conflict. The first is to evaluate each organizational contexts separately in order to decide on the desirable leadership styles. The second view is to adopt different leadership perspectives which transcend the issue of gender.

Al A 'Ali et al. (2024) discuss one of such different perspectives for leadership. It is called the competency model. Women are argued to be change agents . They interact with every situation differently. The interactions are based on women's various competencies. Women's leadership is knowledge based and is on fluid.

Sing et al. (2002) claim that women employ transformative leadership focusing on employees' welfare and wellbeing . This is supported by the findings of Zbihlejova, Frankovsky & Birknerova (2018) exhibiting that males are more authoritative and women are more employee concerns . This as well is illustrated by the argument of Guadagno & Cialdini (2007) . They state that women recruit other enhancement strategies. McKenna & Thomson (2015) argue that the previous pieces of research have shown that the charismatic leaders, regardless of gender, are more engaged in impression management . This is to enable them to improve their self presentations and self- images. Rister (2016) argues that men are more authoritarian and women are more democratic in relation to leadership styles.

This section shows that men and women follow different leadership styles based on their selection of impression management strategies. The selection of strategies mirrors the social and cultural roles of each gender. Women are argued to be democratic, or transformative. They care for employees' well being . This reflects women's strategies of impression management focusing on other enhancement.

Men's leadership styles are claimed to be authoritarian or charismatic. This because of the self enhancement strategies of impression management employed by them.

RESEARCH METHODOLOGY

The impression management subject is contemporary as explained by Vijayabanu et al (2019) and Sanaria (2016) . The later states as well that the link between gender and impression management strategies are not well examined . McGowan & Sekaja (2022) also mention that there are a few studies on impression management and gender. Similar research on impression management is dearth in Middle East in general and in Gulf Corporation Countries in specific. This research therefore is an exploratory in nature . The qualitative methodology can assist to capture the understandings of the subjects being examined. Narrative research method as story telling can allow participants in a given research to disclose their emotions and cognitive concepts simultaneously (Baker & Gower (2010) ; AlSaffar, & Al A'ali, 2021). In-depth interview is the research method to collect information which would be analysed qualitatively. Snowballing method is employed to reach participants. This method declares that no mor interviews will be conducted if no new information is generated.

The Interview conducted seeks to answer the following questions:

Question number one: what is the definition of impression management?

Question number two: what are the strategies of impression management?

Question number three: what are gender differences in relation to the utilisation of strategies of impression management?

Question number four: How impression management strategies influence leadership styles?

ANALYSIS OF COLLECTED INFORMATION

This section presents the discussions and the analysis of collected information from participants to this research. The analysis is a narrative-like and is revolving around a case built. Question one is to define impression management. The discussions of questions two and three are examined simultaneously. This is due for two reasons. The first reason is that the question number two scans the definitions of impression management strategies. Question number three then attempts to contemplate the relationships between gender and impression management strategies. No one of the interviewees was familiar with the concept of impression management due its contemporary nature. The understandings of the strategies and its relationship to gender were attained after submitting the definitions of the strategies to the interviewees. The last question then illustrates the impacts of impression management strategies on gender leadership styles.

The First Interviewee: (Male)

The first question examines the definition of impression management. The interviewee explains that the impression management is a conscious process revolving around a personal vision (image) . The external contexts shape the plans to accomplish the vision (image desired) . This definition is in harmony with the claim of Nayyar and Raja (2012) stating that the impression behavior is shaped by the cultures and the traditions. Such behaviors are planned and deliberate (Sanaria, 2016).

The Second question attempts to define the strategies of Impression management. The interviewee has not submitted definitions of impression management strategies due to his unfamiliarity with the subject. This is supported by the arguments of Vijayabanu et al (2019) and Sanaria (2016) illustrating that the issue of impression management is contemporary and is not fully examined in the eastern part of the world . The third question investigates the gender differences in relation to the employment of strategies of impression management. He at the outset contends that there is no differences between men and women in relation to leadership. He asserts however that women's organizational roles are affected by their social and cultural roles . This is in accordance with the arguments of Rister (2016). After submitting a brief definitions of the strategies, the interviewee presents the discussions below:

Self promotion is the first impression management strategy. The interviewee explains that the masculinity perspective held by the society leads men to express themselves more freely than women. Women conform to their social roles and they are less expressive . This is in harmony with the explanations of Hennig & Jardin (1977) and Larwood & wood (1977) showing that women conform to their social stereotypes. He adds that women do not participate to networks . Gwal (2015) exhibits that women have no access to networks. This makes them less visible . The interviewee believes that self promotion strategy is employed by men more than women. This is similar to the findings of Sing et al. (2002) assuring that men employ the promotion strategy.

The Interviewee affirms that the Ingratiation strategy may be used by both genders . However men are more to ingratiate than women . He clarifies that women are emotional, less expressive and are confined to their social roles. This makes them submissive, passive and conformist in the organisations as well . Men, to the interviewee, are expressive and seek to attain likeness of others more than women .This is stated in the research of Sing et al. (2002) exhibiting that men ingratiate more than women. However, some other pieces of research mention that this is a females 'strategy due to the caring nature of women based on their social roles . This is compatible with the claims of Al-Shatti et al. (2022) and Guadagno and Cialdini (2007) illustrating that feminism perspective stands for women being friendly and caring.

The third strategy Is exemplification. The interviewee claims that self promotion makes men more visible. He illustrates that men, based on their masculinity perspective, are seen to be the dominant gender. (Marshall, 1984). Men 's traits of assertiveness, self confidence and competencies enable them to be seen as role models i.e . Exemplification strategy. This is supported by the findings of Guadagno & Cialdini (2007) and Gwal (2015) mentioning that exemplification is a males' strategy.

The Interviewee assures that supplication, may be classified as a women's strategy . Women are submissive, passive and conformists to their prescribed social and cultural roles. He adds that men are the dominant gender in the society . This is in harmony with the profession of Marshall (1984) regarding the superiority of males in the society . So the interviewee contends that supplication is a females's strategy. This is in accordance with the findings of Al-Shatti, et al. (2022) affirming that women are more inclined to use this strategy.

The last strategy Is intimidation. The interviewee maintains that the social stereotypes dictate how each gender acts. This is similar to the analysis of Larwood & Wood (1977) which stress the impacts of social and cultural stereotypes on genders' behaviours. He therefore determines that men recruit intimidation strategy as reflections of their masculinity nature in the society. This is supported by the findings of Al-Shatti, et al. (2022) and Bolino et al. (2016).

The fourth question explores the impacts of impression management strategies on gender leadership styles. The interviewee declares that leadership is strategic and it is gender free. Leaders are concerned with developing strategies. Strategies employed to achieve the desired visions. He adds that leadership can be viewed through three factors . These factors are made of innovation, integrity and energy. These three factors shapes the impression (the image) which a person develops. The leadership stated by this interviewee is not supported by the literature discussed earlier. Women and men are said to follow different leadership styles based on the use of different strategies of impression management.

The Second Interviewee: (Female)

Question number one pursues the definition of impression management . The interviewee mentions that the impression management is a conscious practice. The practice aims to self promote and self present . This is to develop self image which should be realistic. The self presentation and self image are only related to workplace contexts. This definition is in harmony with the demonstrations of Sanaria (2016) in relation to the desire of an individual to promote a realistic desirable image . It as well conforms with the statements of Nayyar & Raja (2012) mentioning that the external contexts have impacts on the process of impression management .

Question number two scans the strategies of impression management. Question three investigates the impacts of gender on the use of impression management strategies. The two questions overlap because they discuss the issue of strategies of impression management. Their analysis is combined and is presented below.

The first strategy is self promotion. The interviewee explains that women's social stereotypes mould their organizational roles. Men dominate the society hence their abilities to present themselves are greater. This is supported by Marshall (1984) describing the dominance nature of masculinity. The interviewee claims that men therefore employ the self promotion strategy more than women. She clarifies that women are confined by their social stereotypes. This, for her, deprives women from participating to professional networking which men have access to. This is in accordance with the claim of Sing et al. (2002) indicating that women have no access to networks. Bolino et al. (2016) and Al-Shatti et al. (2022) assert that self promotion is more used by men.

The second strategy is ingratiation. The interviewee elucidates that men focus on performance. She adds that women seek to be liked. This is a reflection of females' attitudes for caring about others. They are concerned about coworkers' emotions and feelings. This is upheld by Marshall (1984) exhibiting that women care about others and wholeness. The interviewee argues that this strategy is employed by women. This is supported by Al-Shatti et al. (2022) assuring that ingratiation is a strategy of females. Sing et al. (2002) however believes that the ingratiation is a males' strategy. This is due to the nature of men for being expressive, assertive and self confidence (Larwood & wood, 1977).

The third strategy is exemplification . The interviewee illustrates that all of her role models are women. She believes that this strategy is gender free. This is in agreement with findings of Kurt (2022) displaying that exemplification is a strategy employed by the two genders. Kurt however has not examined the impact of gender on the utilization of strategies of impression management in her research.

The fourth strategy is supplication. The interviewee expresses that men do not show their weaknesses . Showing weakness does not match the images of masculinity. She elaborates that masculinity reflects men's competencies, self confidence, and dominance which is in harmony with the explanations of Marshall (1984). Women's social and cultural roles, for being submissive and passive, permit them to display their weaknesses . This is compatible with the reasoning of the Al-Shatti et al. (2022) indicating that women employ this strategy as result of their prescribed social and cultural roles.

The last strategy is intimidation. The interviewee states that only men employ such strategy of threatening and forcing. She contends that intimidation is a males' strategy . She mentions that men's social and cultural roles justify the use of this strategy by them. This is in accordance with the arguments of Bolino, et al. (2016) explicating that intimidation is a men's strategy.

Question four learns about gender leadership styles in relation to the use of impression management strategies. The interviewee expounds that men are authoritarian based on the use of the self-promotion and intimidation strategies . This is similar to the assertiequally n of Zbihlejova, Frankovsky & Briknerova (2018) elaborating that men are authoritarian . She believes that women are more democratic for using the ingratiation, exemplification and supplication strategies. This as well is supported by the findings of Rister (2016) showing that women are democratic.

The Third Interviewee: (Male)

Question Number one studies the definition of impression management. The Interviewee assures that the impression management is essential to achieve desired images for organisations and for individuals equally. He adds that the impression management is a conscious process. He emphasizes that the images desired should be acceptable to the target audiences. This definition is compatible with the explanations of Vijayabanu, et al, (2019) discussing that the impression (images) have to be accepted others.

Questions number two and three overlap. Question number two seeks to list strategies for impression management and question number three attempts to examine gender differences in relation to such strategies. The analysis of the two questions is jointly presented below.

The first strategy is self promotion . The Interviewee believes that the behaviours leading to self promotion are decided by the genders' social and cultural roles . This is in harmony with the interpretations of Harriman (1985) and Larwood and wood (1977) showing that social and cultural roles shape individuals ' behaviors. Men are usually more expressive than women. They also have access to formal and informal networks. . The deliberations of the Interviewee in relation to men having access to network is in agreement with the conclusion of Sing et al. (2002) . This enables men to engage in self promotion strategy more than women as a result of visibility. He mentions that the strategy of self promotion therefore employed more by men. Men focus on their careers while women care about the entire contexts. This is upheld by the discussions of Gwal (2015) illustrating that men have more abilities to promote themselves.

Ingratiation is the second strategy. The interviewee explicates that ingratiation Is generally used by men more than women. They (men) seek likeness and acceptance by every member in the organization. He elucidates however, that women occasionally use ingratiation strategy with other men. The claim that ingratiation is a males' strategy is in accordance with the arguments of Sing et al. (2002) who explain that men use self-presentation, ingratiation and networking more than women. The statement that women occasionally use ingratiation strategy with men nevertheless is not substantiated by literature.

Exemplification is the third strategy. The interviewee states that the exemplification strategy Is gender-neutral . Men and women can set themselves as models in their own ways. This is in harmony with the findings of Kurt (2022) assuming that men and women rank exemplification strategy as number one. Kurt however did not examine the gender differences in relation to such strategy .

The fourth strategy is supplication. The interviewee expresses that supplication is followed by women more than men. He ascribes this for two reasons. The first is that men focus on job performance and on objectivity . The second is that women are confined to their social and cultural roles . Women's traits emphasize their passivity, submissiveness and conformity as Marshall (1984) postulates. The is supported by the claim of Bolino et al. (2016) stating that women engage in supplication strategy.

The fifth strategy Is intimidation. The interviewee asserts that Intimidation strategy is only recruited by males. Intimidation is to use threats and force to make others comply to orders. He illuminates that men are the dominant gender in the society. Men exhibit their masculinity traits reflecting their superior status in the society. Women nevertheless are are submissive and passive, This is in harmony with the claim of Marshall (1984) illustrating that men are dominant gender and women are the muted group. Women do not use such strategy which is not compatible with their social and cultural roles . This is confirming to the findings of Al-Shatti, et al. (2022) and Guadagno and Cialdini (2007) claiming that intimidation is a males' strategy.

Question number four attempts to capture the definition of leadership based on the use of impression management strategies. The interviewee asserts that leadership is to get things done through people and to cope up with the continuous environmental changes. He affirms that men are charismatic leaders. . This is upheld by the findings of McKenna & Thomson (2015) illustrating that charismatic leadership is the style employed to benefit from impression management strategies. This finding however is not based on examining gender differences. The interviewee adds that women are authoritarian. This is not in harmony with the literature studied above.

The Fourth Interviewee: (Male)

Question number one examines the definition of impression management. The interviewee elaborates that impression management is to project images which change according to the external contexts . The images have impacts on individuals' behaviors. Impression management is a deliberate process to achieve positive self-presentation. This definition is in agreement with the assertions of Vijayabanu, et al, (2019); and Kurt (2022) exhibiting that impression management is related to images evolution. Such images interact with external contexts leading to mould behaviors of individuals.

Questions Number two aims to define strategies of impression management . Questions number three examines the impacts of gender on the use of such strategies. The two questions overlap. The analysis for the two questions therefore is simultaneously presented below.

The first strategy is self promotion . The interviewee explains that men are involved in self promotion more than women. This is due to the different social and cultural roles prescribed to each gender. The masculinity roles are more expressive, assertive and dominant. The feminism roles are being submissive and conformist. This is in harmony with the Marshall's (1984) clarifications claiming that men are the dominant group while women are the muted one. This as well is compatible with the findings of Bolino et al. (2016) ; & Gwal, 2015) claiming that self promotion is a males' strategy.

Ingratiation is the second strategy. The interviewee mentions that men engage in ingratiation strategy more than women. Men due to their social roles attempt to seek likeness and acceptance from the target audience. Women unlike men are submissive, passive, conformist and are not expressive. This matches the descriptions of Larwood and wood (1977) in relation to the learned genders behaviors . This is in harmony as well with the claim of Sing et al. (2002) stating that ingratiation is a males ' strategy.

Exemplification is the third strategy . The interviewee indicates that women attempt to utilize this strategy nowadays . He clarifies that such strategy is more followed by men. Kurt (2022) illustrates that exemplification ranks number one strategy for both genders . Her research nevertheless has not investigated gender differences in relation to impression management strategies. The interviewee expounds that men focus on participating to networks to make themselves visible. This enables them to use exemplification strategy more than women . This is upheld by the descriptions of Gwal (2015) mentioning that men access to networks

Enhance their visibility. Hence they are seen as role models. The discussion of the interviewee is in accordance with the contentions of sing et al. (2002) and of Al-Shatti et al. (2022) arguing that men employ self-entitlement to display their competencies and to introduce themselves as role models.

The fourth strategy is supplication. The interviewee argues that men unlike women never reveal their weakness. This is not a characteristic of masculinity. He elaborates that It is acceptable for women to show their weakness. This matches the social roles of women for being passive, submissive and conformists. This is compatible with the findings of Marshall (1984) affirming that women are the muted group in the society. This is as well upheld by the assertion of Guadagno and Cialdini (2007) exhibiting that supplication is followed by women.

Intimidation is the last strategy. The interviewee propounds that the social and cultural images of men introduce them as the dominant gender. This is supported by the discussions of Marshall (1984). Being the dominant gender allow men to utilize intimidation strategy. The use of intimidation strategy by men is substantiated by the conclusions of Guadagno and Cialdini (2007); Bolino et al. (2016) ; and Al-Shatti, et al. (2022).

Question number four attempts to comprehend the impacts of impression management strategies on gender leadership styles. The interviewee asserts that men and women are alike when it comes to leadership . Both genders follow the authoritarian leadership styles. The literature affirms that men are authoritarian as discussed by Rister (2016). However the claim that women are authoritarian is not in accordance with the findings of the literature examined.

The Fifth Interviewee: (Female)

Question number one attempts to learn about the definition of impression management. The interviewee delineates that impression management is a set of deliberate behaviours exhibited by individuals . The behaviors are directed to self promote . The self promotion aims to develop desirable images validated by the concerned culture. This is in agreement with the discussions of Vijayabanu, et al, (2019); and Kurt,(2022) illustrating that impression management is concerned with individuals' behaviors to reflect self- images which have to be accepted by others.

It is mentioned above that questions two and three overlap. The analysis of the two questions therefore is combined and is presented below.

The first strategy is self promotion. The interviewee explains that this strategy should not be gender based . However the genders' prescribed social and cultural roles make it easier for men to promote themselves. She adds that women due to their prescribed social roles are less engaged in this strategy for being passive, submissive and conformists. This is in harmony with the arguments of Rister (2016) ;Marshall (1984); and McGowan & Sekaja (2022). They mention that women are confined by their social roles . The argument that men engage in self promotion more than women is upheld by the explanations of Sing et al. (2002) illustrating that self promotion is a males' strategy.

The second strategy is ingratiation. The Interviewee expounds that ingratiation is a males' strategy. She states that men have latitude in expressing themselves. Men dominate the society therefore they are superior to women (Marshall, 1984). The interviewee contends that men's ingratiation with others are socially and culturally acceptable. This is compatible with sing et al. (2002) arguing that men use ingratiation more than women .

The third strategy is exemplification. The interviewee expounds that exemplification is believed to be a males' strategy . She elucidates that It is easier for men to exhibit and to display self- confidence, assertiveness and competencies. These traits reflect masculinity as Marshall (1984) postulates. The masculinity hence leads to increase men visibility in the organisations. This is in accordance with the assertions of Guadagno & Cialdini (2007) stating that men recruit self- enhancement strategies. She adds that men dominate networks. This is in agreement with the affirmations of Gwal (2015) claiming that women do not have access to networks. She clarifies that the social and cultural roles assigned to women make them less conspicuous . This corresponds to the claim of Marshall (1984) classifying women as the muted group. Kurt (2022) nevertheless illustrates that exemplification can be exhibited by the two genders. Her research however has not studied the impacts of gender in relation to the utilisation of this strategy.

The fourth strategy Is supplication. The interviewee declares that women employ this strategy more than men. She adds that women are passive, submissive and conformists due to their social roles. . This is in agreement with the claim of Bolino et al. (2016) mentioning that women follow strategies which match their social stereotypes. Al-Shatti et al. (2022) as well find that the supplication is a females' strategy. She however reveals that men exhibit two impression management tactics. The first tactic is sandbagging which claims barriers to affect the performance. The second is self handicapping that impedes achievement by creating obstacles . This is supported by the arguments of Guadagno & Cialdini (2007) and Jones & Pittman (1982) discussing that males illustrate sandbagging and self handicapping. The nterviewee contends that such tactics are not being noticed by others in the organizations.

The last strategy is intimidation. The interviewee interprets that intimidation is a males' strategy . Employees are subjected to threats and forces to implement their leadership's demands. Threats making is compatible with the masculinity traits and characteristics. This mirrors the claim of Marshall (1984) illustrating that men are the dominant gender in the society. The findings of Al-Shatti, et al. (2022) and Guadagno and Cialdini (2007) support the interviewee' s view that intimidation is a males' strategy.

Question number four examines the impacts of impression management strategies on gender leadership styles. The interviewee indicates that men follow authoritarian leadership style. This is due to their dependence on self promotion and intimidation strategies as stated above. The interviewee 's assertion that men follow authoritarian style is supported by Zbihlejova, Frankovsky & Briknerova (2018) arguing that males are authoritative. She however asserts that women display concerns for the feelings and emotions of others. Besides women care for the wholeness of the team. She summarises her discussion by stating that women follow the transformative leadership style . This is in harmony with the findings of Sing et al. (2002) stating that women employ transformative leadership.

CONCLUSION

There is a lack of research about the issue of impression management globally and in the Gulf Corporation Countries especially . The research in this chapter investigates the issue of gender differences concerning the impression management strategies and leadership. There is hardly similar research to the one presented in this chapter in this region, Qualitative research is the methodology employed. Five interviews are conducted with two females and three males leaders in the private sector. In-depth interview is the research method to collect information. Information collected is analyzed and is presented in a case-built. Four questions are investigated.

Question number one seeks the definition of impression management. The responses of all participants have common themes. Interviewees state that the impression management is a conscious and a deliberate process . The process is directed to promote self-images. The images change based on the external contexts. No variation appears between men and women in relation to responses for question number one. The literature discussed above supports such responses.

Questions number two and three are analyzed simultaneously. The two questions attempt to learn about the strategies of impression management and their impacts on genders.

There seems to be general understandings between men and women interviewees concerning the first strategy in relation to self promotion. All interviewees argue that this is a males' strategy. This is due to the masculinity perspective in the society. The masculinity perspective exhibits the males' traits of assertiveness, competitiveness, self confidence and competencies . Men as well dominate networks. This is compatible with the literature reviewed.

The second strategy is ingratiation. Interviewees' responses vary in relation to this second strategy. The three males and one female interviewees agree that ingratiation is a males' strategy. This is due to their social and cultural roles allowing them to express themselves freely. Women nonetheless are passive, submissive and conformists to their social roles. Such roles make them inferior to men . One female interviewee however claims that women social roles reflect kindness and caring for the teams. This means that women use this strategy for it matches to their social roles. The interviewees' replies are in harmony with the literature reviewed.

The third strategy Is exemplification strategy. Three interviewees claim that exemplification is a males' strategy. These are two men and one female. The rest of interviewees consisting of one male and one female argue that exemplification is gender-neutral. This is compatible with the literature review which shows no conclusive findings about this strategy.

The fourth strategy is supplication. All interviewees insist that women only employ supplication . This strategy is upheld by the social and cultural roles of women displaying passivity. Submissiveness and conformity. One female interviewee adds that men as well engage in tactics illustrating their weaknesses. These are sandbagging and self handicapping which are not noticed by others. The literature reviewed supports that women follow supplication. But the majority of literature reviewed has not referred to tactics used by men.

The last strategy Is intimidation. There seems to be consent among interviewees regarding this last strategy. The interviewees assure that this is a males' strategy. This is in accordance with the literature reviewed above. Man are seen to be the dominant gender in the society due to their social and cultural roles.

The last question investigates the impacts of strategies of impression management on leadership styles. The analysis of this last question shows variations in relation to the responses of the interviewees. One male interviewee claims that leadership is gender free and both genders follow strategic leadership. This claim is not supported by the literature discussed above. Another male interviewee assumes that both genders are authoritarian. One more male interviewee expresses the view that women are authoritarian. So the total of two male interviewees claim that women are authoritarian. The literature stated above however does not agree with the arguments referring to females as being authoritarian . There are two female interviewees who agree with the assumption that males are authoritarian. It is the total of three interviewees who ague that men are authoritarian. This is in harmony with literature discussed above. These are two females and one male as mentioned earlier. One female interviewee mentions that females employ transformative leadership and the another female interviewee postulates that women engage in democratic leadership style. One male interviewee believes that men are charismatic leaders. All these different responses are reinforced by the literature examined above.

FUTURE SUGGESTED RESEARCH

This chapter shows the scarcity of research on the issue of impression management strategies globally and in the Gulf corporation Countries specifically. Therefore there is a need to conduct more research to study this issue in order to promote better comprehensions of the subject of strategies of impression management and gender leadership. Based on the conclusions of the research presented in this chapter, the suggested future studies are as follows:

- Replicating the same research on different places and countries may result in different findings . This is to examine the cultural Impacts on the use of impression Management strategies.
- Repeating the same research in the same context but using quantitative methodology may result in different outcomes
- Conducting research to examine factors Influencing strategy choices by each gender

ACKNOWLEDGMENT

We would like to express thanks to all participants for their valuable contributions in this research especially Mrs. Fatima Alalwai, Chief Executive Officer, Bahrain Islamic Bank. We would like also to extend our gratitude to Mr. Adnan Ahmed Yousif, President and Chief Executive of Lemrair Consultancy Company for his continuous support and his significant contributions in this and in the previous works

REFERENCES

Al-A'ali, E. (1991) The phenomenon of women in Management: An alternative perspective and its implication in the case of Bahrain (Lancaster, U.K. University of Lancaster, unpublished Ph.D. thesis)

Al A'Ali, E. & Alazali 2018) . Gender Differences in Relation to organization Sources of power: An exploratory Research of individuals and Contextual issues in E. Al A'Ali, M. Al-Shammari & H. Masri (Eds.)Arab Women and Their Evolving Roles in the Global Business Landscape (pp.1-25). IGI GlOBAL. DOI:DOI: 10.4018/9781-1-5225-3710-6.ch001

Al A'Ali, E., Masmoudi, M., & AlSaffar, G. (2024). Women Leadership in Digital Era: The Competency Model. In Al A'Ali, E., Masmoudi, M., & AlSaffar, G. (Eds.), *Transformative Roles of Women in Public and Private Sectors* (pp. 18–30). IGI GLOBAL., DOI: 10.4018/979-8-3693-3208-5.ch002

Al-Shatti, E., Ohana, M., Odou, P., & Zaitouni, M. (2022). Impression Management on Instagram and Unethical Behavior: The Role of Gender and Social Media Fatigue. *International Journal of Environmental Research and Public Health, 19*(16), 9808. DOI: 10.3390/ijerph19169808 PMID: 36011435

AlSaffar, G., & Al A'ali, E. (2021), Psyciatry in the Midst of the Pandemic: A narrative perspective in E. Al-A'Ali & M. Masmoudi, (Eds.), Global perspective on Change Management and Leadership in the Post-COVID-19 Era. (pp. 24-34). IGI GLOBAL. DOI:DOI: 10.4018/978-1-7998-6948-1.ch.2

Baker, R. T., & Gower, K. (2010). Strategic Application of Storytelling in Organizations: Toward Effective Communication in a Diverse World. The Journal of Business Communication (1973), 47(3), 295-312., DOI: 10.1177/0021943610369782

Bois, S. (1978) The Art of Awareness (3rd Ed) Wm. C. Brown Company

Bolino, M., Long, D., & Turnley, W. (2016). Impression management in organizations: Critical questions, answers, and areas for future research. *Annual Review of Organizational Psychology and Organizational Behavior, 3*(1), 377–406. DOI: 10.1146/annurev-orgpsych-041015-062337

Debus, M. E. (2024). Ingold, Pia V.; Gross, C.; & Bolino, M.C., (2024). Researching the top? Profile of impression Management and Career. *Journal of Business and Psychology, 39*, 1284–1301. DOI: 10.1007/s10869-024-09954-7

Edeh, F. O., Zayed, N. M., Darwish, S., Nitsenko, V., Hanechko, I., & Islam, K. M. A. (2023) Impression Management and Employee Contextual Performance in service Organizations (Enterprises).Emerging Science Journal. Vol.7, No. 2, April, 2023. DOI: http://dx. Doi. Org/DOI: 10.28991/ESJ-2023-07-02-05

Guadagno, R. E. & Cialdini, R. B. (2007) Gender Differences in Impression Management is in Organizations: A qualitative Review in Sex Roles published by Springer Natur, 56(7):483-494.DOI:DOI: 10.1007s11199-007-9187-3

Gwal R. (2015). Tactics of Impression Management: Relative Success on Workplace Relationship. International Journal of Indian Psychology, 2 (2), DOI: , DIP: 18.01.064/20140202DOI: 10.25215/0202.064

Hennig, M., & Jardin, M. (1977). *The Managerial Women*. John Wiley and Sons Inc.

Jones, E., & Pittman, T. (1982). Toward a General Theory of Strategic Self Presentation. In psychological perspectives on Self. In Souls, I. J. (Ed.), (pp. 231–262). Hillsdale Lawrence Erlbaum Assoc.

Kurt, Y. (2022). MANAGING IMPRESSION IN THE WORKPLACE: A RESEARCH ON AIRPORT PROFESSIONALS. *International Journal of Aviation, Aeronautics, and Aerospace, 9*(2). Advance online publication. DOI: 10.15394/ijaaa.2022.1687

Larwood, L., & Wood, M. (1977) women in Management. Lexington: Lexington Books

Marshall, J. (1984). *Women Managers: Travellers in a Male World*. John Wiley and Sons Inc.

McGowan, N. A., & Sekaja, L. (2022). A diary study of the impression management strategies utilised by industrial and organizational psychology interns. SA Journal of Industrial Psychology/SA Tydskrif vir Bedryfsielkunde, 48(0),a1902. DOI: 10.4102/sajip.v48i0.1902

Nayyar, S., & Raja, T. N. (2012). The Impact of Impression Management Behavior on Organizational Politics. *Interdisciplinary Journal of Contemporary Research in Business*, *3*(9), 914–923.

Sanaria, A. D. (2016). A Conceptual Framework for Understanding the Impression Management Strategies Used by Women in Indian Organizations. *SA Journal of Human Resource Management*, *3*(1), 25–39. DOI: 10.1177/2322093716631118

Sing, V., Kumra, S., & Vinnicombe, S. (2002) Gender and Impression Management: Playing the Promotional Game in Journal of Business Ethics, Netherlands: Kluwer Academy Publisher, 37:77-89

Tedeschi, J. T. (1990). Self Presentation and Social Influence:An Interactionist perspective. In Cody, M. J., & McLaughlin, M. L. (Eds.), *The psychology of Tactical Coo* (pp. 301–323). Multilingual Matters.

Vijaybanu, C., Theresa, Ch., & Daisy, A. (2019). Impression Management Tactics booster for the communication of IT employees SMART PLS Approach. *Revista de Psicología*, *47*(2), 683–707. DOI: 10.18800/psico.201902.012

Zbihlejová, L., Frankovsky, M., & Birknerova, Z. (2018). Leadership Styles if Managers from Perspective of Gender. *International Journal of Organizational Leadership*, *7*(4), 340–347. DOI: 10.33844/ijol.2018.60216

Chapter 2
Individuals and the Use of Image and Impressions Management

Indranil Mutsuddi
https://orcid.org/0000-0002-4202-8744
JIS University, India

ABSTRACT

Impression management refers to how individuals shape others' perceptions by adjusting behavior, communication, and appearance to fit social or situational norms. Influenced by cultural, environmental, and organizational factors, this process can be intentional or automatic. While skillful impression management can aid in social belonging, career advancement, and personal achievement, it may also trigger identity conflicts, psychological stress, and emotional fatigue—especially when one's public image diverges from their true self. The rise of social media and AI further complicates self-presentation, raising issues around transparency, ethics, and mental health. Current research highlights both advancements and gaps in understanding these dynamics, with implications for inclusive leadership and HR practices. This chapter underscores the need for ethical, culturally aware impression management strategies that balance self-presentation with authenticity to promote well-being and trust in diverse, hybrid environments.

INTRODUCTION

People from all walks of life, often without realizing it, engage in the act of impression management — shaping how others perceive them through their words, behavior, and appearance. This process can be intentional or automatic. Whether

DOI: 10.4018/979-8-3373-5519-1.ch002

it's blending in with a group, being friendly and agreeable, or highlighting personal strengths, individuals use various strategies to influence how they come across to others. Perception, however, isn't shaped in isolation. It's affected by more than just what someone says or does. The environment, cultural context, social roles, and even the expectations or assumptions of others all play a role in how impressions are formed.

At its core, impression management isn't just about being liked — it's about connection, belonging, and achieving personal or professional goals. A well-managed impression can lead to deeper friendships, romantic interest, job offers, or leadership opportunities. On the flip side, poor or conflicting impressions can result in misunderstandings, tension, or missed chances. Over time, how others see us — and how we manage that image — can shape our mental health, social relationships, and overall life satisfaction. In today's digital world, platforms like social media have added a new dimension to how people manage their image. Online, individuals often carefully curate how they present themselves — from the photos they post to the way they communicate — all in an effort to create a specific, often idealized, impression. Yet, this constant self-presentation can sometimes feel disconnected from one's true identity. Striking a balance between adjusting to social expectations and staying authentic is crucial for maintaining well-being and building genuine relationships.

This chapter aims to offer a comprehensive review of the literature on impression and image management, highlighting the existing research and identifying gaps in our current understanding. It will explore how individuals manage impressions both in their personal lives and professional environments. These insights are especially valuable for HR professionals and people managers, helping them better understand employees from diverse cultural backgrounds and create inclusive, performance-driven organizational cultures.

REVIEW OF LITERATURE

Impression management plays a role across various business settings, including financial reporting, marketing, recruitment, and job interviews. Because it's centered on influencing how others view a person or organization—whether through genuine or selective portrayals—it often raises questions about ethics (Provis, 2023). In management research, the term typically refers to deliberate efforts by individuals or companies to create a positive image in the eyes of others. The concept of impression management has its roots in earlier theories focused on how both individuals and organizations construct and maintain their identities and public images, including efforts related to branding and reputation. In its modern form, it incorporates perspectives from areas like public relations, organizational communication, and strategic management (Henderson, 2017). It also takes into account how quickly relationships can shift—both inside organizations and with external audiences—in an interconnected and rapidly evolving global environment. In professional settings, employees often engage in impression management—intentional efforts to affect how they are viewed by others in the organization, such as managers, colleagues, subordinates, or clients (Bozeman & Kacmar, 1997). These individuals, sometimes seen as "actors," use various tactics to shape the perceptions of those around them (Rosenfiled et al., 1994), referred to as "targets." This can include developing a new professional identity or reinforcing an existing one (M. C. Bolino et al., 2008), often aiming to be seen as capable, friendly, or in need of assistance. Such actions are frequently purposeful, as employees are found to tailor their behavior and image to support their personal or career-related objectives (Bolino et al., 2016).

The study conducted by (Wang et al., 2020) pointed out that using consumption as a way to influence others' perceptions has become a widespread approach to impression management, particularly highlighting its relevance to broader social challenges. Their study shed light on the unique pressures female professionals face, especially regarding how they manage and present their image in professional settings. Similarly, (Sun et al., 2021) noted that employees increasingly turn to Enterprise Social Media Platforms (ESMPs) to curate and control how they're viewed by colleagues, using these tools to build and maintain their professional identity. These platforms function as digital environments where employees interact, offering opportunities to shape peer perceptions through deliberate self-presentation (Rui & Stefanone, 2013). Adding to this, (Ji et al., 2025) noted that as profile images have become more significant in shaping how individuals are perceived online especially in social media platforms. Social media platforms provided users more control over how they presented themselves visually, allowing for more deliberate and strategic impression management over others. Impression management—can have significant psychological effects and may even contribute to unethical behavior. Guided by the stressor–strain–outcome framework, the study conducted by (Al-Shatti et al., 2022) investigated how impression management pressures impacted individual well-being and, subsequently, the likelihood of unethical actions in their behavior. The study also explored whether curating one's image on social media platforms like Instagram led to emotional fatigue that carries over into unethical behavior in the workplace. On the other hand, the study conducted by (Liu & Lei, 2025) examined how self-presentation on social media relates to the effectiveness of impression management (IME). It broke down IME into five key areas: strategies for shaping one's identity, managing how others perceive them, expressing themselves clearly, protecting their image, and overall confidence in presenting themselves online.

Employees relied on impression management (IM) strategies to shape how they're being perceived in their workplace (Debus et al., 2024). While there's plenty of research on how IM affects things like job interviews and performance reviews, its long-term impact on career growth and advancement remains unclear and not well understood. The study also revealed that employees who frequently used positive impression management tactics—such as self-promotion, expressing appreciation for others, and setting a strong example—tended to report the highest levels of personal career satisfaction. These behaviors were also linked to greater recognition from supervisors, including stronger recommendations for rewards, suggesting a connection to tangible career advancement. Additionally, (Brouer et al., 2016) found that an individual's skill in managing resources played a key role in how effective their positive impression management efforts were. Specifically, those who are better at handling their resources tended to gain more social support and connections as a result of using these strategies. On the other hand, job seekers and employees often used impression management strategies to present themselves in a more favorable light, hoping to highlight their skills or contributions at work. However, much of the existing research in this area has focused mainly on specific techniques like flattery and promoting one's own achievements (Curtis et al., 2023).

From a software developer connecting with a teammate via video chat to a carpenter texting clients between jobs, remote communication is now a regular part of how work gets done (Blunden & Brodsky, 2024). Whether it's for casual updates or high-stakes interviews, managing impressions in virtual settings has become an integral aspect of today's professional environment (Raghuram et al., 2019). Researchers such as (Wang et al., 2020) have noted that individuals try to influence how others perceive them as part of their daily routines. However, the effects of this behavior on personal well-being remain largely unclear. Individuals with a strong tendency for self-monitoring are highly aware of how they present themselves in daily interactions and often modify their behavior to suit the social context. This skill of interpreting and responding to others' cues is closely connected to the practice of managing impressions (Koslowsky et al., 2022). In virtual interactions, employees lose access to many of the nonverbal signals—such as gestures and facial expressions—that typically help them understand others. As a result, they rely more heavily on verbal communication and language style to interpret and form impressions during online exchanges (Switzer, 2008). In essence, impression management involves influencing how others view us by employing different methods to shape perceptions, whether in personal relationships or professional environments.

On the other side, (Park et al., 2024) showed that leaders who effectively used impression management were more likely to be perceived by their team members as trustworthy and consistent in their actions. This perception, in turn, was linked to improved follower performance—but primarily among those team members who also engaged in impression management themselves. These findings suggest that when both leaders and followers participate in impression management, it enhances their sense of connection and reinforces the belief that the leader demonstrates genuine behavioral integrity. Impression management was found to be a crucial factor in shaping the way ethical leadership encourages environmentally responsible behavior within the organization. In other words, the way leaders and employees manage how they are perceived helps bridge the connection between ethical leadership practices and the adoption of green initiatives, making it an essential part of promoting sustainable actions at work (Tuna & Gül, 2024). A study focusing on South Korean sports celebrities found that their impression management strategies on social media were diverse and intentional. Some athletes used their platforms to build closer connections with fans by sharing personal moments and expressing themselves in ways that fostered relatability and emotional connection. In contrast, others maintained a sense of distance by posting content that highlighted their financial success or social and cultural status (Yoo, 2022). This research showed that people had different motivational and behavioral intentional while using impression management strategies in their day to day personal and professional endeavours.

CRITICAL REVIEW OF LITERATURE AND RESEARCH GAP ANALYSIS

The above literature indicates that, impression management plays an important role in many business settings, including areas like financial reporting, hiring, daily workplace interactions, and leadership, where individuals and organizations actively work to create positive perceptions. Studies reveal that this practice spans both traditional in-person communication and modern digital platforms such as social media and internal enterprise networks, with employees and managers using various strategies to shape how others see them. Research also points to the psychological and ethical challenges involved, including stress, possible unethical actions, and difficulties in balancing genuine self-presentation with strategic image crafting. Although there is considerable focus on short-term effects like interview success, performance reviews, and online self-presentation, there is still a lack of insight into the long-term consequences for career progression, how impression management differs between virtual and face-to-face settings, and the influence of cultural and gender differences. Moreover, the relationship between impression management and leadership approaches in promoting ethical behavior and sustainability within organizations is not well explored, nor is the development of impression management skills throughout one's career. Further in-depth research is needed to better understand these gaps and to create models that reflect the evolving digital environment and varied personal motives behind impression management.

OVERVIEW OF IMPRESSION MANAGEMENT

Impression management involves the deliberate efforts individuals make to shape how others perceive them, particularly in social and online environment. It revolves around the idea of shaping one's identity by selecting what information to share, highlight, or withhold. On platforms like social media, for instance, users often fine-tune their profiles—choosing which details to make visible and which to keep hidden—effectively sending signals about who they are and how they want to be perceived. The process involved in impression creation and tendency to maintain the same isn't always deliberate. While some people intentionally craft their image to gain acceptance, foster relationships, or pursue specific goals like employment or recognition, others might affect perceptions without even realizing it. People engage in this form of social navigation using a variety of approaches. They may showcase their strengths and successes (a form of self-promotion), express admiration or agree with others to win favor (known as ingratiation), or lower expectations in anticipation of challenges (called self-handicapping). The choice of strategy depends heavily on context—the social setting, the role someone is playing, and what matters to the audience they are trying to influence. At its heart, impression management is about taking control over how one is perceived, aligning outward behavior with internal objectives and the social norms of the moment.

Everyday Occurrences of Impression Management

Impression management is something we all engage in—sometimes on purpose, other times without even realizing it. It refers to the ways individuals try to influence how others perceive them. Whether they are meeting someone for the first time or posting on social media, people often shape their behavior, appearance, or communication to leave a certain impression. The goal is usually to be seen in a favorable light, to gain approval, or to avoid judgment or criticism. Today, social media is a major space where impression management plays out. Platforms such as Instagram, Facebook, and LinkedIn allow users to present carefully chosen aspects of their lives. People often highlight achievements, happy moments, or aesthetically pleasing content, while leaving out struggles or less flattering experiences. This can create an unrealistic portrayal of a person's life—making it seem more perfect or effortless than it actually is.

In the field of sociology, intention towards making impression on others is recognized as a social strategy aimed at shaping how others interpret people, their actions, or even the things people do or own. Impression management can be intentional, like rehearsing what to say in an interview, or it can happen automatically, such as adjusting the tone in a conversation without thinking about it. Often, impression management is tied to personal motivations—like the need to fit in, to be respected, or to craft a certain identity which people desire.

Social Contexts of Impression Management

Impression management is a key part of how people interact with others. It refers to the ways people intentionally—or sometimes unintentionally—shape how they come across in different situations. This often means adjusting their behavior, expressions, or the information they share to influence how they're perceived by those around them. Whether at work, in social settings, or online, people regularly shift how they present themselves depending on the context, the people they're interacting with, cultural expectations, and what they hope to achieve. At its core, this process reflects a basic human need: the desire to be seen positively. How others view individuals can have a powerful impact on the kinds of relationships and opportunities they actually have access to. What's considered appropriate behavior can differ widely from one situation to another, so most people learn to adapt. For example, someone might speak more formally and dress more professionally in a business meeting, while feeling free to be more casual and open with close friends.

Outside of the office, impression management also plays out in everyday social life. People use different techniques—like talking about their achievements, downplaying certain things, or carefully choosing what they say—to influence how others see them. These behaviors help people form friendships, build trust, maintain social harmony, or even start romantic relationships. The image people project shapes not only how others treat them but also what opportunities or challenges they encounter in their day to day social interactions. Presenting oneself in a positive way can help open doors, while missteps in social presentation can have the opposite effect. Being able to understand and adjust to different social environments is an essential skill—it helps people stay connected, avoid conflict, and form deeper, more meaningful bonds. Fig 1 illustrates the social perspectives of impression management.

Figure 1. **Social Contexts of Impression Management**

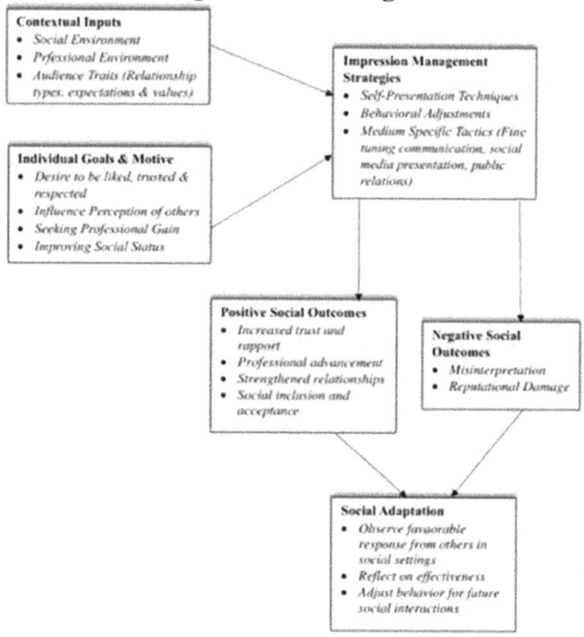

(Source: Author)

Role of Environment, Culture, and Social Expectations on Impression Management

Impact of the Environment

The environment plays an influential role in how individuals manage the impressions they leave on others. Both the social and physical context surrounding a person can shape their behavior, communication, and overall self-presentation. People often—whether intentionally or instinctively—adjust how they act in response to what they believe is expected of them, particularly when they seek acceptance, validation, or success in personal and professional settings. Different social settings, such as workplaces, friend groups, or community gatherings, tend to promote specific behaviors aligned with their values and norms. For example, someone may present themselves with greater formality in a business meeting but adopt a more relaxed and informal tone when spending time with close friends. The awareness of being observed—either by a real audience or a perceived one—can amplify the desire to make a favorable impression. This may result in intentional actions, like displaying eco-friendly behavior in public to project a responsible or considerate image. Cultural norms and group expectations can subtly but powerfully shape how people behave. There's often a strong tendency to mirror the actions, dress, and language of a particular group in order to feel included. Physical environments also affect behavior; in public settings, individuals might engage in more socially acceptable or visible positive actions due to a sense of being watched or judged.

Impact of Organizational Culture

The culture within an organization significantly influences how employees present themselves at work. In workplaces where the environment is supportive, inclusive, and grounded in shared values, people are more likely to feel connected, motivated, and secure. This psychological safety encourages authenticity—employees feel free to express their true selves without fear of judgment or repercussion. In such cultures, there is little need for employees to deliberately shape or control how others perceive them. However, when the organizational atmosphere is tense, defensive, or overly hierarchical, employees may begin to feel vulnerable. In these settings, impression management (IM) can become a protective strategy. Workers may find themselves constantly monitoring how they are viewed by peers and leadership, adjusting their behavior not out of authenticity, but out of concern for criticism, exclusion, or negative consequences. In these environments, personal image can start to matter more than genuine performance or collaboration. Toxic cultures, especially those marked by low trust and poor communication, can even foster more aggressive forms of IM. Employees may resort to intimidation, manipulation, or other tactics to gain influence or shield themselves in unpredictable situations.

Impact of Social Expectation

People's everyday behavior is frequently shaped, whether intentionally or unintentionally, by the social context in which they live. People naturally adapt their words, actions, and even their appearance in response to what they think is expected or accepted in a given social setting. This adaptive behavior, often referred to as impression management, is shaped by cultural expectations, community standards, and the specific roles people occupy in the society. These adaptations can take many forms. Some individuals might lean into established gender norms without realizing it, while others might change their tone, posture, or expression depending on who they're speaking to. In work-related situations, the goal might be to come across as capable and dependable. In social scenarios, the emphasis might shift toward being friendly or approachable. Underlying these shifts is a shared human motivation: the drive to belong, to be valued, and to make a positive impact on others. Impression management is often used as a strategy people use—whether purposefully or instinctively—to gain acceptance, influence others' views, or protect their sense of identity in a social setting. Achieving goals like forming connections, earning trust, or maintaining one's reputation often depends on how successfully someone navigates these social expectations. Further, in today's digital world, managing how people are seen has expanded beyond face-to-face interaction. Social media platforms have become a stage for people to carefully craft how they appear to others.

Connection, Belonging, and Personal/Professional Goals and Impression Management

Social Connections and Impression Management

Forming and maintaining social relationships and networks involves more than just frequent interaction—it requires intentional effort in how people present themselves to others. People often adjust their behavior, language, and demeanor based on the social setting, aiming to influence how they are perceived. Whether someone is trying to appear approachable in a new social group, competent in a job interview, or authentic on social media, these subtle shifts in presentation help shape the way others respond. A well-managed impression can increase trust, likability, and social acceptance, ultimately strengthening personal and professional relationships. Rather than being a superficial act, managing one's image is a meaningful social tool that helps individuals navigate the complexities of human interaction.

Belongingness and Impression Management

The desire to belong is one of the most deeply rooted and influential human drives. People are inherently drawn to social groups and relationships where they feel recognized, accepted, and appreciated. When this need goes unfulfilled—whether through rejection, isolation, or simply feeling invisible—it often evokes a powerful emotional reaction. As a result, individuals might become more aware of others' perceptions and modify their behavior or appearance to feel accepted again. This involves intentionally crafting how one is seen by others. When people feel excluded, they might go out of their way to seem more approachable, capable, or in tune with group norms. This can show up through subtle shifts in tone, body language, or even personal opinions and actions—all intended to re-establish connection and acceptance within the group. The link between the need to belong and impression management reveals just how closely people's social instincts are tied to the way they present themselves. Impression management isn't always about ambition or image—sometimes, it's an emotional strategy to cope with the pain of being left out. In environments where individuals feel secure and included, they tend to act more authentically.

Personal Goals and Impression Management

People often adjust how they come across to others in order to pursue personal aims or aspirations. This behavior, commonly referred to as impression management, is typically motivated by the need for acceptance, approval, or recognition. Two major forms of this are how individuals present themselves personally and how they display what they associate with—such as their achievements, products, or professional work. Shaping one's image can be either a deliberate or automatic act, depending on the situation. Whether someone is trying to make a strong first impression, fit into a group, or move forward in their career, they may change how they act, speak, or appear to align with their intentions. Sometimes this is done to avoid negative judgments, while other times it serves as a way to reflect one's personality or beliefs. Though impression management can help people succeed socially or professionally, it's important to approach it with care. There's a balance between adapting to social norms and staying honest with oneself. Being authentic not only promotes emotional resilience but also helps build lasting, meaningful connections with others.

Professional Goals and Impression Management

In the workplace, the way individuals present themselves can significantly influence their professional growth. Impression management refers to the deliberate effort to shape others' perceptions by highlighting qualities like competence, reliability, and integrity. When applied thoughtfully, these efforts can lead to valuable career benefits such as new job opportunities, promotions, and stronger professional networks. Employees often adopt various impression strategies to positively influence how they are seen by colleagues and supervisors. Studies have shown that genuine and constructive use of these tactics is often linked to greater acknowledgment from leadership, including improved evaluations and a higher likelihood of receiving rewards—key markers of career advancement.

THEORETICAL PERSPECTIVE OF IMPRESSION MANAGEMENT

Goffman's Dramaturgical Approach & Impression Management

Erving Goffman's theory of social interaction (Goffman, 1959) draws a comparison between everyday life and a theatrical performance. According to this perspective, individuals behave much like actors, deliberately managing how they present themselves to others. They adjust their actions and control what information is shared in order to meet social norms and shape how they are viewed. Goffman points out that these performances don't always reflect a person's true thoughts or emotions. People often play certain roles because the situation demands it, not because it aligns with their personal beliefs. For example, he mentions a scenario where a doctor gives a patient a placebo—not out of faith in the treatment, but because the patient expects a more involved response. Figure 2 illustrates how behaviors can be driven more by social expectations than by genuine intent. A key idea in this framework is the notion of the "front"—the parts of a person's behavior that are regularly used to define a situation for those observing. Through repeated social encounters, individuals create and refine their sense of self (Self Identity). For Goffman, self identity for an individual is not something static or inherent; rather, it emerges and evolves through ongoing interaction with others.

Figure 2. **Goffman's Dramaturgical Approach & Impression Managemen**

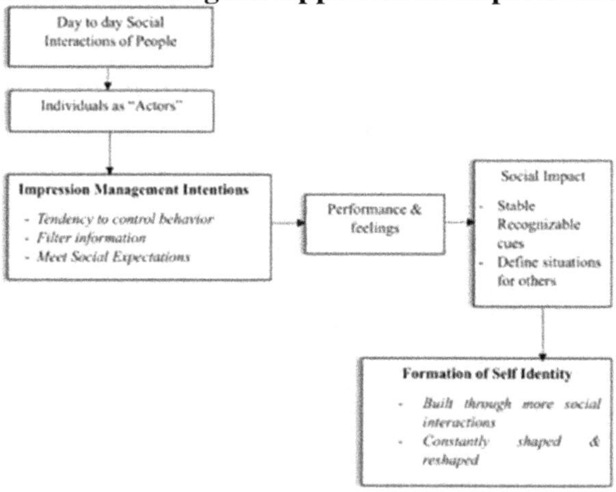

(Source: Author)

Signalling Theory & Impression Management

Further, signalling theory also offers a useful lens for understanding impression management by exploring how individuals or organizations—who possess private information—communicate it credibly to others in the face of information asymmetry. According to the theory, senders use visible behaviors or characteristics (signals) to convey their genuine qualities or intentions, while receivers interpret these cues to inform their judgments and decisions.

Self-Presentation Theory & Impression Management

Within the field of social psychology, the ideas of self-presentation and impression management are closely connected. Impression management involves the range of behaviors—both deliberate and unintentional—that people use to influence how others view them. Self-presentation is a more intentional form of this process, where individuals carefully shape their behavior or appearance to create a desired impression, especially in situations where social perception plays a key role. Self-presentation theory explains how people manage the way they're perceived by others. It focuses on the efforts people make to leave a positive impression and gain approval in social situations. The idea is that people don't just passively interact—they actively shape their behavior, words, and appearance to reflect the image they want others to see. This could mean showcasing individual level talents, trying to come across as friendly, or acting in ways that highlight people's culture and values. The theory often compares social life to a performance, where individuals play different roles depending on who they are with and what outcomes they are aiming for.

Expectation Theory & Impression Management

In exploring impression management, it's important for researchers to consider contrasting theories. Expectancy theory views behavior as driven by beliefs about effort, performance, and valued outcomes. In contrast, impression management focuses on how individuals consciously or unconsciously shape others' perceptions through social behavior, highlighting external rather than internal motivators.

PSYCHOLOGICAL CONSEQUENCES OF IMPRESSION MANAGEMENT

While carefully shaping how others see people can make social interactions smoother, this strategy often comes at a psychological cost. The continuous effort to maintain a favorable image can lead to increased anxiety, self-deception, and a sense of losing touch with one's authentic self (Fig 3).

The Stress of Constant Performance

At the core of impression management is a strong desire to be perceived in specific ways—be it competent, friendly, confident, or dependable. But striving to uphold these impressions, particularly in high-pressure settings like job interviews or public presentations, can provoke significant stress. The fear of negative judgment or failing to meet expectations can make even casual conversations mentally taxing. Over time, this sustained tension can develop into chronic social anxiety, making it increasingly difficult to engage comfortably in both professional and personal contexts.

Blurring the Lines Between Self and Persona

Frequently curating one's identity to win approval or sidestep criticism can lead individuals to confuse this constructed image with their true self. As this alternate persona becomes more dominant, it may distort personal values, thoughts, and emotions. The disconnect between who one really is and who they believe they should be can result in identity confusion and inner unease.

Figure 3. **Psychological Consequences of Impression Management**

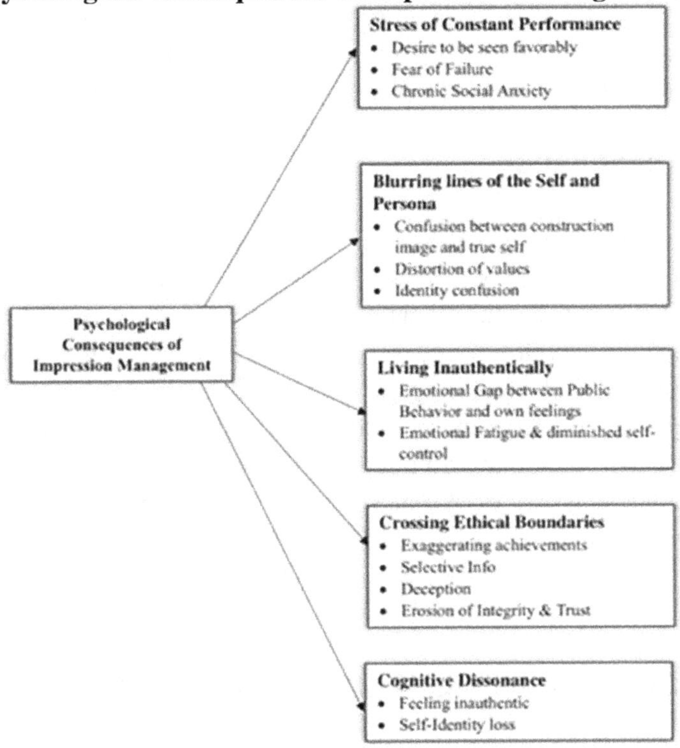

(Source: Author)

Living Inauthentically and its Consequences

Perhaps one of the most profound effects of ongoing image control is the emotional divide it creates between one's public behavior and private feelings. When this gap widens, it often leads to a persistent sense of being inauthentic. This internal mismatch can spark cognitive dissonance—the discomfort that arises when our actions clash with our beliefs. For instance, someone who constantly acts extroverted to fit in might feel exhausted or insincere if they are naturally more reserved. Over time, suppressing genuine emotions and traits requires sustained mental effort, leading to emotional fatigue and diminished self-control.

Crossing Ethical Boundaries

In some situations, especially on social media where appearances are tightly managed, the urge to maintain a flawless image can cross ethical lines. The intense need to be seen as successful or morally upright might drive individuals to exaggerate achievements, selectively present information, or even deceive others. These choices—though sometimes subtle—can gradually erode personal integrity and strain relationships, ultimately affecting one's credibility and trustworthiness.

Cognitive Dissonance

Trying to control how others see an individual can sometimes cause a clash inside, especially when the person people show to the world doesn't match who they really feel are deep down. When there's a gap between an individual's outward image and his/her true values or sense of self, it can leave them feeling uneasy or unhappy. It might feel like that they are putting on a disguise, and that others only see a carefully crafted version of the individual rather than the real person beneath. Over time, this difference between public and private selves can lead to a sense of not being genuine, and may even make us question who people really are. Finding a balance between fitting in socially and staying authentic to who people are inside is a challenging but vital part of maintaining their emotional well-being.

IMPRESSION MANAGEMENT BEHAVIOR OF PEOPLE

How people present themselves to others is a fundamental part of their personal and professional endeavors. Whether people are meeting someone for the first time, collaborating with coworkers, or simply chatting with friends, people often change the way they act and communicate to leave a particular impression. These deliberate or instinctive attempts to shape others' perceptions can help individuals form connections, establish trust, and achieve their personal and professional objectives. People tend to use a variety of methods—such as choosing their tone, controlling facial expressions, or emphasizing certain qualities—to shape the image they want to convey. This continual process of managing impressions is essential for navigating social situations smoothly and can play a significant role in achieving success across different areas of life (Table 1).

Table 1. **Impression Management Behavioral Tendencies of People** *(Source: Author)*

Impression Management Behavioral Tendencies	Features
Effort to please others	This refers to the way people often try to gain approval and acceptance from those around them. This usually involves deliberately using certain behaviors, like giving sincere compliments, showing admiration, or agreeing with others' viewpoints, to make a favorable impression. These actions help to create a sense of connection, build trust, and encourage others to respond positively. Such behavioral tendencies (ingratiation) could be both manipulative or authentic – depending on the true intention of the person.
Threatening and Bullying	At times, individuals rely on intimidation to gain control or steer the thoughts and actions of others. This might involve using harsh language, aggressive gestures, or dominant behavior to create an atmosphere of tension or fear. The intention behind such actions is often to push others into compliance or to influence their mindset by making them feel uneasy or overpowered
Tendency to reflect	This approach includes purposefully presenting oneself as especially committed, ethical, or admirable—almost like trying to set an example for others. The intention behind this behavior is usually to gain admiration and respect by appearing exceptionally well-rounded or morally upright.
Imploration	At times, individuals attempt to influence how they're perceived by exposing their struggles or emotional hardships. They may present themselves as overwhelmed, dependent, or emotionally fragile in order to stir feelings of sympathy. This strategy relies on evoking empathy, encouraging others to respond with care, support, or a willingness to help. It's a gentle yet intentional way of gaining assistance by appealing to people's instinct to be compassionate toward those who seem to be hurting
Forthrightness	This involves expressing one's thoughts clearly and establishing limits with calm confidence. It may also include sharing personal experiences and highlighting his/her strengths, experience and intellectual insights.
Self-Presentation	It involves how people present themselves by carefully sharing signals and behaviors that shape the image they wish others to perceive. The main purpose is often to earn acceptance and favorable responses from those they interact with.

IMPRESSION MANAGEMENT IN PROFESSIONAL SETTINGS

In today's professional world, the ability to manage how others perceive you—known as impression management—is an essential skill. It goes beyond simply making a good first impression; it involves thoughtfully shaping the way you present yourself in everyday interactions at work. Whether you're in a meeting, giving a presentation, or navigating office dynamics, how you carry yourself can significantly influence how others view your competence, credibility, and character. This process is deeply psychological, rooted in understanding social cues and expectations. By being intentional about your behavior, communication style, and even appearance, you can actively guide how you're perceived by colleagues, supervisors, and clients, ultimately playing a key role in career growth and workplace relationships.

Strategies used by Employees & Managers by creating Impressions

Employees often remain aware of how they are perceived by colleagues and supervisors, intentionally or unintentionally altering their behavior to shape opinions about their skills, character, and contributions to the team. Some employees might focus on promoting their achievements to demonstrate their abilities, while others may use friendliness or compliments to build positive relationships. There are also more subtle approaches, such as going above and beyond to set a strong example or, in certain situations, using their authority to establish control. The approach someone takes usually depends on their goals—whether they want to earn a promotion, build trust, or simply blend in with the group.

Down-to-the-Earth Approach

The down-to-earth style in impression management emphasizes being genuine, humble, and approachable. Rather than relying on authority or showmanship, these leaders connect with others through honesty, empathy, and openness about both successes and challenges. By fostering trust and encouraging authenticity, they create a supportive work environment where respect is earned naturally. This grounded approach helps build strong relationships and often results in teams that are more motivated, loyal, and engaged.

Confident Expert Approach

The confident expert approach in impression management involves showcasing strong knowledge and skills while staying calm and approachable. Those who use this style communicate their expertise clearly and with humility, earning trust without seeming arrogant. They prepare well, support their views with facts, and openly admit when they don't know something, which boosts their credibility. Confident experts also engage others by listening and respecting different opinions, building solid professional relationships based on mutual respect. This balance of competence and approachability helps them influence decisions, stand out in meetings, and open doors for career advancement. Rather than dominating conversations, they project steady confidence that encourages collaboration and trust.

Supportive Team-Oriented Approach

The supportive team oriented approach in impression management focuses on fostering genuine relationships through cooperation and care. Instead of highlighting personal success, these individuals prioritize collaboration, trust, and helping others thrive. They listen attentively, offer assistance selflessly, and celebrate team achievements, creating an inclusive and positive work environment. This style reflects strength in kindness and reliability, as supportive team players consistently honor commitments and stand by their colleagues during challenges. By demonstrating empathy and teamwork, they naturally earn respect and trust. In the workplace, this approach builds strong connections and encourages collective effort, often leading to greater influence and career opportunities.

Going Above and Beyond Approach

The "going above and beyond" approach in impression management means putting in extra effort to make a real difference, not just meeting basic requirements. People who adopt this style actively seek ways to add value, help their team, and solve problems beyond what's expected. This mindset comes from a genuine wish to contribute, whether by staying late, assisting colleagues, or suggesting improvements. Consistently doing more builds a reputation for reliability and dedication, earning trust naturally. This approach also reflects pride and responsibility, showing that success involves lifting the whole team.

Role in of Impression Management in Recruitment, Performance, and Career Advancement

The following Table (Table 2) illustrates the impact of impression management in recruitment, employee performance and their career advancement endeavours in an organization.

Table 2. **Impression Management in Recruitment, Performance, and Career Advancement**

Impression Management in various aspects of professional endeavours	**Details**
Recruitment	In the hiring process, especially during interviews, managing impressions plays a vital role. Job seekers often adopt different approaches to put their best foot forward—they emphasize their strengths, share meaningful experiences, come across as friendly, and try to minimize any shortcomings. However, it's not only the applicants who influence perceptions. Interviewers also communicate messages—sometimes deliberately, sometimes unintentionally—that shape how candidates view the company and the position. These exchanges can greatly affect the overall outcome of recruitment.
Employee Performance	The way employees present themselves at work plays a major role in their performance, particularly regarding how supervisors and teammates view them. Positive impression management techniques can improve performance by strengthening workplace relationships and highlighting an individual's abilities. However, if these efforts seem insincere or manipulative, they may damage trust and ultimately hinder job success.
Employee Career Advancement	The way employees shape others' perceptions of them plays a significant role in their professional development. Their workplace reputation, influenced by these impressions, often determines their potential for promotions and acknowledgment. When employees intentionally display confidence and professionalism, they increase their likelihood of receiving positive feedback and advancing within the organization. Making a genuine and strong impression can open the door to increased responsibilities, career advancement, and involvement in key initiatives.

(Source: Author)

IMPRESSION MANAGEMENT IN THE DIGITAL WORLD

Individuals are increasingly mindful of how they portray themselves online, whether intentionally or instinctively. This includes choosing what aspects of their lives to reveal, curating their digital profiles, and adjusting their communication style to influence how others perceive them. People often aim to make a good impression or connect with certain groups, so they tend to highlight the best parts of themselves and leave out anything that might not look as good. For instance, someone might carefully pick their profile picture, write a bio that fits their desired image, and include details that support the story they want to tell about themselves. They also adjust the way they write or speak online, choosing words and tones that help send the message they want others to receive.

Influence of Social Media and Enterprise Platforms in Impression Management

In the modern digital world, both social media and enterprise platforms play a vital role in how people and organizations present themselves publicly. These digital tools offer various ways for users to create and control their online presence, such as setting up personalized profiles, sharing photos or videos, interacting with others, and choosing who can see their information. This control allows individuals and organizations to carefully shape how they are seen by others, influencing perceptions whether someone is promoting their professional identity or a business is managing its reputation.

When people look specifically at Enterprise Social Media Platforms (ESMPs), these are internal networks designed for communication and teamwork within companies. Unlike public social platforms, ESMPs provide a private space where employees connect, exchange updates, acknowledge accomplishments, and collaborate professionally. Beyond these functions, ESMPs offer a unique setting for employees to manage their professional image. Through deliberate choices about what to share or emphasize, employees can influence how coworkers, supervisors, and leadership perceive them. Within these platforms, employees can choose which achievements or skills to highlight, and decide what parts of their personality or work to keep private. This thoughtful approach helps them build credibility, increase their visibility in the organization, and potentially advance their careers. Because ESMPs mix formal workplace communication with more casual social interaction, employees must carefully balance being open and engaged with maintaining professional boundaries and not oversharing.

Impression Management and Digital Communication

In the digital age, the ability to influence how others perceive people—whether as individuals or as organizations—has become a vital skill often referred to as impression management. This involves intentionally shaping and controlling an individual's online presence to present an image that is both appealing and genuine. For example, this can include developing well-crafted professional profiles on platforms like LinkedIn, staying mindful of the digital footprints they leave behind, and communicating clearly and thoughtfully in all online interactions, from emails to social media posts.

Social media, in particular, serves as a central stage for this careful presentation and communication leading to effective online impression management. Rather than simply sharing random moments, many people use these platforms to carefully design how their lives are seen by others, emphasizing positive achievements, meaningful experiences, or relatable stories. Each update, photo, or comment acts like a piece of a larger narrative that people create about themselves. Whether it's showcasing career highlights, celebrating personal milestones, or sharing engaging content, both individuals and brands put significant effort into managing their online reputations to foster trust, build credibility, and connect with others.

Online Self-Presentation and Profile Management

Online self-presentation is about how people control the way they appear to others on the internet. Whether it's through social media accounts or personal profiles, individuals carefully decide what to share and how to share it, including the photos and other visuals they choose. It's essentially about managing the information they put out there to create the impression they want others to have. When people build their online profiles, they often spend time shaping a version of themselves that reflects how they want to be seen. This usually means highlighting their best qualities and being mindful about what details they reveal, leaving out anything that might not show them in the best light.

Psychological Effects of Digital Impression Management

At first, managing how people present themselves on the internet might seem straightforward or even enjoyable. However, it can have a much bigger impact on the mental health than what people realize. The pressure to always display an idealized, flawless version of the self can trigger feelings of anxiety and stress. Constantly trying to appear perfect or likable demands a lot of mental and emotional energy, which over time can lead to burnout and emotional fatigue. Instead of feeling self-assured, many people start to experience doubt about themselves and see their confidence decline. A major challenge in carefully crafting an online persona is the growing gap between that public image and who people truly are inside. When the online persona someone presents doesn't reflect their true feelings or beliefs, it can lead to an internal struggle known as cognitive dissonance. In these situations, individuals may feel conflicted—wanting to express themselves more genuinely but fearing criticism or social rejection. Over time, the pressure to uphold this false image can become mentally draining, resulting in emotional fatigue.

IMPRESSION MANAGEMENT IN ETHICAL LEADERSHIP

In any workplace or organization, leaders are not only responsible for making strategic decisions—they also influence how others view them. The way a leader presents themselves, whether to team members, peers, or external stakeholders, plays a critical role in shaping relationships and organizational culture. Because of this, leaders must be thoughtful and intentional in how they manage their public image. When approached ethically, managing one's image isn't about creating a false persona—it's about highlighting authentic qualities in a way that builds trust and encourages respect. Leaders who manage impressions with honesty and integrity can foster stronger connections, reinforce their credibility, and set a positive example for others to follow.

Ethical leaders understand that trying to appear competent or principled is not the same as actually being so. They recognize the importance of staying grounded in their values, ensuring that their outward behavior matches their internal beliefs. Authenticity, in this context, means being consistent, open, and sincere—not putting on a performance. Used with integrity, impression management can help leaders communicate confidence, competence, and a clear moral compass. These qualities are reassuring to those who follow them.

Conversely, when a leader prioritizes image over integrity—fabricating stories of success, or projecting an ethical stance they don't live up to—they undermine the very trust they seek to build. What may appear as strong leadership on the surface can quickly unravel once the truth comes to light, affecting morale, relationships, and the leader's reputation. Ultimately, ethical leaders don't focus on image for its own sake. They lead with purpose and transparency, knowing that lasting influence comes not from looking good, but from doing good. Staying true to one's values, showing respect for others, and choosing honesty over convenience—these are the real cornerstones of ethical and effective leadership.

IMPRESSION MANAGEMENT ACROSS DIVERSE GROUPS

Many individuals practice impression management, often without even realizing it. Whether they're meeting someone for the first time or trying to fit into a social environment, people naturally adapt how they present themselves. This might involve altering their tone, behavior, or body language based on the context, the expectations of a particular role, or the cultural norms at play. The underlying goal is typically to gain respect, create a favorable impression, or avoid being judged negatively.

Diversity and Impression Management

Impression management and diversity are often interrelated, as both individuals and organizations may actively manage their image to reflect a commitment to inclusivity and awareness of diversity. Sometimes, these efforts are deliberate and designed to create a positive public image, even if they don't accurately represent the organization's actual level of diversity. This superficial approach—commonly referred to as diversity washing—emphasizes outward displays of inclusivity while neglecting the underlying structural problems that persist behind the scenes. With growing public scrutiny on representation and equity in the workplace, organizations are under increasing pressure to demonstrate diversity. In response, some adopt impression strategies that focus more on image than impact. For example, they might highlight a few diverse hires in senior roles or emphasize diversity in branding, even when their internal practices don't support meaningful inclusion.

A common tactic is to match external diversity efforts with what is socially expected, not necessarily out of genuine commitment, but to avoid backlash or being seen as out of touch. While this can temporarily shield an organization from criticism, it risks long-term consequences, such as a loss of trust among employees, customers, and partners. When diversity becomes more about optics than action, true progress toward fairness and belonging is slowed. These performative efforts raise ethical questions, especially when they mislead others into believing the organization is more inclusive than it actually is. This not only undermines the integrity of the organization but also disrespects the very values of inclusion it claims to support.

FUTURE TRENDS IN IMAGE AND IMPRESSION MANAGEMENT

In the near future, managing visuals and shaping online presence will be increasingly influenced by advancements in AI and automation. These tools will enable instant image adjustments, the creation of realistic digital content, and deeper insights into how audiences respond to visuals. This shift will lead to more tailored marketing strategies, reduced costs, and greater emphasis on eco-friendly image processing. When it comes to online reputation, AI-powered platforms will become essential for monitoring social media interactions and public perception. As a result, both individuals and organizations will be better equipped to fine-tune their digital strategies and build more meaningful connections with their audiences.

Impact of Emerging Technologies on Impression Management

Advances in technology are changing the way individuals and organizations shape their image and present themselves online. Whether through social media platforms or virtual meetings, these tools provide new opportunities to influence how others see us. Artificial intelligence is becoming increasingly important in communication, helping to customize messages, personalize interactions, and oversee our digital presence more effectively. The ability to edit and save conversations means that what we share online can be more intentional and lasting. At the same time, technology is altering the social and emotional cues we rely on, affecting how relationships are built and maintained in virtual settings. AI-powered communication tools are now playing a bigger role in managing how we are perceived, often automating parts of our conversations. For example, smart email assistants that suggest or even send responses can make our communication appear smoother and more professional. Virtual environments give us even more control over how we present ourselves since messages can be revised, videos re-shot, and interactions don't always need to happen instantly. This flexibility allows people to carefully craft their online identity and keep it consistent over time.

Evolving Social Norms and Expectations

As cultures and communities evolve, so do the silent guidelines that influence how we're expected to behave. These changing social norms shape the way people choose to present themselves, especially in both public and professional settings. From clothing choices to speech patterns and even the way people share their thoughts, individuals often modify their behavior to align with the values of those around them. This adaptation can be intentional or happen without much thought, particularly when responding to expectations tied to gender or social roles. Adding on, in today's digital world, managing how people appear online has become just as important as how they present themselves in person. The online profiles and interactions of individuals can shape others' opinions, affecting relationships and opportunities. As societal values shift due to cultural changes and social movements, people may feel the need to adjust their self-presentation to stay relevant or accepted.

Changing paradigms in AI-driven Virtual Identities for Impression Management

AI-driven virtual identities are reshaping how individuals and organizations manage their image. With communication tasks increasingly handled by AI, perceptions are now shaped not just by people, but by intelligent systems. In contrast to conventional impression management that depends on deliberate self-presentation, AI leverages data to customize interactions and shape perceptions. Tools like chatbots and virtual influencers personalize messages and mimic human-like dialogue, playing a growing role in consumer engagement and brand building. However, this shift raises concerns about authenticity. Many question whether AI-generated communication feels genuine, especially as emotional understanding in AI remains limited. Interactions can sometimes seem robotic, affecting trust and connection. As reliance on AI grows, the distinction between human and automated messaging continues to blur, prompting a reevaluation of how impressions are formed in the digital age.

Impression Management: The Road Ahead

The growing role of AI in managing impressions creates new opportunities for research, such as understanding how people perceive and trust interactions mediated by AI versus those handled by humans, and how relationships develop in digital environments where emotional signals are limited and communication is often delayed. Different cultures and contexts influence how individuals adapt their impression strategies online. As societal expectations around inclusivity, professionalism, and authenticity change, people modify their online behaviors accordingly. At the same time, ethical challenges arise, including concerns about distinguishing genuine self-presentation from manipulation, protecting privacy and obtaining informed consent, and addressing potential biases embedded in AI systems. Furthermore, the use of AI to simulate emotional engagement may affect authentic human connection and raises important questions about responsibility and openness in AI-driven communications.

IMPLICATIONS OF THE STUDY

Theoretical Implications of the Study

This research emphasizes impression management as an essential social mechanism connected to identity and interpersonal communication. Building on concepts such as Goffman's dramaturgy and self-presentation theory, it illustrates how individuals both deliberately and unintentionally adjust their actions and shared information to align with social expectations and accomplish objectives in diverse contexts, including digital platforms and professional environments. The discussions made in the chapter emphasize that impression management is influenced by cultural, environmental, and technological factors, affecting perceptions of authenticity and ethics. It also reveals the psychological challenges—such as emotional strain—that arise when personal identity conflicts with the projected image. Additionally, the research explores how AI and digital tools are transforming impression management, creating new challenges for authentic self-expression and trust in today's social landscape.

Practical Implications of the Study

This study's practical implications span personal, professional, and digital spheres. Recognizing how people shape their identity to influence others underscores the need for self-awareness and authentic self-presentation while balancing social expectations. For professionals, effective impression management supports career growth by building trust and credibility. Organizations can leverage this understanding to foster ethical leadership and positive workplace culture instead of superficial image control. In the digital age, being mindful of impression management helps prevent psychological stress, ethical issues, and identity confusion, especially as AI and technology shape interactions. Overall, this insight helps individuals and organizations navigate social dynamics while maintaining integrity and well-being.

Social Implications of the Study

The discussions made in this chapter indicates that impression management plays a crucial role in how individuals portray themselves and engage with others across social, professional, and online settings. Through intentional or instinctive efforts to manage their image, people impact how they are perceived, build relationships, gain acceptance, and access career opportunities—all while adapting to cultural and situational norms. Although this process helps build connections and achieve goals, it can also cause psychological strain, identity conflicts, and ethical challenges when the presented image conflicts with one's true self. In rapidly changing digital and organizational settings, managing impressions is essential but can lead to stress and impact mental health. Additionally, impression management intersects with issues of diversity and authenticity, exposing the tension between outward appearances and inner realities. Overall, understanding impression management sheds light on how people balance self-presentation with genuine identity in today's complex social world.

SCOPE OF FURTHER STUDY

Future empirical studies on impression management should explore how both intentional and unintentional efforts to influence others' perceptions operate in social, workplace, and digital environments. Research is needed to understand the mental health impacts of ongoing impression management, including issues like anxiety, identity struggles, and internal conflicts, especially related to social media use. Greater attention should be given to how cultural, environmental, and organizational factors shape these behaviors, particularly in increasingly diverse and interconnected societies. Moreover, the role of advancing technologies—such as AI and automation—in reshaping online self-presentation warrants investigation, alongside the ethical concerns surrounding AI-generated virtual personas and their effect on genuine self-expression. Lastly, studying impression management in the context of ethical leadership and its effect on fostering or hindering diversity and inclusion efforts can provide important perspectives on how individuals and groups manage their identities amid rapid social and technological shifts.

CONCLUSIONS

Impression management is an essential social process in which individuals, often without realizing it, influence how they are perceived in personal, professional, and online contexts. By adapting their behavior and communication to align with social and cultural norms, people shape their identity, interact effectively within various environments, and work toward achieving their objectives. This study reveals that impression management is not always intentional but deeply tied to our need for acceptance and belonging. Environmental factors, organizational culture, and social norms play key roles in influencing self-presentation. While impression management aids social and career success, it can also cause stress, identity conflicts, and feelings of inauthenticity when there is a disconnect between one's true self and public image. Ethical challenges arise, especially for leaders and digital users, where the desire to appear flawless may compromise honesty. Advancements in digital technology and AI are changing how people manage impressions, creating new opportunities and concerns about authenticity. Understanding impression management requires balancing its advantages with attention to psychological well-being and ethical behavior. Ongoing research should focus on how evolving technologies and social norms impact these practices to promote genuine and responsible self-presentation.

REFERENCES

Al-Shatti, E., Ohana, M., Odou, P., & Zaitouni, M. (2022). Impression Management on Instagram and Unethical Behavior: The Role of Gender and Social Media Fatigue. *International Journal of Environmental Research and Public Health, 19*(16), 9808. DOI: 10.3390/ijerph19169808 PMID: 36011435

Blunden, H., & Brodsky, A. (2024). A Review of Virtual Impression Management Behaviors and Outcomes. *Journal of Management, 50*(6), 2197–2236. DOI: 10.1177/01492063231225160

Bolino, M., Long, D., & Turnley, W. (2016). Impression Management in Organizations: Critical Questions, Answers, and Areas for Future Research. *Annual Review of Organizational Psychology and Organizational Behavior, 3*(1), 377–406. DOI: 10.1146/annurev-orgpsych-041015-062337

Bolino, M. C., Kacmar, K. M., Turnley, W. H., & Gilstrap, J. B. (2008). A Multi-Level Review of Impression Management Motives and Behaviors. *Journal of Management, 34*(6), 1080–1109. DOI: 10.1177/0149206308324325

Bozeman, D. P., & Kacmar, K. M. (1997). A Cybernetic Model of Impression Management Processes in Organizations. *Organizational Behavior and Human Decision Processes, 69*(1), 9–30. DOI: 10.1006/obhd.1996.2669

Brouer, R. L., Gallagher, V. C., & Badawy, R. L. (2016). Ability to Manage Resources in the Impression Management Process: The Mediating Effects of Resources on Job Performance. *Journal of Business and Psychology, 31*(4), 515–531. DOI: 10.1007/s10869-015-9426-5

Curtis, S. R., Carre, J. R., Mueller, S. M., & Jones, D. N. (2023). Hiding your dark side: Anticipatory impression management of communal traits. *Current Psychology (New Brunswick, N.J.), 42*(22), 18720–18730. DOI: 10.1007/s12144-022-03039-5

Debus, M. E., Ingold, P. V., Gross, C., & Bolino, M. C. (2024). Reaching the Top? Profiles of Impression Management and Career Success. *Journal of Business and Psychology, 39*(6), 1283–1301. DOI: 10.1007/s10869-024-09954-7

Goffman, E. (1959). *The Presentation of Self in Everyday Life. Doubleday: Garden City, New York, 1959*. Doubleday.

Henderson, A. (2017). Impression Management. In *The International Encyclopedia of Organizational Communication* (pp. 1–6). Wiley., DOI: 10.1002/9781118955567.wbieoc104

Ji, X., Li, C., Law, R., & Liu, X. (2025). Profile image album management and users' online sharing behavior. *Tourism Management, 109*, 105159. DOI: 10.1016/j.tourman.2025.105159

Koslowsky, M., Pindek, S., & Reizer, A. (2022). Impression Management in Everyday Life. In *Theories in Social Psychology* (2nd ed., pp. 350–371). Wiley., DOI: 10.1002/9781394266616.ch14

Liu, Y., & Lei, K. (2025). Development and validity test of impression management efficacy scale based on self-presentation behavior of Chinese youth on social media. *Frontiers in Psychology, 16*, 1494083. Advance online publication. DOI: 10.3389/fpsyg.2025.1494083 PMID: 39950071

Park, H., Leroy, H., Dragoni, L., Simons, T., & Yun, S. (2024). Does Leaders' Impression Management Help or Hurt? It Depends on the Perspective of the Follower. *Journal of Leadership & Organizational Studies, 31*(4), 473–490. DOI: 10.1177/15480518241273322

Provis, C. (2023). Impression Management and Business Ethics. In *Encyclopedia of Business and Professional Ethics* (pp. 1127–1130). Springer International Publishing., DOI: 10.1007/978-3-030-22767-8_1212

Raghuram, S., Hill, N. S., Gibbs, J. L., & Maruping, L. M. (2019). Virtual Work: Bridging Research Clusters. *The Academy of Management Annals, 13*(1), 308–341. DOI: 10.5465/annals.2017.0020

Rosenfiled, P., Giacalone, R., & Riordan, C. A. (1994). Impression Management Theory and Diversity. *The American Behavioral Scientist, 37*(5), 601–604. DOI: 10.1177/0002764294037005002

Rui, J., & Stefanone, M. A. (2013). Strategic self-presentation online: A cross-cultural study. *Computers in Human Behavior, 29*(1), 110–118. DOI: 10.1016/j.chb.2012.07.022

Sun, Y., Fang, S., & Zhang, Z. (2021). Impression management strategies on enterprise social media platforms: An affordance perspective. *International Journal of Information Management, 60*, 102359. DOI: 10.1016/j.ijinfomgt.2021.102359

Switzer, J. S. (2008). Impression Formation in Computer-Mediated Communication and Making a Good (Virtual) Impression. In *Handbook of Research on Virtual Workplaces and the New Nature of Business Practices* (pp. 98–109). IGI Global. DOI: 10.4018/978-1-59904-893-2.ch008

Tuna, Ö., & Gül, İ. (2024). *The Role of Impression Management in the Impact of Ethical Leadership on Green Organizational Behavior.*, DOI: 10.4018/979-8-3693-5298-4.ch017

Wang, W., Zhou, K., Yu, Z., & Li, J. (2020). <p>The Cost of Impression Management to Life Satisfaction: Sense of Control and Loneliness as Mediators</p>. *Psychology Research and Behavior Management, 13*, 407–417. DOI: 10.2147/PRBM.S238344 PMID: 32440240

Yoo, E. (2022). Impression management of South Korean sports stars through image-based social media. *Sport in Society, 25*(9), 1734–1755. DOI: 10.1080/17430437.2021.1878146

Chapter 3
From Policy to Plate:
Impression Management, Food Security, and Culinary Image Formation in the Hospitality Industry

Shivansu Sachan
https://orcid.org/0000-0002-9893-8018
CSJM University, India

ABSTRACT

The hospitality industry is increasingly shaped by the complex interplay between food security governance, policy imperatives, and the strategic presentation of culinary experiences. This paper explores how hospitality stakeholders—hotels, resorts, and tourism establishments—engage in impression management to align with food security goals while enhancing their culinary image. By examining the transition "from policy to plate," the study analyzes how regulations related to sustainable sourcing, food safety, nutrition, and local procurement are translated into visible practices that influence guest perception and satisfaction. Drawing upon theories of symbolic interactionism and institutional isomorphism, the paper argues that food-related policies are not only operational frameworks but also tools for image-building and competitive positioning in the global hospitality market.

INTRODUCTION

The hospitality industry, a multifaceted global sector encompassing hotels, restaurants, tourism, and events, plays a pivotal role in economic development, cultural exchange, and social well-being. Its intricate operations are not merely about

DOI: 10.4018/979-8-3373-5519-1.ch003

providing accommodation and sustenance; they are deeply intertwined with complex dynamics of perception, policy, and practice. In an increasingly interconnected and discerning world, the success and sustainability of hospitality enterprises hinge not only on the quality of their core services but also on their ability to manage impressions, adhere to robust governance frameworks, and cultivate a compelling culinary image. This chapter delves into these critical, yet often disparate, dimensions, exploring their interconnections and collective impact on the contemporary hospitality landscape. The formation of a compelling culinary image has emerged as a powerful differentiator in the competitive hospitality market. Beyond mere sustenance, food in the hospitality context is an experience, a cultural expression, and a critical component of brand identity. The culinary image encompasses everything from the quality and provenance of ingredients to the creativity of menu design, the skill of the chefs, the presentation of dishes, and the overall dining ambiance. A strong culinary image can elevate a restaurant, hotel, or destination, attracting discerning clientele and generating positive word-of-mouth. This image, however, is not static; it is constantly shaped by consumer trends, media representation, and, increasingly, by the industry's demonstrated commitment to ethical and sustainable food practices.

IMPORTANCE OF THE HOSPITALITY INDUSTRY

The hospitality industry is a cornerstone of the global economy, contributing significantly to Gross Domestic Product (GDP) and employment worldwide. It is a dynamic and diverse sector, encompassing a wide array of businesses such as hotels, resorts, restaurants, cafes, bars, catering services, event management companies, and travel agencies. Beyond its direct economic contributions, the industry serves as a vital conduit for cultural exchange, fostering understanding and connection between people from different backgrounds. It facilitates tourism, which in turn stimulates local economies, supports traditional crafts, and preserves cultural heritage. The industry's reach extends beyond direct service provision, influencing a vast network of suppliers, from agricultural producers and food processors to linen manufacturers and technology providers. Moreover, the hospitality industry is a significant employer, offering a wide range of job opportunities across various skill levels. It provides livelihoods for millions globally, often serving as an entry point into the workforce for young people and those seeking flexible employment. The industry's growth and resilience are therefore critical for social stability and economic prosperity. However, its inherent characteristics, such as high customer interaction, perishable products (especially food), and reliance on global supply chains, expose it to unique challenges related to impression management, food security, and maintaining a consistent culinary image. The recent global health crises, for instance, starkly highlighted the vulnerabilities of the industry, underscoring the need for robust governance frameworks and adaptive strategies to ensure long-term sustainability and resilience.

LITERATURE REVIEW

The hospitality industry's expanding scope has prompted extensive scholarly inquiry into the interplay between perception, policy, and practice, particularly regarding impression management, food security governance, and culinary image formation. Impression Management (IM), rooted in Goffman's (1959) dramaturgical theory and the broader self-presentation framework, has been extensively studied in organizational behavior and service research (Leary & Kowalski, 1990; Bolino et al., 2016). Scholars emphasize that IM within hospitality extends beyond surface behavior to encompass emotional labor, authenticity, and brand consistency (Groth & Grandey, 2012; Kim & Baker, 2019). Frontline employees serve as key impression agents, shaping guest perceptions and reinforcing organizational image through affective displays and interactional competence. Parallelly, food security governance has evolved from a state-centric concern to a multi-actor framework emphasizing sustainability, resilience, and ethical responsibility (FAO, 2021; Ericksen, 2008). Research underscores the importance of hospitality institutions in supporting local food systems, reducing waste, and promoting equitable access to food (Hall & Gössling, 2017; Hede & Watne, 2013). Governance mechanisms such as Hazard Analysis and Critical Control Points (HACCP) and sustainable sourcing policies are central to operational credibility and consumer trust (Mensah & Julien, 2011; Gossling et al., 2016).Culinary image formation, meanwhile, has emerged as a distinct research stream linking gastronomy, marketing, and destination branding (Binkley, 2018; Cohen & Avieli, 2004). Scholars conceptualize culinary image as a composite of authenticity, innovation, sensory quality, and narrative identity that shapes consumer evaluations and destination appeal (Sims, 2009; Hjalager & Richards, 2002). The chef's philosophy, menu design, service aesthetics, and ambiance collectively form the symbolic capital of hospitality brands, aligning gastronomic experiences with cultural heritage and sustainability values. Studies in culinary tourism (Everett & Slocum, 2013; Ellis et al., 2018) reveal how food authenticity and ethical consumption increasingly drive travel motivations, positioning cuisine as both a market differentiator and a socio-environmental statement. Despite the maturity of these individual domains, gaps remain in understanding their synergistic interdependence. Existing research largely treats impression management, food governance, and culinary branding as discrete constructs, overlooking how governance-driven practices (e.g., sustainable sourcing or waste reduction) influence culinary imagery and stakeholder impressions (Freeman et al., 2010; Jones et al., 2021). The integrated approach proposed in this chapter responds to this lacuna by bridging these spheres into a cohesive model of responsible hospitality. It reflects a paradigm shift in hospitality studies—from transactional performance to transformational engagement—where ethical governance enhances organizational impression and culinary excellence. Such integration, as suggested by contemporary scholarship, represents the future of hospitality competitiveness grounded in authenticity, transparency, and sustainability (Bohdanowicz & Zientara, 2008; Gossling & Hall, 2019).

OBJECTIVES

While impression management, food security governance, and culinary image formation have each been extensively studied within their respective domains, there remains a significant research gap in understanding their synergistic interplay within the hospitality industry. Existing literature often treats these concepts in isolation, overlooking the complex ways in which they influence and reinforce one another. For instance, how do a hotel's food waste reduction policies (food security governance) impact its public perception (impression management) and, consequently, its culinary reputation (culinary image formation)? Conversely, how can a strong culinary image be leveraged to promote sustainable food practices and enhance a hospitality brand's overall impression?

This chapter aims to bridge this gap by providing a comprehensive and integrated analysis of these three critical dimensions. Specifically, the objectives of this chapter are to:

1. Examine the theoretical underpinnings and practical applications of impression management within the hospitality industry, highlighting its significance in shaping customer perceptions and organizational reputation.
2. Analyze the multifaceted aspects of food security governance in the hospitality sector, including regulatory compliance, sustainable sourcing, food waste management, and community engagement.
3. Investigate the key drivers and processes involved in culinary image formation, exploring how hospitality establishments cultivate and maintain a distinctive gastronomic identity.
4. Unpack the intricate interconnections and reciprocal relationships among impression management, food security governance, and culinary image formation, demonstrating how these elements collectively contribute to the success and sustainability of hospitality businesses.

5.Provide practical implications and strategic recommendations for hospitality practitioners and policymakers seeking to optimize their approaches to impression management, food security, and culinary branding.
6.Identify avenues for future research to further deepen our understanding of these complex and evolving dynamics.

IMPRESSION MANAGEMENT IN THE HOSPITALITY INDUSTRY

Defining Impression Management (IM)

Impression Management (IM) is a fundamental concept in social psychology and organizational behavior, referring to the conscious or unconscious efforts by individuals or organizations to control the impressions that others form of them (Binkley, 2018). It is a pervasive social phenomenon, integral to human interaction and organizational functioning. At its core, IM is about strategic self-presentation, where actors (individuals or entities) attempt to influence the perceptions of their audience (others) regarding their attributes, behaviors, or intentions. This influence is typically aimed at achieving specific goals, such as gaining social approval, enhancing status, securing resources, or maintaining a positive reputation (Bohdanowicz & Zientara, 2008). In the hospitality industry, both self-enhancement and ingratiation are common self-presentation strategies employed by frontline employees to enhance customer satisfaction and secure positive reviews or tips. Organizational self-presentation, on the other hand, often focuses on projecting an image of competence, social responsibility, and trustworthiness to attract investors, customers, and talented employees.

IM Strategies Employed by Hospitality Organizations and Employees

Impression management in the hospitality industry is a dynamic and multilayered process, enacted at both individual (employee) and organizational levels. These strategies are meticulously designed to shape perceptions, build trust, and ultimately enhance the guest experience and brand reputation. The effectiveness of these strategies often lies in their seamless integration into daily operations, making them appear natural and authentic rather than contrived.

Impact of IM on Customer Perception and Experience

The strategic deployment of impression management by hospitality organizations and their frontline employees profoundly influences customer perception and shapes the overall service experience. Customer perception is not merely a reflection of the tangible aspects of a service (e.g., a clean room, a well-cooked meal) but is heavily mediated by the intangible cues and signals conveyed through IM. A positive perception, cultivated through effective IM, can lead to enhanced customer satisfaction, loyalty, and positive word-of-mouth, all of which are critical for business success in the highly competitive hospitality landscape. One of the primary impacts of IM is on customer satisfaction. When employees successfully project an image of professionalism, attentiveness, and genuine care, customers are more likely to feel valued and respected. For instance, a hotel guest who is greeted warmly, whose requests are anticipated, and whose concerns are addressed promptly and empathetically, will likely report higher levels of satisfaction. This satisfaction stems not only from the resolution of a need but also from the positive emotional experience created by the employee's impression management efforts. Similarly, in a restaurant, a server who is knowledgeable about the menu, anticipates dining needs, and handles any issues with grace and efficiency contributes significantly to a positive dining experience, even if minor culinary imperfections exist. Beyond immediate satisfaction, effective IM contributes to customer loyalty and repeat business. When customers consistently have positive experiences shaped by well-managed impressions, they develop trust in the brand and are more likely to return. This trust is built on the perception of reliability, competence, and a genuine commitment to service excellence. A customer who feels consistently well-cared for and impressed by the service will not only become a repeat patron but may also develop an emotional attachment to the brand, making them less susceptible to competitive offerings. This long-term relationship building is a direct outcome of sustained positive impression management.

IM also plays a role in managing customer expectations. Through strategic communication and presentation, hospitality establishments can set realistic yet appealing expectations for their services. For example, a restaurant's elegant decor, sophisticated menu descriptions, and the refined demeanor of its staff all contribute to an impression of high-end dining, thereby setting expectations for a premium experience. When the actual service delivery aligns with or exceeds these carefully crafted expectations, customer perception is further enhanced. However, a mismatch between the projected image and the reality can lead to disappointment and negative perceptions, regardless of the objective quality of the service.

Challenges and Ethical Considerations in IM

While impression management is a vital tool for success in the hospitality industry, its implementation is not without challenges and significant ethical considerations. Navigating these complexities is crucial for organizations to maintain authenticity, build genuine trust, and avoid the pitfalls of superficiality or manipulation.

One of the primary challenges lies in maintaining authenticity and consistency. In a service-oriented industry, customers are increasingly discerning and can quickly detect insincerity. If the projected image, carefully crafted through IM strategies, does not align with the actual service experience or organizational values, it can lead to a perception of deception. This discrepancy can severely damage trust and reputation. For instance, a hotel that heavily promotes its eco-friendly image but fails to implement genuine sustainability practices may face backlash from environmentally conscious guests. Consistency is also challenging across multiple touchpoints and a diverse workforce. Ensuring that every employee, from the front desk to housekeeping, consistently embodies the desired brand image requires continuous training, clear communication, and a strong organizational culture.

FOOD SECURITY GOVERNANCE IN THE HOSPITALITY INDUSTRY

Defining Food Security and its Dimensions (Availability, Access, Utilization, Stability)

Food security is a multifaceted concept that has evolved significantly over time, moving beyond a narrow focus on food supply to encompass a broader understanding of individuals' ability to obtain and utilize food. The most widely accepted definition, provided by the Food and Agriculture Organization (FAO) of the United Nations, states that "Food security exists when all people, at all times, have physical, social and economic access to sufficient, safe and nutritious food that meets their dietary needs and food preferences for an active and healthy life" (Everett & Slocum, 2013). This comprehensive definition highlights four key dimensions that are essential for achieving and maintaining food security:

Food Availability: This dimension refers to the physical presence of food, whether from domestic production, imports, or food aid. It considers the quantity and quality of food supplies at various levels, from global and national to local markets. For the hospitality industry, food availability is crucial as it dictates the range and consistency of ingredients that can be sourced for culinary operations. Factors influencing availability include agricultural production, climate conditions, trade policies, and food processing and storage infrastructure.

Role of Governance in Food Security

Governance plays a pivotal role in shaping the landscape of food security, providing the frameworks, institutions, and processes through which decisions are made and implemented across the food system. It moves beyond mere policy-making to encompass the complex interplay of state, market, and civil society actors in addressing food security challenges. Effective food security governance is characterized by its ability to foster coordination, ensure accountability, promote participation, and adapt to changing circumstances (Food and Agriculture Organization of the United Nations (FAO), 2021).

For example, a hotel chain's decision to source ingredients from local, sustainable farms not only supports local economies (contributing to food access and stability for producers) but also reduces its carbon footprint (addressing climate change impacts on food availability). Similarly, implementing robust food waste reduction programs within restaurants and catering operations directly contributes to the utilization dimension of food security by minimizing edible food loss. These actions, while driven by business imperatives, are also acts of responsible governance within the broader food system.

Food Security Governance Frameworks and Policies in Hospitality

The hospitality industry operates within a dense web of food security governance frameworks and policies, ranging from international guidelines to local ordinances. These frameworks are designed to ensure food safety, promote public health, and increasingly, to encourage sustainable and ethical practices across the food supply chain. Compliance with these regulations is non-negotiable, forming the bedrock of responsible food operations within hotels, restaurants, and catering services.

Sustainable Sourcing and Supply Chain Management

Beyond basic regulatory compliance, a critical aspect of modern food security governance in the hospitality industry involves sustainable sourcing and robust supply chain management. This goes beyond simply ensuring food safety to encompass environmental, social, and economic considerations throughout the entire journey of food, from farm to plate. Sustainable sourcing aims to minimize negative impacts while maximizing positive contributions to food security and broader sustainability goals (Goffman, 1959).

Key elements of sustainable sourcing and supply chain management in hospitality include:

Local and Seasonal Sourcing: Prioritizing the procurement of ingredients from local farmers and producers, especially those that are in season, offers multiple benefits. It reduces the carbon footprint associated with long-distance transportation, supports local economies and livelihoods, and often ensures fresher, higher-quality produce. By strengthening local food systems, hospitality businesses contribute to the food availability and stability dimensions of food security within their immediate communities. This also allows for greater transparency and traceability of ingredients, enhancing food safety and quality control. For example, a restaurant might proudly feature a "farm-to-table" menu, highlighting the specific local farms from which their ingredients are sourced, thereby building trust and appealing to environmentally conscious consumers.

Ethical Sourcing and Fair Trade: Sustainable sourcing extends to ensuring that food products are produced under ethical labor conditions and that producers receive fair compensation. This is particularly relevant for commodities sourced from developing countries, such as coffee, tea, chocolate, and certain seafood. Adhering to fair trade principles or certifications helps to address social inequities within the food system, contributing to the economic access dimension of food security for marginalized communities. Hospitality companies might partner with certified fair trade suppliers or conduct due diligence to ensure their supply chains are free from exploitative labor practices.

Environmentally Responsible Production: This involves sourcing from suppliers who employ environmentally sound agricultural and fishing practices. This includes minimizing pesticide use, conserving water, promoting biodiversity, avoiding deforestation, and preventing overfishing. Certifications such as organic, MSC (Marine Stewardship Council) for sustainable seafood, or Rainforest Alliance can guide sourcing decisions. By supporting such practices, the hospitality industry contributes to the long-term sustainability of food production systems, which is vital for future food availability and stability.

Waste Reduction in the Supply Chain: While food waste within the hospitality establishment is a major concern (discussed in the next section), sustainable supply chain management also focuses on reducing waste upstream. This involves working with suppliers to minimize packaging, optimize delivery schedules to reduce spoilage, and explore opportunities for utilizing "ugly" or imperfect produce that might otherwise be discarded. Collaborative efforts across the supply chain can significantly reduce food loss and improve resource efficiency.

CULINARY IMAGE FORMATION IN THE HOSPITALITY INDUSTRY

Defining Culinary Image and its Components (e.g., authenticity, innovation, quality)

The culinary image of a hospitality establishment is a complex, multi-dimensional construct that extends far beyond the mere act of serving food. It represents the collective perception and reputation of a restaurant, hotel, or destination's food and beverage offerings, encompassing the entire gastronomic experience. This image is not solely about taste; it is a holistic impression shaped by a myriad of tangible and intangible elements that contribute to a diner's overall satisfaction and memory of the experience. A strong culinary image is a powerful asset, driving customer choice, fostering loyalty, and contributing significantly to brand equity.

Key components that contribute to the formation of a compelling culinary image include:

Quality: This is arguably the most fundamental component. Quality in a culinary context refers to the excellence of ingredients, the precision of preparation, and the consistency of execution. It encompasses the freshness, provenance, and inherent characteristics of raw materials, as well as the skill and care applied in transforming them into dishes. High-quality food is the bedrock upon which a positive culinary image is built. This includes not only the taste but also the texture, aroma, and visual appeal of the dishes.

Authenticity: In an increasingly globalized world, authenticity has become a highly valued aspect of culinary experiences. It refers to the perceived genuineness and fidelity of a dish or cuisine to its cultural or regional origins. This can manifest in the use of traditional recipes, cooking methods, and ingredients, as well as the cultural narrative surrounding the food. For example, an Italian restaurant might emphasize its use of imported San Marzano tomatoes and hand-made pasta to convey authenticity. Authenticity can also relate to the transparency of sourcing and preparation, where customers perceive the food as being true to its natural state or origin.

Value Perception: This component relates to the customer's assessment of the benefits received versus the cost incurred. Value is not just about price; it encompasses the entire experience, including food quality, service, ambiance, and the overall emotional return on investment. A strong culinary image often implies a high perceived value, even if prices are premium, because customers feel they are receiving an exceptional and worthwhile experience.

Factors Influencing Culinary Image Formation

The culinary image of a hospitality establishment is not formed in a vacuum; it is the result of a complex interplay of various internal and external factors. These factors, when strategically managed, contribute to a cohesive and compelling gastronomic identity that resonates with consumers. Understanding these influences is crucial for businesses aiming to cultivate a strong and positive culinary reputation.

Menu Design and Food Presentation

Menu design and food presentation are foundational elements in shaping a restaurant or hotel's culinary image. They are often the first tangible points of interaction a diner has with the food offering, setting expectations and communicating the establishment's culinary philosophy. These elements go beyond mere aesthetics; they are strategic tools for conveying quality, creativity, and authenticity.

Chef's Reputation and Culinary Philosophy

The chef, particularly the executive chef or head chef, is often the artistic visionary and driving force behind a hospitality establishment's culinary identity. Their reputation and underlying culinary philosophy profoundly influence the formation and perception of the culinary image. In many cases, the chef becomes synonymous with the restaurant or hotel, drawing diners based on their personal brand and gastronomic approach.

Chef's Reputation: A chef's reputation is built on a combination of factors, including their culinary skill, experience, awards and accolades (e.g., Michelin stars, James Beard Awards), media presence, and critical reviews. A highly acclaimed chef brings immediate credibility and prestige to an establishment, elevating its culinary standing. Diners, especially in the fine dining segment, are often drawn to restaurants specifically to experience the creations of a renowned chef. This phenomenon highlights the personal branding aspect of culinary image formation, where the chef's individual identity becomes intertwined with the establishment's appeal.

Restaurant Ambiance and Service Quality

Beyond the food itself, the physical ambiance of a restaurant and the quality of its service are integral to the formation of its culinary image. These elements create the context in which the food is experienced, profoundly influencing a diner's perception of the meal and the overall establishment. A harmonious blend of captivating ambiance and impeccable service can elevate even simple dishes, while their absence can detract from the most exquisite cuisine.

Restaurant Ambiance: Ambiance refers to the overall atmosphere and character of a dining space, shaped by its design, decor, lighting, music, and even scent. It sets the mood and communicates the restaurant's identity and target market. Different types of ambiance contribute to distinct culinary images:

Marketing and Branding Strategies (e.g., food photography, social media)

In the contemporary hospitality landscape, effective marketing and branding strategies are indispensable for shaping and disseminating a compelling culinary image. In an increasingly digital and visually driven world, how a restaurant or hotel communicates its gastronomic identity to the public is almost as important as the food itself. These strategies leverage various channels to create desire, build anticipation, and reinforce the desired perception of culinary excellence.

Food Photography and Videography: Visual content is paramount in culinary marketing. High-quality food photography and videography are crucial for showcasing dishes in an appetizing and appealing manner. This involves:

Brand Storytelling: Beyond individual dishes, a compelling brand story can differentiate an establishment and resonate with diners. This narrative might focus on the restaurant's history, the chef's journey, the inspiration behind the cuisine, or its commitment to specific values (e.g., sustainability, community). A well-crafted story creates an emotional connection and adds depth to the culinary image.

Customer Reviews and Word-of-Mouth

In the digital age, customer reviews and word-of-mouth (WOM) have become arguably the most powerful forces in shaping a hospitality establishment's culinary image. Unlike traditional marketing, which is controlled by the business, reviews and WOM are generated by consumers themselves, lending them an unparalleled level of credibility and influence. The collective voice of diners, amplified by online platforms, can make or break a culinary reputation.

Online Customer Reviews: Platforms such as Yelp, TripAdvisor, Google Reviews, OpenTable, and specialized food blogs serve as public forums where diners share their experiences, rate establishments, and provide detailed feedback on food quality, service, ambiance, and value. These reviews are a primary source of information for potential customers researching dining options. Key aspects of their influence include:

THE ROLE OF CULINARY TOURISM AND DESTINATION IMAGE

Culinary tourism, also known as gastronomic tourism or food tourism, has emerged as a significant and rapidly growing segment of the tourism industry. It refers to travel for the purpose of experiencing unique and memorable food and drink. This phenomenon plays a crucial role in the formation of a destination's overall image, with the culinary offerings of a region or city becoming a primary draw for visitors. For the hospitality industry, understanding this symbiotic relationship is key to leveraging culinary assets for broader economic and reputational gains.

Culinary Tourism as a Motivator for Travel: Food and drink are no longer just ancillary components of a trip; for many travelers, they are the central motivation. Tourists seek authentic culinary experiences, from street food stalls and local markets to Michelin-starred restaurants and cooking classes. This desire to explore local flavors, traditions, and food cultures drives travel decisions and influences destination choice. A destination renowned for its distinctive cuisine or vibrant food scene can attract a specific demographic of travelers, thereby boosting tourism revenue and supporting local food producers and hospitality businesses.

Culinary Image as a Component of Destination Image: The culinary image of a region or city directly contributes to its broader destination image. Destination image is the sum of beliefs, ideas, and impressions that a person has of a place. When a destination is perceived as having a rich, diverse, and high-quality culinary offering, it enhances its attractiveness and competitiveness in the global tourism market. For example, cities like Paris, Rome, or Tokyo are synonymous with world-class cuisine, and their culinary reputation is a significant part of their appeal to tourists. Similarly, regions known for specific food products (e.g., Napa Valley for wine, Bologna for pasta) leverage these culinary assets to define their identity and attract visitors.

Interconnections: Policy, Impression Management, Food Security, and Culinary Image

The preceding chapters have individually explored impression management, food security governance, and culinary image formation within the hospitality industry. While each concept holds significant importance on its own, their true impact and strategic relevance become apparent when examining their intricate interconnections. These three dimensions are not isolated silos but rather form a dynamic ecosystem where policies, perceptions, and practices mutually influence and reinforce one another. This section will delve into these synergistic relationships, illustrating how a holistic approach to their management can drive sustainable success and competitive advantage in the hospitality sector.

How Food Security Policies Influence Impression Management and Culinary Image

Food security policies, whether enacted by governments or adopted voluntarily by organizations as part of their governance framework, have a profound and often indirect influence on both impression management and culinary image formation within the hospitality industry. These policies, designed to ensure the availability, access, utilization, and stability of food, shape operational practices that, in turn, become visible or communicable aspects of a hospitality brand's identity.

The Role of Impression Management in Communicating Food Security Efforts and Enhancing Culinary Image

Impression management serves as a crucial bridge between a hospitality establishment's genuine food security efforts and the perceptions formed by its various stakeholders, particularly customers. It is through strategic communication and presentation that the often-complex and behind-the-scenes work of food security governance is translated into a compelling narrative that enhances both the overall brand impression and the specific culinary image. Without effective impression management, even the most robust food security policies might go unnoticed or unappreciated by the target audience. In essence, impression management transforms internal food security policies and practices into external perceptions. By strategically communicating their commitment to food safety, sustainable sourcing, and waste reduction, hospitality businesses can cultivate an image of responsibility, integrity, and culinary excellence. This proactive communication not only builds trust and attracts discerning customers but also reinforces the authenticity and appeal of their gastronomic offerings, demonstrating that good governance can indeed lead to good impressions and a superior culinary image.

Culinary Image as a Driver for Sustainable Food Practices and Improved Food Security

The relationship between culinary image and food security is not unidirectional; a strong and positive culinary image can, in turn, become a powerful driver for the adoption of sustainable food practices and contribute significantly to improved food security outcomes. When culinary excellence is intrinsically linked to ethical sourcing, waste reduction, and community engagement, it creates a virtuous cycle where gastronomic appeal reinforces responsible practices, and responsible practices enhance gastronomic appeal. This symbiotic relationship positions the hospitality industry as a key influencer in shaping a more sustainable and food-secure future.

Firstly, a culinary image built on authenticity and provenance can directly encourage sustainable sourcing. When a restaurant or hotel prides itself on using local, seasonal, or ethically sourced ingredients, this commitment becomes a core part of its culinary identity. Diners are increasingly interested in knowing where their food comes from and how it was produced. By highlighting these aspects on menus, through chef narratives, and in marketing materials, establishments educate consumers and create demand for sustainably produced food. This increased demand provides an economic incentive for farmers and producers to adopt more sustainable agricultural practices, thereby contributing to the long-term availability and stability of food supplies. For example, a restaurant celebrated for its "ocean-friendly" seafood menu, featuring only sustainably caught species, not only enhances its culinary image but also actively supports responsible fishing practices that contribute to marine food security.

Secondly, a culinary image that emphasizes innovation and creativity in waste reduction can transform food waste from a problem into an opportunity. Chefs who are celebrated for their "nose-to-tail" or "root-to-stem" cooking philosophies, or for their ability to create exquisite dishes from ingredients that might otherwise be discarded, elevate the concept of waste reduction to an art form. This innovative approach to food waste not only minimizes environmental impact but also showcases culinary ingenuity, enhancing the establishment's reputation for creativity and resourcefulness. When diners see delicious and aesthetically pleasing dishes created from what they might perceive as scraps, it shifts their perception of food waste and encourages more mindful consumption. This contributes to the utilization dimension of food security by maximizing the value of every ingredient.

Thirdly, a culinary image that is perceived as socially responsible and community-oriented can drive initiatives that directly address food access and utilization. Restaurants and hotels that are known for their community engagement, such as donating surplus food to food banks, supporting local food education programs, or providing culinary training to disadvantaged individuals, build a strong ethical culinary image. This image attracts socially conscious diners and employees who are drawn to businesses that make a positive societal impact. The financial success generated by this positive image can then be reinvested into further community initiatives, creating a sustainable model for addressing local food insecurity. For instance, a popular bakery known for its delicious artisanal breads might also gain renown for its daily donations of unsold bread to local shelters, reinforcing its culinary appeal with a strong sense of social purpose.

Fourthly, the influence of celebrity chefs and culinary media can significantly amplify the message of sustainable food practices. When influential chefs, who are central to culinary image formation, champion causes like sustainable seafood, plant-based diets, or food waste reduction, their advocacy can inspire widespread adoption of these practices across the industry and among consumers. Culinary shows, food magazines, and social media platforms can highlight establishments that excel in both culinary artistry and sustainable practices, making these practices aspirational and desirable. This media attention helps to normalize and popularize sustainable food choices, contributing to a broader cultural shift towards more food-secure behaviors.

Finally, a strong culinary image can foster customer loyalty and advocacy for sustainable food systems. When diners have consistently positive experiences with establishments that integrate sustainable practices, they become advocates for those practices. They might seek out similar establishments, encourage friends and family to support them, and even demand more sustainable options from other food providers. This consumer-driven demand creates market pressure for the entire hospitality industry to adopt more responsible food practices, ultimately contributing to a more resilient and equitable food system.

CASE STUDIES/EXAMPLES ILLUSTRATING INTERCONNECTIONS

To further illustrate the intricate interconnections among impression management, food security governance, and culinary image formation, this section presents several hypothetical yet representative case studies from the hospitality industry. These examples demonstrate how strategic decisions and operational practices in one area can ripple through and impact the others, highlighting the need for a holistic and integrated approach.

Case Study 1: The Luxury Hotel Chain and Sustainable Seafood

Scenario: A global luxury hotel chain, "Grandeur Resorts," decides to implement a stringent sustainable seafood policy across all its properties. This policy dictates that only seafood certified by organizations like the Marine Stewardship Council (MSC) or Aquaculture Stewardship Council (ASC) can be purchased and served. This is a direct manifestation of their food security governance commitment, aiming to combat overfishing and support healthy marine ecosystems for long-term food availability.

Impact on Culinary Image: The policy immediately influences the culinary offerings. Chefs at Grandeur Resorts are challenged to innovate with a more limited, but sustainably sourced, selection of seafood. They begin to highlight the origin and sustainability certifications of their seafood on menus, in-room dining guides, and even through QR codes that link to information about the fishing practices. This commitment to responsible sourcing becomes a unique selling proposition, enhancing the hotel chain's culinary image as one that values both exquisite taste and environmental stewardship. Diners, particularly those who are environmentally conscious, perceive the food as not only delicious but also ethically superior, adding a layer of moral appeal to the gastronomic experience.

Interconnection: Here, a policy decision rooted in food security governance directly shapes the culinary image by influencing ingredient selection and menu presentation. This enhanced culinary image, in turn, provides a strong narrative for impression management, allowing the hotel to project an image of responsibility and attract a values-aligned customer base. The positive impression then reinforces the business case for maintaining and even expanding the sustainable sourcing policy.

Case Study 2: The Urban Bistro and Food Waste Reduction

Scenario: "The Green Plate," a popular urban bistro, implements a comprehensive food waste reduction program. This involves meticulous inventory management, creative "nose-to-tail" and "root-to-stem" cooking techniques, composting all organic waste, and donating edible surplus food to a local food bank. These actions are driven by a commitment to food security governance, aiming to minimize environmental impact and contribute to local food access.

Impact on Culinary Image: The bistro's chefs embrace the challenge of waste reduction as an opportunity for culinary innovation. They introduce a rotating "Zero-Waste Special" on their menu, featuring dishes crafted from ingredients that might otherwise be discarded (e.g., vegetable trimmings transformed into flavorful broths, fruit peels into infusions). This approach positions The Green Plate as a highly creative and resourceful culinary destination, enhancing its culinary image. Diners are intrigued by the innovative dishes and appreciate the bistro's commitment to sustainability, viewing the food as both delicious and conscientiously prepared. The narrative around their food becomes one of ingenuity and responsibility.

Impact on Impression Management: The Green Plate actively promotes its food waste reduction efforts on its social media channels, website, and through in-restaurant signage. They share statistics on the amount of food diverted from landfills and the number of meals donated to the food bank. This transparent communication is a key impression management strategy, cultivating an image of environmental leadership and community engagement. The bistro gains a reputation as a responsible and ethical business, attracting a loyal customer base that values sustainability. Local media often feature The Green Plate in articles about sustainable businesses, further amplifying its positive impression. The impression conveyed is one of genuine care for the environment and the community, which resonates deeply with modern consumers.

Interconnection: In this case, a food security governance initiative (waste reduction) directly sparks culinary innovation, which in turn enhances the bistro's culinary image. This unique and responsible culinary image then becomes a powerful tool for impression management, attracting customers and positive media attention, thereby reinforcing the bistro's commitment to sustainable practices.

Case Study 3: The Family Restaurant and Allergen Management

Scenario: "Family Feast," a large, popular family restaurant, invests heavily in robust food security governance around allergen management. This includes comprehensive staff training on allergen protocols, dedicated preparation areas, clear menu labeling for common allergens, and a system for communicating with guests about their dietary needs. This goes beyond basic compliance to ensure the safety and well-being of all diners.

Impact on Culinary Image: While not directly related to taste, the restaurant's meticulous allergen management significantly enhances its culinary image for a specific and growing segment of the population: those with food allergies or sensitivities. Family Feast becomes known as a safe and trustworthy dining option for families where members have dietary restrictions. This reputation for safety and inclusivity adds a crucial dimension to its culinary appeal, making it a preferred choice over competitors who may not offer the same level of assurance. The food is perceived as not just tasty, but also safe and accessible to a wider audience.

Impact on Impression Management: Family Feast actively communicates its allergen management protocols on its website, through staff interactions, and in its marketing materials. They highlight their commitment to guest safety and comfort, which is a powerful impression management strategy. Parents, in particular, are highly appreciative of the peace of mind offered by the restaurant's thorough approach, leading to strong positive word-of-mouth and glowing online reviews. The restaurant projects an image of care, responsibility, and attentiveness to customer needs, building deep trust and loyalty. This impression extends to the entire dining experience, making it a go-to for many families.

Interconnection: Here, a proactive food security governance measure (allergen management) directly improves the culinary image by making the food accessible and safe for a vulnerable group. This enhanced culinary image then serves as a powerful basis for impression management, fostering trust and loyalty among a key demographic, which in turn reinforces the restaurant's commitment to comprehensive food safety.

DISCUSSION AND FUTURE DIRECTIONS

Synthesis of Findings

This chapter has systematically explored the intricate relationships among impression management, food security governance, and culinary image formation within the dynamic context of the hospitality industry. Our synthesis reveals that these three seemingly distinct domains are, in fact, deeply interconnected and mutually influential, forming a complex ecosystem that shapes the success, sustainability, and societal impact of hospitality businesses. The key findings can be summarized as follows:

Firstly, impression management is a pervasive and strategic imperative for hospitality organizations and their employees. Rooted in theories like Goffman's dramaturgical perspective and self-presentation, IM extends beyond superficial aesthetics to encompass every touchpoint of the customer journey. Frontline employees engage in emotional labor and various self-presentation tactics to create positive service encounters, while organizations employ branding, CSR initiatives, and crisis communication to cultivate a desired corporate image. Effective IM directly influences customer perception, satisfaction, loyalty, and positive word-of-mouth, underscoring its critical role in competitive differentiation and brand building. However, the pursuit of favorable impressions must be balanced with authenticity and ethical considerations to avoid perceptions of deception and to mitigate employee burnout.

Secondly, food security governance is a fundamental and evolving responsibility for the hospitality sector. Moving beyond mere regulatory compliance (e.g., HACCP, local health codes), robust food security governance encompasses sustainable sourcing, comprehensive food waste reduction and management, and proactive community engagement. The industry's role in addressing global and local food security challenges, such as climate change impacts, supply chain vulnerabilities, and food access disparities, is increasingly recognized. Implementing strong food security governance not only ensures public health and legal compliance but also drives operational efficiencies through waste reduction and enhanced supply chain resilience. This commitment to responsible food practices is no longer a niche concern but a strategic imperative that contributes to both financial viability and societal well-being.

Thirdly, culinary image formation is a holistic process that extends beyond the taste of food to encompass the entire gastronomic experience. It is shaped by a multitude of factors, including meticulous menu design and food presentation, the reputation and philosophy of the chef, the ambiance of the dining environment, and the quality of service. Furthermore, strategic marketing and branding, particularly through high-quality food photography and social media engagement, play a crucial role in disseminating and reinforcing the desired culinary perception. Critically, customer reviews and word-of-mouth have emerged as powerful, credible forces in shaping and validating a culinary image, highlighting the importance of consistent excellence and responsive reputation management. The rise of culinary tourism further underscores the significance of a strong culinary image in contributing to a destination's overall appeal and economic vitality.

Finally, and most importantly, our analysis reveals the profound interconnections and synergistic relationships among these three concepts. Food security policies, such as those promoting sustainable sourcing or waste reduction, directly influence the operational practices that become integral to an establishment's culinary image. For instance, a commitment to local sourcing (food security governance) can enhance the authenticity and freshness of dishes, thereby elevating the culinary image. This enhanced culinary image, in turn, provides compelling narratives for impression management, allowing businesses to project an image of responsibility, quality, and innovation. Conversely, strategic impression management is essential for effectively communicating food security efforts to stakeholders, translating internal policies into external perceptions of trustworthiness and ethical conduct. Moreover, a strong culinary image can itself become a powerful driver for sustainable food practices, as consumer demand for ethically sourced and responsibly prepared food encourages the industry to adopt more food-secure behaviors. The case studies presented illustrate these dynamic feedback loops, demonstrating that a holistic approach to managing these dimensions leads to superior outcomes in terms of reputation, customer loyalty, and sustainable business growth.

Theoretical and Practical Implications

The integrated analysis of impression management, food security governance, and culinary image formation in the hospitality industry yields significant theoretical and practical implications for academics, industry practitioners, and policymakers.

Theoretical Implications

This chapter contributes to existing academic literature by providing a novel, integrated framework that bridges traditionally separate domains. By demonstrating the synergistic relationships among impression management, food security governance, and culinary image, it offers a more holistic understanding of how hospitality businesses operate and succeed in a complex environment. Specifically:

Enriching Impression Management Theory: We extend impression management theory by illustrating how organizational practices related to food security (e.g., sustainable sourcing, waste reduction) serve as powerful, authentic signals for impression formation, moving beyond purely communicative or symbolic gestures. This suggests that genuine commitment to ethical and sustainable practices can be a more robust basis for long-term impression management than superficial tactics. Future research could explore the perceived authenticity of IM strategies rooted in operational sustainability versus purely marketing-driven approaches.

Expanding Food Security Governance Research: This chapter highlights the critical, yet often overlooked, role of the private sector, particularly the hospitality industry, in food security governance. It moves beyond state-centric views to emphasize the agency of businesses in shaping food systems through their procurement, operational, and communication strategies. It also underscores how business-driven food security initiatives can yield reputational and financial benefits, providing a strong incentive for greater private sector engagement. This opens avenues for research into the effectiveness of different governance models within the industry and their measurable impact on food security indicators.

Limitations of Current Research

While this chapter provides a comprehensive and integrated analysis of impression management, food security governance, and culinary image formation in the hospitality industry, it is important to acknowledge certain limitations in the current body of research and, by extension, in the scope of this chapter. Recognizing these limitations is crucial for guiding future research efforts and for a more nuanced understanding of the complex dynamics at play.

Firstly, much of the existing research, particularly in impression management and culinary image formation, tends to be qualitative or case-study based, offering rich insights into specific contexts but sometimes lacking the generalizability that quantitative studies can provide. While valuable for exploring complex social phenomena, a greater emphasis on large-scale empirical studies, potentially employing advanced statistical methods, could offer more robust evidence of the causal relationships and interdependencies proposed in this chapter. For instance, while we argue that sustainable sourcing enhances culinary image, the precise magnitude and conditions under which this occurs could benefit from quantitative validation across diverse hospitality settings.

Secondly, there is a relative paucity of longitudinal studies that track the long-term impacts of food security governance initiatives on impression management and culinary image. Reputational shifts and changes in consumer perception often unfold over extended periods. Cross-sectional studies, while providing snapshots, may not fully capture the dynamic and evolving nature of these relationships. Longitudinal research could provide deeper insights into the sustainability of positive impressions and the enduring effects of responsible food practices.

Thirdly, the research often focuses on established markets and larger hospitality entities, potentially overlooking the unique challenges and opportunities faced by small and medium-sized enterprises (SMEs) or those operating in developing economies. SMEs, which constitute a significant portion of the hospitality industry, may have different resource constraints, regulatory environments, and consumer bases, which could influence their approach to impression management, food security, and culinary branding. Future research should strive for greater geographical and organizational diversity to ensure the applicability of findings across the entire spectrum of the industry.

Fourthly, while this chapter highlights the importance of consumer perception, there is a need for more nuanced research into the specific psychological mechanisms through which food security practices translate into positive culinary images and impressions. For example, how do different communication strategies regarding sustainable sourcing impact consumer trust and willingness to pay a premium? What are the cognitive and emotional processes involved when a consumer perceives a restaurant as "ethical" or "responsible" based on its food practices? Understanding these underlying mechanisms could lead to more effective communication and marketing strategies.

Fifthly, the role of technology in mediating these interconnections warrants further in-depth investigation. While we touched upon social media and online reviews, the rapid advancements in areas like blockchain for supply chain transparency, AI for waste management, and personalized digital marketing offer new avenues for impression management, food security governance, and culinary image formation. Research could explore the effectiveness and ethical implications of these emerging technologies in shaping consumer perceptions and driving sustainable practices. Finally, the chapter, while broad in its scope, cannot delve into the granular details of every sub-sector within the hospitality industry (e.g., cruise lines, institutional catering, fast food). Each sub-sector may have unique operational realities and stakeholder dynamics that influence the interplay of these concepts. Future research could focus on specific sub-sectors to provide more tailored insights and recommendations. These limitations do not diminish the value of the integrated framework presented but rather serve as a roadmap for future scholarly inquiry, encouraging researchers to address these gaps and contribute to a more comprehensive and empirically robust understanding of the complex relationship between policy, perception, and plate in the hospitality industry.

CONCLUSION

This chapter has undertaken a comprehensive exploration of the intricate and often overlooked interconnections among impression management, food security governance, and culinary image formation within the dynamic landscape of the hospitality industry. Our central argument posits that these three domains, while distinct in their theoretical underpinnings and practical applications, are in fact deeply synergistic, collectively shaping the success, sustainability, and societal impact of hospitality enterprises. The journey "from policy to plate" is thus revealed as a complex interplay where strategic decisions and operational practices in one area profoundly influence the others.We established that impression management is a fundamental and pervasive aspect of hospitality operations, enacted by both individuals and organizations to strategically shape perceptions among diverse stakeholders. Its effectiveness directly correlates with customer satisfaction, loyalty, and brand reputation, underscoring its role as a critical determinant of competitive advantage. However, we emphasized the imperative for authenticity and ethical conduct to ensure long-term trust and avoid the pitfalls of superficiality.

Our analysis of food security governance highlighted its evolution beyond mere regulatory compliance to encompass a holistic commitment to sustainable sourcing, rigorous food waste reduction, and meaningful community engagement. The hospitality industry, as a significant player in the global food system, bears a substantial responsibility in addressing challenges related to food availability, access, utilization, and stability. We demonstrated that robust food security governance not only ensures public health and legal adherence but also yields tangible operational efficiencies and enhances organizational resilience.The core contribution of this chapter lies in unraveling the profound interconnections among these three concepts. We illustrated how food security policies, such as those promoting sustainable sourcing or waste reduction, directly inform and enhance the culinary offering, thereby elevating the culinary image. This enhanced culinary image, in turn, provides compelling narratives for strategic impression management, allowing businesses to project an image of responsibility, quality, and innovation. Conversely, effective impression management is crucial for transparently communicating food security efforts, translating internal policies into external perceptions of trustworthiness and ethical conduct. Moreover, a strong culinary image can itself become a powerful driver for sustainable food practices, as consumer demand for ethically sourced and responsibly prepared food encourages the industry to adopt more food-secure behaviors. The case studies presented provided concrete examples of these dynamic feedback loops, underscoring the need for an integrated approach.

REFERENCES

Binkley, S. (2018). *The business of authenticity: An ethnography of post-industrial markets*. Routledge.

Bohdanowicz, P., & Zientara, P. (2008). Corporate social responsibility in hospitality: Issues and implications. *Hospital Management*, *27*(4), 724–738. DOI: 10.1016/j.ijhm.2007.09.001

Bolino, M. C., Long, D., & Turnley, W. H. (2016). Impression management in organizations: Critical questions, answers, and areas for future research. *Annual Review of Organizational Psychology and Organizational Behavior*, *3*(1), 377–406. DOI: 10.1146/annurev-orgpsych-041015-062337

Cohen, E., & Avieli, N. (2004). Food in tourism: Attraction and impediment. *Annals of Tourism Research*, *31*(4), 755–778. DOI: 10.1016/j.annals.2004.02.003

Ellis, A., Park, E., Kim, S., & Yeoman, I. (2018). What is food tourism? *Tourism Management*, *68*, 250–263. DOI: 10.1016/j.tourman.2018.03.025

Ericksen, P. J. (2008). Conceptualizing food systems for global environmental change research. *Global Environmental Change*, *18*(1), 234–245. DOI: 10.1016/j.gloenvcha.2007.09.002

Everett, S., & Slocum, S. L. (2013). Food and tourism: An effective partnership? A UK-based review. *Journal of Sustainable Tourism*, *21*(6), 789–809. DOI: 10.1080/09669582.2012.741601

Food and Agriculture Organization of the United Nations (FAO). (2021). *The State of Food Security and Nutrition in the World 2021: Transforming food systems for food security, improved nutrition and affordable healthy diets for all*. FAO.

Freeman, R. E., Harrison, J. S., Wicks, A. C., Parmar, B., & De Colle, S. (2010). *Stakeholder theory: The state of the art*. Cambridge University Press. DOI: 10.1017/CBO9780511815768

Goffman, E. (1959). *The presentation of self in everyday life*. Anchor Books.

Gössling, S., & Hall, C. M. (2019). *Sustainable hospitality and tourism as motors for development: Case studies from developing regions*. Routledge.

Gössling, S., Hall, C. M., & Scott, D. (2016). *Tourism and sustainability: Principles to practice* (4th ed.). Routledge.

Groth, M., & Grandey, A. A. (2012). From bad to worse: Negative exchange spirals in employee–customer service interactions. *Organizational Psychology Review*, *2*(3), 208–233. DOI: 10.1177/2041386612441735

Hall, C. M., & Gössling, S. (2017). *Food tourism and regional development: Networks, products and trajectories*. Routledge.

Hede, A. M., & Watne, T. (2013). Leveraging the human side of sustainability in hospitality through local sourcing and social entrepreneurship. *International Journal of Hospitality Management*, *34*, 108–116. DOI: 10.1016/j.ijhm.2013.02.002

Hjalager, A. M., & Richards, G. (2002). *Tourism and gastronomy*. Routledge.

Jones, P., Hillier, D., & Comfort, D. (2021). Sustainability in the global hotel industry. *International Journal of Contemporary Hospitality Management*, *33*(6), 1999–2016. DOI: 10.1108/IJCHM-09-2020-1053

Kim, H., & Baker, M. (2019). The impact of emotional labor on customer satisfaction and organizational outcomes in hospitality. *International Journal of Hospitality Management*, *81*, 1–10. DOI: 10.1016/j.ijhm.2019.02.003

Leary, M. R., & Kowalski, R. M. (1990). Impression management: A literature review and two-component model. *Psychological Bulletin*, *107*(1), 34–47. DOI: 10.1037/0033-2909.107.1.34

Mensah, I., & Julien, P. A. (2011). Implementation of food safety management systems in hotels: The case of Greater Accra Region, Ghana. *International Journal of Hospitality Management*, *30*(1), 161–167. DOI: 10.1016/j.ijhm.2010.04.008

Sims, R. (2009). Food, place and authenticity: Local food and the sustainable tourism experience. *Journal of Sustainable Tourism*, *17*(3), 321–336. DOI: 10.1080/09669580802359293

Chapter 4

Cultural Values and Impression Management in the Bahraini Public Sector:

Insights From an HRM Framework

Asma Ayari
https://orcid.org/0000-0002-2134-0624
Independent Researcher, Bahrain

ABSTRACT

Cultural diversity has a profound influence on organizational behavior, yet empirical evidence from the public sector in the Arab Gulf remains limited. This chapter investigates how nationality, religion, and other diversity factors influence cultural values and impression management within Bahrain's Works Affairs Institution. Using Hofstede's Values Survey Module 2013 (VSM13) and SPSS-based quantitative analysis, the study examines fifteen diversity variables, nine of which showed statistically significant—though mostly moderate—associations with Hofstede's cultural dimensions. Nationality and religion emerged as the strongest predictors of cultural orientation, while generational cohort had a negligible impact, countering the popular narrative of generational determinism. The findings reveal an organizational culture marked by extreme collectivism, low power distance, and high indulgence, reflecting both traditional norms and evolving modernization patterns.

DOI: 10.4018/979-8-3373-5519-1.ch004

1. INTRODUCTION

For the last two decades, scholars have been engaged in exploring the role of cultural diversity in the workplace by addressing key questions: Does it exist? What are its driving forces? Moreover, how does it shape employee behavior about organizational goals? With increasing globalization, cultural diversity has emerged as a defining organizational phenomenon, particularly in Human Resource Management (HRM) (Budhwar & Mellahi, 2012; Yadav & Lenka, 2020). Diversity encompasses a wide range of demographic variables, including religion, ethnicity, nationality, age, education, and language, all of which influence workplace interactions and outcomes (Loden & Rosener, 1991; Jehn, Northcraft, & Neale, 1999). The significance of understanding these dimensions becomes more pressing in today's knowledge-based economy, where innovation and adaptability are deeply tied to human capital (Parry, 2014; Costanza et al., 2012).

While diversity has the potential to enhance creativity, job satisfaction, and employee retention, it also presents challenges, including communication barriers, conflicting work values, and integration difficulties (Webber & Donahue, 2001; Scutariu & Bodnărescu, 2023). These effects—both positive and negative—require thoughtful HR strategies that accommodate and leverage diversity for institutional effectiveness (Boxall, 1994; Budhwar & Mellahi, 2012). Mismanaged diversity can lead to increased turnover, interpersonal conflict, and reduced employee morale, whereas well-managed diversity can contribute to a culture that is inclusive, innovative, and performance oriented (Saxena, 2014; Roberge & Van Dick, 2010). Thus, HR leaders must develop an acute awareness of the cultural variables that define their workforce.

Despite the extensive literature on workplace diversity, there is a notable lack of research focused on the public sector, especially within the Arab Gulf context. Most diversity studies are concentrated in Western countries and private sector environments, leaving a critical gap in understanding how public sector institutions in non-Western societies address the issue (Ali, 1995; Al-Rasheed, 2001). The Gulf Cooperation Council (GCC) countries, including Bahrain, have undergone rapid socio-economic transformations driven by diversification agendas, a surge in foreign labor, and public administration reforms (Barakat, 1993; Yaghi, Yaghi, & Yaghi, 2025). These shifts have not only made workforce diversity a reality but also a defining feature of governance.

This chapter aims to address this gap by examining the primary diversity factors that influence cultural values within Bahrain's public workforce. Special attention is given to generational cohorts to understand their impact on shared workplace values and behaviors (Joshi, Dencker, & Franz, 2011; Wang & Duan, 2025). The Ministry of Works, Municipalities Affairs, and Urban Planning (MoWMAUP) serves as the case study, offering a comprehensive view of diversity dynamics in one of Bahrain's most prominent public institutions. This ministry comprises a diverse group of professionals across various functions, including engineering, planning, infrastructure, and municipal services, making it an ideal setting to examine intergroup dynamics and value systems.

The research utilizes Hofstede's cultural dimensions framework, offering a solid theoretical basis for assessing and contrasting cultural values across demographic variables (Hofstede, 1984; Hofstede & Minkov, 2010). The application of Hofstede's Values Survey Module 2013 (VSM13) facilitates the quantification of six principal cultural dimensions—power distance, individualism versus collectivism, masculinity versus femininity, uncertainty avoidance, long-term orientation, and indulgence versus restraint—and assesses their correlation with variables such as nationality, religion, educational attainment, language, and age (Hofstede & Minkov, 2013).

This analysis is particularly relevant for HR managers responsible for balancing organizational cohesion and responsiveness in an increasingly complex environment (Berman, Bowman, West, & Van Wart, 2016). While private companies may adjust quickly to talent demands, public institutions face structural rigidities, bureaucratic inertia, and a broader mandate of public accountability. In such a setting, impression management becomes a strategic tool not only at the individual level but also for institutional image-building (Goffman, 1959/1990). How employees perceive one another, how they align with organizational goals, and how the institution presents itself to citizens and stakeholders are all shaped by internal cultural dynamics.

Moreover, the chapter aligns with the broader theoretical perspective of impression management, which focuses on how individuals and organizations actively shape perceptions to influence social and professional outcomes (Pettigrew, 1979; Goffman, 1959/1990). In public institutions, the stakes are exceptionally high, as these bodies are expected to embody neutrality, inclusiveness, and competence. When public employees come from varied cultural backgrounds and hold divergent values, the risk of internal fragmentation increases. This, in turn, can damage the organization's external image. As such, managing impressions becomes intertwined with managing internal diversity.

The cultural composition of Bahrain's public workforce, characterized by a mix of Bahrainis and expatriates from South Asia and other Arab countries, introduces further complexity (Barakat, 1993; Ali, 1995). Language, educational background, and generational orientation all contribute to workplace heterogeneity. This chapter examines whether these factors reinforce or undermine standard value systems and how they influence employee engagement, collaboration, and alignment with institutional norms.

Ultimately, the aim of this chapter is twofold. First, it contributes to filling a significant academic gap by offering an empirically grounded case study on cultural values and impression management in the public sector of the Gulf region. Second, it provides actionable recommendations for public sector HR practitioners in Bahrain and similar contexts. These recommendations are designed to assist policymakers, department heads, and HR managers in developing targeted strategies to enhance employee integration, improve workplace communication, and support the organization's mission while maintaining its public image. By examining the intersection of cultural values and impression management, this chapter provides public sector HR managers with evidence-based insights and practical guidance for motivating, managing, and retaining a diverse workforce. It provides a structured framework for understanding how individual characteristics, such as age, religion, and nationality, interact with broader institutional dynamics (Triandis, 1988; Komisarof & Akaliyski, 2025). This knowledge is essential for fostering organizational unity, maintaining institutional credibility, and enhancing service delivery in an increasingly pluralistic and scrutinized public sector environment.

2. LITERATURE REVIEW

The literature on cultural diversity and impression management is extensive yet fragmented across disciplines such as organizational behavior, sociology, and public administration. Scholars have long debated the extent to which diversity variables—such as age, nationality, education, and religion—shape cultural orientations in the workplace (Loden & Rosener, 1991; Jehn et al., 1999; Yadav & Lenka, 2020). Hofstede's (1984) cultural dimensions remain a foundational framework, though later critiques highlight the risks of overgeneralization and ecological fallacy (McSweeney, 2002; Komisarof & Akaliyski, 2025). At the same time, impression management theory provides a complementary perspective, emphasizing how individuals and institutions actively construct and project identities (Goffman, 1990). More recent research has integrated these perspectives, showing how national culture and organizational settings jointly influence employee behavior and institutional image (Costanza et al., 2012; Yaghi et al., 2025; Wang & Duan, 2025). By synthesizing these contributions, the present review establishes a theoretical foundation for examining how cultural values shape both workplace dynamics and impression management practices within Bahrain's public sector.

2.1 Cultural Diversity and Organizational Behavior

Cultural diversity has become a prominent topic in organizational research due to its dual impact—both beneficial and challenging—on Human Resource Management (HRM). It refers to the variety of cultural or ethnic groups within a society or organization, encompassing differences in nationality, ethnicity, language, religion, gender, and generational identity (Loden & Rosener, 1991; Williams & O'Reilly, 1998). Research has shown that such diversity can enhance creativity, innovation, and decision-making but can also lead to friction, miscommunication, and fragmentation when left unmanaged (Jehn et al., 1999; Saxena, 2014; Scutariu & Bodnărescu, 2023).

In the context of Bahrain's public sector, cultural diversity is reflected in the coexistence of local and expatriate populations working together. The dynamics of collaboration and conflict in this workforce make understanding diversity essential for institutional cohesion and effectiveness (Yadav & Lenka, 2020). Hofstede's cultural dimensions offer a foundation for examining these cultural differences through a structured theoretical lens (Hofstede, 1984; Hofstede & Minkov, 2013). More recent studies highlight that cultural dimensions remain relevant for explaining employee behavior, but new empirical evidence stresses the moderating role of proactive behavior and generational factors in shaping workplace values (Zheng et al., 2025).

2.2 Impression Management in Public Sector HRM

Impression management, conceptualized initially by Goffman (1959), refers to the process by which individuals attempt to control the perceptions others form about them. In public organizations, impression management extends beyond the individual level to include the institution's image, legitimacy, and perceived integrity. Given the public sector's accountability to citizens, trust and credibility become paramount (Pettigrew, 1979; Bolzonella, 2024). Thus, managing internal cultural values is critical to fostering consistent and positive external perceptions.

In culturally diverse environments, public employees bring varying expectations, values, and communication styles, which can influence how they present themselves and interpret the behavior of others (Jehn et al., 1999; Scutariu & Bodnărescu, 2023). Misalignment in these perceptions may lead to unintentional breaches in institutional decorum or conflicting interpretations of professional conduct.

As such, HR managers in public institutions must pay attention not only to policy and performance but also to how cultural values shape employees' self-presentation, behavior, and alignment with organizational goals. Impression management strategies—such as promoting shared values, inclusive communication styles, and culturally sensitive leadership—can bridge value gaps and reinforce a cohesive institutional image (Komisarof & Akaliyski, 2025; Zheng et al., 2025).

2.3 Theoretical Foundation: Hofstede's Cultural Dimensions

This study employs Hofstede's cultural value framework, which identifies six dimensions to explain cultural values:

I. Power Distance Index (PDI)

The Power Distance Index (PDI), created by Hofstede (1984), quantifies the degree to which subordinate members of organizations acquiesce to unequal power allocation. In high PDI cultures, authority is centralized, hierarchy is rigid, and subordinates are discouraged from questioning decisions. Superiors enjoy privileges and are often unapproachable, making upward communication difficult. This environment supports impression management strategies focused on projecting control and order, which may enhance public perceptions of authority but suppress internal innovation and feedback (Hofstede, 2002; Hofstede & Minkov, 2010).

Conversely, low PDI cultures view hierarchical roles as flexible. Power is decentralized, communication is encouraged, and leadership is seen as participative. Such workplaces support impression management approaches that highlight inclusivity, shared values, and employee engagement—qualities that can boost institutional trust and attract diverse talent (Pettigrew, 1979; Zheng et al., 2025).

In Bahrain's public sector, high PDI tendencies reflect traditional norms but may hinder modernization efforts. HR managers must recognize how power dynamics shape employee perceptions and external image. Effective impression management in this context requires not only policy reform but also visible leadership behaviors—such as transparency, dialogue, and accessibility—that shift perceptions from authoritarian to accountable (Bolzonella, 2024).

- ***Hypothesis 1.*** *There are significant differences across generational cohorts in their orientation toward Power Distance within Bahrain's public institutions.*

II. Individualism vs. Collectivism (IDV)

In collectivist organizational cultures, employees adopt a "we" mindset, prioritizing group loyalty and interpersonal relationships over individual tasks. Personal ties and in-group belonging often influence workplace behavior and hiring practices, where family or social affiliations may take precedence over qualifications (Hofstede, 1984; Hofstede & Minkov, 2010). By contrast, individualist cultures emphasize personal achievement and autonomy, framing the workplace as a transactional environment where performance and results drive decision-making (Triandis, 1988; Soares et al., 2007).

Impression management also differs significantly between these cultural contexts. Collectivist environments discourage direct feedback to preserve group harmony, while individualist contexts reward self-promotion and individual visibility (Komisarof & Akaliyski, 2025). These differences shape how employees present themselves, respond to authority, and perceive recognition within organizations.

Building on the cultural contrast between collectivism and individualism, and its implications for workplace relationships and impression management, the following hypothesis is proposed:

- ***Hypothesis 2.*** *The older generation is expected to exhibit a lower level of individualism compared to the younger generation.*

III. Masculinity vs. Femininity (MAS)

Hofstede's masculinity–femininity dimension delineates the degree to which societies prioritize traditionally "masculine" attributes—such as assertiveness, competition, and achievement—over "feminine" attributes, which encompass modesty, caring, and quality of life (Hofstede, 1984; Hofstede & Minkov, 2010). In masculine societies, gender roles are clearly defined, organizational awards are linked to quantifiable performance, and conflict is often addressed through competition. In contrast, feminine cultures prioritize equality, collaboration, and conflict resolution via negotiation and compromise (Soares, Farhangmehr, & Shoham, 2007).

These orientations influence impression management strategies in the workplace. Masculine environments often promote self-presentation centered on status, assertiveness, and visible achievement, whereas feminine cultures encourage relational harmony, modest self-presentation, and collective rather than individual success (Budhwar & Mellahi, 2012; Wiese, Lehmann, & Beckmann, 2024).

This cultural contrast is particularly relevant in intergenerational contexts, where older employees may gravitate toward traditional masculine norms, while younger employees increasingly display more collaborative and egalitarian behaviors (Joshi, Dencker, & Franz, 2011; Parry, 2014; Wang & Duan, 2025). For public institutions, recognizing these shifts is crucial to managing both internal dynamics and external perceptions effectively.

- **Hypothesis 3:** *The older generation is expected to have a higher masculinity culture compared to the younger generation.*

IV. Uncertainty Avoidance Index (UAI)

The **Uncertainty Avoidance Index (UAI)**, developed by Hofstede, measures how societies cope with ambiguity and unknown situations. It reflects a cultural inclination toward structured routines or flexible adaptability. High UAI cultures tend to value stability, clear rules, and detailed planning to manage anxiety about uncertain outcomes. In contrast, low UAI cultures are more comfortable with ambiguity, allowing greater freedom, experimentation, and relaxed work norms (Hofstede, 1984; Hofstede & Minkov, 2010).

In the workplace, these differences manifest in how employees approach change, follow procedures, and react to novel situations. High UAI cultures foster formality, strict protocols, and an aversion to risk, aligning with bureaucratic systems and top-down management. Low UAI cultures, however, encourage innovation, open communication, and flexible thinking (Soares et al., 2007; Wiese et al., 2024). From an impression management standpoint, organizations in high-UAI contexts may emphasize reliability, predictability, and order to maintain public confidence. At the same time, those in low-UAI settings often present themselves as agile, creative, and responsive to change (Scutariu & Bodnărescu, 2023).

Given the link between age and preference for certainty observed in Hofstede's IBM study, older employees often align more closely with high-UAI values (Hofstede, 1984; Joshi et al., 2011). Accordingly, the hypothesis is:

- **Hypothesis 4**: *The older generation is expected to exhibit a higher level of uncertainty avoidance compared to the younger generation.*

V. Long-Term vs. Short-Term Orientation (LTO)

Hofstede's fifth cultural factor, Long-Term Orientation (LTO), came from Michael Bond's 1987 Chinese Value Survey.Long-term orientation focuses on benefits in the future, dedication and realistic planning. Short-term orientation, on the other hand, focuses on tradition, obligations to society, and quick results. Long-term oriented cultures value thrift, persistence, and adaptability, while short-term cultures prioritize respect for historical values, stability, and fulfilling current expectations.

In organizational settings, these orientations influence decision-making, change management, and employee development. Long-term-oriented institutions are more likely to invest in capacity-building and sustainable strategies, while short-term-oriented ones may focus on immediate outcomes and symbolic gestures. From an impression management lens, institutions with a long-term focus craft an image of strategic vision and responsibility. In contrast, those with a short-term orientation often align with maintaining public approval and cultural continuity.

Given that long-term values often stem from accumulated life experiences and traditional norms, it is anticipated that older employees will exhibit a stronger long-term orientation than younger ones.

- **Hypothesis 5:** *The older generation is expected to have a higher long-term orientation culture compared to the younger generation.*

VI. Indulgence vs. Restraint (IND)

The degree to which individuals endeavour to regulate their desires and impulses. This cultural dimension, though relatively new, has gained traction in cross-cultural studies for distinguishing how societies manage gratification and control of basic human desires. Indulgent cultures permit the free expression of enjoyment, such as leisure, consumption, and personal happiness, while restrained cultures emphasize self-control, social norms, and duty over desire. These values shape not only individual behavior but also institutional norms.

In organizational settings, indulgent cultures foster freedom of expression and autonomy, empowering employees to voice their opinions and prioritize their well-being. Such environments tend to promote open communication, which enhances internal impression management and aligns with an image of employee-centric governance. In contrast, restrained cultures are marked by rigidity, formality, and reluctance to speak up—factors that hinder open dialogue and contribute to a more reserved organizational image. Employees in restrained settings may stay silent even when dissatisfied, which can distort internal impressions and external perceptions of workplace harmony.

These differences extend to customer service, where indulgent cultures expect visible displays of friendliness, while restrained cultures consider overly emotional expressions inappropriate. Such nuances directly affect how the public and stakeholders perceive institutions.

Given these dynamics, especially their impact on generational behavior and impression management, the following hypothesis is proposed:

- **Hypothesis 6:** The older generation is expected to have a higher restraint culture compared to the younger generation.

The hypotheses established herein provide the basis for the practical section of this study.

2.4 Critiques and Defense of Hofstede's Framework

Hofstede's cultural model remains foundational in cross-cultural research, though it has sparked significant critique. McSweeney (2002) highlighted methodological shortcomings, noting its reliance on historical IBM data from 1967 to 1973 and the use of national averages as proxies for culture, which may misrepresent the evolving and varied cultural landscapes. Similarly, Ailon (2008) and d'Iribarne (2009) criticized the ecological fallacy of attributing national-level scores to individual behaviors, emphasizing instead the internal diversity and contextual subtleties of culture.

Responding to these critiques, Hofstede and colleagues defended the model's validity and robustness through longitudinal replications, while acknowledging its limitations in capturing organizational cultures and temporal shifts (Hofstede, 2002; Hofstede & Minkov, 2010). More recently, scholars have advanced the debate. Jackson (2020) called for more nuanced and dynamic frameworks that reflect contemporary complexity, while policy analysts have argued for greater precision through individual-level diagnostics alongside national indicators (Bolzonella, 2024).

These debates also carry implications for impression management. If culture is multi-layered and context-specific, so too are the strategies people and institutions use to craft their image. Relying solely on national averages risks oversimplifying the variation in impression management across regions, organizations, or generational cohorts. Research in cross-cultural business communication has shown that mixed-method approaches—combining qualitative case studies with quantitative measures—offer richer insights into how cultural values influence self-presentation, communication norms, and organizational branding (Soares et al., 2007).

Despite these limitations, Hofstede's framework remains widely utilized due to its comparability, clarity, and enduring relevance across fields such as marketing, psychology, and public administration. It continues to provide a useful starting point for exploring how dimensions like power distance, uncertainty avoidance, or collectivism shape institutional reputation and stakeholder perceptions in the public sector, including Bahrain.

This chapter therefore adopts Hofstede's model pragmatically, while supplementing it with critiques and qualitative insights to enrich the understanding of impression management. By integrating generational and organizational variability, it develops a more contextually sensitive interpretation rather than treating cultural dimensions as static labels.

2.5 Diversity Factors Affecting Cultural Values

The literature recognizes a wide array of diversity factors influencing cultural values. Loden and Rosener (1991) distinguished between primary dimensions (e.g., age, ethnicity) and secondary dimensions (e.g., education, income). Jehn et al. (1999) introduced the categories of social category, informational, and value diversity. More recently, Yadav and Lenka (2020) emphasized the importance of studying multiple diversity variables in tandem rather than isolating one or two factors.

To thoroughly understand the cultural values of public sector employees, it is essential to identify the diversity factors influencing those values. Research shows that a definitive consensus on the definition of diversity is lacking. Loden and Rosener (1991) characterized diversity as the factors that distinguish one group of individuals from another across primary and secondary dimensions. Thomas (1996) defined diversity as "any mixture of items characterized by differences and similarities." According to Williams and O'Reilly (1998), it is defined as "differences between individual characteristics and attributes that lead to a perception that the other person is different from me." Van Knippenberg et al. (2004) defined diversity from a social psychological perspective as "differences between individuals on any attribute that may lead to the perception that another person is different from self."

Multiple researchers have suggested classifications for the categorization of diversity. Loden and Rosener (1991) delineated primary dimensions, including race, gender, and age, alongside secondary dimensions such as educational background and religion. Arredondo and Glauner (1992) expanded this by adding culture, language, and social class, as well as introducing a tertiary dimension that reflects the historical moments experienced by individuals. Jehn et al. (1999) categorized diversity into three types: social group diversity, educational diversity, and monetary diversity. Webber and Donahue (2001) differentiated between relations-oriented diversity and task-oriented diversity. Maier (2003) proposed more than 38 possible diversity dimensions, conceptualizing individuals as "kaleidoscopes" and likening diversity to an iceberg—visible and invisible layers that shape identity. Saxena (2014) developed a model including key variables such as age, caste, gender, religion, attitudes, and language. Yadav and Lenka (2020) conducted a systematic review of 65 research studies, highlighting the significance of analysing the combined impact of multiple diversity variables instead of focusing on isolated factors.

In line with these classifications, this study investigates fifteen diversity factors that may influence cultural values in the workplace. These include gender, age, generational cohort, disability, ethnicity, nationality, educational background, field of study, job category, years of experience, monthly household income, religion, language, family status, and whether the individual has children. These factors were selected for their theoretical relevance and potential influence on the cultural dimensions proposed by Hofstede (1984, 2010, 2013). Their inclusion enables a comprehensive analysis of the interplay between demographic diversity and cultural value orientation in Bahrain's public sector. Furthermore, understanding these diversity dimensions is essential for shaping organizational strategies that improve internal cohesion, employee engagement, and the institution's ability to manage its external image effectively. This alignment with impression management theory (Goffman, 1959) allows us to explore not only how employees internalize values but also how institutions project professionalism, inclusivity, and cultural sensitivity.

2.6 Theoretical Framework

This study adopts Hofstede's cultural dimensions as the primary theoretical lens, complemented by Goffman's dramaturgical theory of impression management. Hofstede's framework enables the analysis of individual value orientations across dimensions such as power distance, individualism, and uncertainty avoidance (Hofstede, 1984; Hofstede & Minkov, 2010, 2013). At the same time, Goffman's (1959) dramaturgical theory provides a means to understand the performative aspects of behavior within institutional settings. This integrated perspective enables a nuanced examination of how public sector employees in Bahrain construct, manage, and project culturally influenced professional identities—both within their organizations and to the broader public.

As a result of the above literature review, the following research model (Figure 1) will be examined during the field study to identify the correlations and the impact of each diversity factor on Hofstede's cultural dimensions.

Figure 1. Relationship Between Diversity Variables and Hofstede's Cultural Dimensions

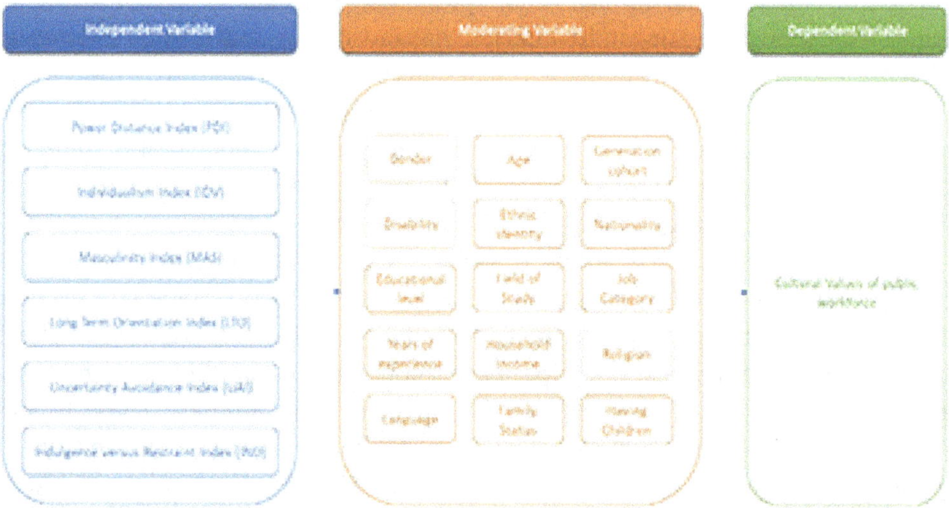

2.7 Research Model and Application

The conceptual framework maps the relationship between fifteen diversity variables and Hofstede's six cultural dimensions, with particular attention to generational cohorts as a moderating factor in these relationships (Hofstede, 1984; Hofstede & Minkov, 2010, 2013). In addition, the framework incorporates the concept of impression management to explore how internal cultural diversity shapes institutional behavior and, by extension, public perception (Pettigrew, 1979). The primary aim of this framework is to support HR professionals in developing informed strategies that foster cultural harmony, strengthen the internal image of public institutions, and protect their external reputation (Berman et al., 2016; Budhwar & Mellahi, 2012). By identifying the diversity variables most influential in shaping workplace values and behaviors, the study contributes both theoretically and practically to the discipline of HRM within the Bahraini public sector.

3. RESEARCH METHODOLOGY

This section defines the research methodology used in the current study, which investigates the correlation between workforce diversity and cultural values in Bahrain's public sector. The methodology employs a quantitative, exploratory design, utilizing structured survey instruments and established cultural models to analyse the dynamics of diversity and perception in institutional contexts.

The study employs a quantitative, exploratory case study design to examine the influence of multiple diversity variables on employees' cultural values within a public institution. The exploratory nature of the research is suitable given the complexity and contextual specificity of cultural values about workforce diversity (Creswell & Creswell, 2017). While the findings are not intended to be generalized beyond the specific case studied, the quantitative approach provides a structured and statistically grounded framework for analyzing patterns and relationships within the collected data.

3.1 Research Instrument

This study uses the 24-item paper-based Values Survey Module 2013 (VSM 13) to compare national variations and culturally influenced values across nations (Hofstede, Geert; Minkov, 2013). Hofstede claimed that the VSM questionnaire, originally designed to assess national differences, allows for meaningful computation and comparison of dimension scores across genders (female versus male) and generations (grandparents versus parents versus children). VSM topic questions are scored on a five-point Likert scale. The computation gives results in six dimensions: power distance, indulgence against restraint, masculinity versus femininity, individuality versus collectivism, uncertainty avoidance, and long-term versus short-term orientation. The literature review detailed the six dimensions.

This study utilizes the most recent version, VSM13. This study utilized officially published authorized versions of the VSM 13 in various languages, including Arabic and English. Both the English and Arabic versions of the VSM 13 were distributed to all participants via email. Additionally, nine questions were incorporated into the original VSM to investigate the Particular Arabic cultural values relevant to the context of the Kingdom of Bahrain. Additionally, the VSM survey originally included five demographic profile questions: gender, age, years of formal education, job title, and nationality. To examine the impact of various diversity dimensions, ten demographic questions were incorporated into the original questionnaire. These questions pertain to educational background, age cohort, work experience, monthly household income, religion, language, disability, family status, number of children, and ethnic identity. Consequently, a total of 15 diversity dimensions were assessed in this research.

3.2 Population and Sampling

This study's target population comprised 1,080 full-time employees from the Work Affairs department in the Kingdom of Bahrain. The survey was electronically distributed through the institution's internal email portal across three rounds in February 2025: the first on February 4, the second on February 11, and the third on February 18. Of the 100 responses received, two were excluded for not meeting the inclusion criteria (i.e., they were not current employees), yielding a final valid sample size of N = 98 (Table 1). The observed response rate aligns with the methodological guidelines established by Hofstede and Minkov (2013), which suggest a minimum of 50 responses to facilitate meaningful statistical analysis among relatively homogeneous subgroups. The study encountered limitations in achieving equal subgroup representation across the 15 diversity dimensions; however, the final dataset offers a robust foundation for analysis (Creswell & Creswell, 2017).

Table 1. Survey Distribution and Response Summary for Work Affairs Institution

Total Population	Distributed surveys		Retained surveys	Rejected surveys	Analyzed surveys	
	No.	Percentage%			No.	Percentage%
1080	1080	100	100	2	98	9

3.3 Data Collection Procedure

To facilitate accessibility and data precision, the VSM13 questionnaire was digitized using Microsoft Forms, with versions provided in both English and Arabic. Prior to formal distribution, the instrument was pilot tested with a small cohort of employees demographically similar to the target sample to ensure clarity and comprehension (Creswell & Creswell, 2017).

The survey was conducted anonymously, and participation was voluntary. Respondents were informed of the study's objectives, the confidentiality of their responses, and their right to withdraw at any point. This information was presented in an introductory statement at the beginning of the online questionnaire, in line with established research ethics guidelines (Berman et al., 2016).

All valid responses were exported from Microsoft Forms into Excel and subsequently imported into IBM SPSS Statistics (Version 26) for analysis, which allowed both descriptive and inferential statistical techniques to be applied (Cleff, 2014).

3.4 Data Analysis Techniques

The research was executed in two consecutive rounds to provide an accurate evaluation of cultural influences and rigorous statistical validation. The first phase utilized data from the Values Survey Module 2013 (VSM13), created by Hofstede and Minkov (2013), to calculate indices for each of the six cultural dimensions: Power Distance, Individualism vs. Collectivism, Masculinity vs. Femininity, Uncertainty Avoidance, Long-Term Orientation, and Indulgence vs. Restraint. This meant putting all the answers together and normalizing them using the standardized VSM13 procedures to get quantitative scores that showed the group's cultural inclinations.

During the second phase, the calculated indices underwent statistical analysis utilizing the Statistical Package for the Social Sciences (SPSS). This included descriptive statistics to examine distributional patterns and inferential tests such as t-tests, one-way ANOVA, and regression analysis to explore relationships between cultural values and identified diversity characteristics (e.g., age, gender, job category). The integration of these two phases established a comprehensive methodological framework, enabling both the measurement of cultural profiles and the empirical testing of the study's hypotheses (Creswell & Creswell, 2017).

3.4.1 Calculation of Cultural Indices

The responses to the VSM13 items were processed using the official formulas provided by Hofstede and Minkov (2013) for each of the six cultural dimensions. These formulas rely on weighted differences between paired survey items, adjusted by a constant (C) to position results on the standardized 0–100 scale commonly applied in Hofstede's cultural framework. However, in this study the constant (C) could not be applied because Bahrain was not separately represented in the original IBM dataset from the 1960s, which formed the basis for Hofstede's calibration. Consequently, the analysis emphasized internal relative comparisons of cultural scores within the Bahraini public sector workforce rather than direct benchmarking against other national profiles.

3.5.2 Statistical Analysis with SPSS

Three main statistical tests were conducted using SPSS:

- ***Reliability Analysis***: pertains to the assessment of the consistency of the instrument, specifically the VSM13, in the context of this study. Cronbach's alpha is commonly employed to assess whether the items of an instrument measuring the same construct accurately reflect the intended construct (Trochim & Donnelly, 2001). The coefficient evaluates the internal consistency of the instrument, producing Cronbach's alpha values between 0 and 1. Cronbach's alpha generally increases with higher correlations among the items. An alpha coefficient of 0.7 is typically considered to reflect acceptable reliability (Hofstede, Geert; Minkov, 2013), whereas an alpha of 0.8 or higher indicates good reliability. High reliability (0.95 or above) is not necessarily beneficial, as it may indicate redundancy among the items (Boyle, 1991).
- ***Spearman's rank correlation coefficient*** is a non-parametric statistical measure that uses a monotonic function to evaluate the strength of the relationship between two variables. Pearson's correlation assesses linear relationships, while Spearman's correlation analyses monotonic relationships, irrespective of their linearity. The Spearman correlation test is frequently utilized to evaluate relationships between ordinal variables.
- ***One-Way ANOVA:*** This test was conducted to examine whether generational cohort (e.g., Baby Boomers, Generation X, Millennials) had a statistically significant impact on cultural values.

These statistical tools were chosen for their importance to research questions and their ability to uncover patterns within a diverse organizational population.

3.6 Ethical Considerations

This study was performed in compliance with strict ethical standards, following recognized institutional and academic protocols. Participants received comprehensive information regarding the study's objectives, their involvement in the research, and their rights, which included the option to participate and withdraw at any time without negative repercussions. The survey instrument was carefully crafted to remove any potentially disrespectful, biased, or discriminatory language, thereby ensuring a respectful and inclusive methodology. Stringent measures were implemented to ensure the anonymity and confidentiality of all participants. No identifiable information was collected, and all data were managed with the highest level of confidentiality. Throughout the research process, from data collection to analysis, objectivity and transparency were maintained to uphold the integrity of the findings.

4. FINDINGS

This chapter delineates the principal findings of the study, which examined the correlation between workforce diversity characteristics and cultural aspects within Bahrain's public sector, particularly the Works Affairs organization. Quantitative data analysis was performed utilizing IBM SPSS, and cultural values were assessed employing Hofstede's VSM13 technique.

4.1. Instrument Reliability

The survey instrument's internal consistency was evaluated using Cronbach's Alpha, yielding a coefficient of .702 across 47 items.(Table 2). According to psychometric standards (Boyle, 1991; Cronbach, 1951), this value indicates satisfactory reliability and supports the instrument's appropriateness for measuring cultural aspects among a diverse respondent population.

Table 2. Reliability Statistics for the Research Instrument

Cronbach's Alpha	Cronbach's Alpha Based on Standardized Items	N of Items
.702	.710	47

4.2. Calculated Cultural Dimensions

The computed indices indicate that the Bahraini public workforce demonstrates a low Power Distance (PDI = 30), exceedingly low Individualism (IDV = 1), moderate Masculinity (MAS = 18), negative Uncertainty Avoidance (UAI = -25), negative Long-Term Orientation (LTO = -23), and a high degree of Indulgence (IND = 63).

Figure 2. Comparison of Hofstede's Cultural Dimensions: Arab Countries vs. Bahrain

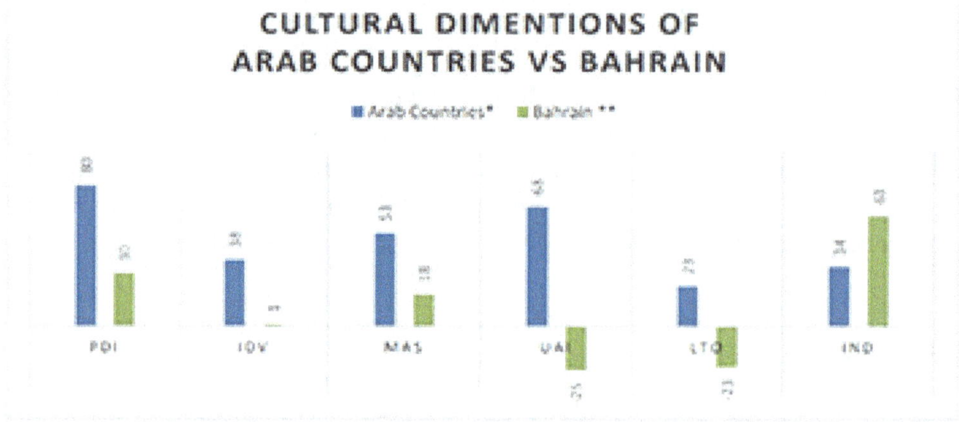

These findings significantly differ from Hofstede's (Hofstede, 1984; Hofstede & Minkov, 2010) overall statistics for Arab nations, indicating a distinct cultural profile within Bahrain's public sector, which may be shaped by institutional norms, modernization trends, and the demographic diversity of its personnel (Figure 2 & Table 3).

Table 3. Comparison of Hofstede's Cultural Dimensions: Arab Countries vs. Bahrain

	PDI	*IDV*	*MAS*	*UAI*	*LTO*	*IND*
*Arab Countries**	80	38	53	68	23	34
*Bahrain ***	30	1	18	-25	-23	63

* Referencing to Hofstede data matrix for Arab Countries (UAE, Lebanon, Saudi Arabia, Kuwait, Egypt, Iraq, Libya)

** Values obtained by Author from the research study analysis

4.3. Demographic Sample

The survey sample (n = 98) represented a heterogeneous workforce, encompassing a broad spectrum of nations, age demographics, generational cohorts, educational attainments, occupational classifications, income levels, and ethnic identities (Table 4). The predominant demographic consisted of males (73.5%), Bahraini nationals (61.2%), and professionals (80.6%), with notable participation from Generation X (42.9%) and Generation Y (48%).

Table 4. Demographic and Socio-Economic Characteristics of the Respondents

Factor	Subgroup	Frequency	Percent	Cumulative Percent
Gender	Male	72	73.5	73.5
	Female	26	26.5	100.0
Nationality	Bahraini	60	61.2	61.2
	European	5	5.1	66.3
	Indian	12	12.2	78.6
	Pakistani	2	2.0	80.6
	Pilipino	9	9.2	89.8
	Malaysian	2	2.0	91.8
	others	8	8.2	100.0
Age	20-29	13	13.3	13.3
	30-39	35	35.7	49.0
	40-49	25	25.5	74.5
	50-59	23	23.5	98.0
	60-69	2	2.0	100.0
Generation cohort	Baby Boomers	9	9.2	9.2
	Generation X	42	42.9	52.0
	Generation Y	47	48.0	100.0
Educational level	High school	4	4.1	4.1
	Diploma	12	12.2	16.3
	Bachelor	57	58.2	74.5
	Master	22	22.4	96.9
	High Diploma	3	3.1	100.0
Field of study	Arts and humanities	1	1.0	1.0
	Social sciences, journalism, and information	2	2.0	3.1
	Business, administration, and law	10	10.2	13.3
	Natural sciences, mathematics, and statistics	2	2.0	15.3
	Information and Communication Technologies	9	9.2	24.5
	Engineering, manufacturing and construction	67	68.4	92.9
	Health and welfare	1	1.0	93.9
	Services	1	1.0	94.9
	Others	5	5.1	100.0
Job category	Professionals	79	80.6	80.6
	Managerial	6	6.1	86.7
	Senior Management	2	2.0	88.8
	Admin/ Support Jobs	11	11.2	100.0

continued on following page

Table 4. Continued

Factor	Subgroup	Frequency	Percent	Cumulative Percent
Work experience	Below 5 years	11	11.2	11.2
	Between 5 to 10 years	23	23.5	34.7
	Between 10 to 15 years	12	12.2	46.9
	Between 15 to 20 years	14	14.3	61.2
	Between 20 to 25 years	15	15.3	76.5
	Between 25 to 30 years	10	10.2	86.7
	Above 30 years	13	13.3	100.0
Monthly household income	Below BHD 500	3	3.1	3.1
	BHD 501 – BHD 1000	24	24.5	27.6
	BHD 1001 – BHD 1500	23	23.5	51.0
	BHD 1501 – BHD 2000	15	15.3	66.3
	BHD 2001 – BHD 2500	7	7.1	73.5
	Above BHD 2500	8	8.2	81.6
	Prefer not to say	18	18.4	100.0
Religion	Muslim	75	76.5	76.5
	Christian	13	13.3	89.8
	Hindu	5	5.1	94.9
	Prefer not to say	4	4.1	99.0
	other	1	1.0	100.0
Language	Arabic	67	68.4	68.4
	English	4	4.1	72.4
	Urdu	5	5.1	77.6
	Hindi	1	1.0	78.6
	Tagalog	9	9.2	87.8
	other	12	12.2	100.0
Disability	Not Disable	98	100.0	100.0
Family status	Single	21	21.4	21.4
	Married	74	75.5	96.9
	Divorced	1	1.0	98.0
	Prefer not to say	2	2.0	100.0
No. of children	No Children	26	26.5	26.5
	One Child	11	11.2	37.8
	Two Children	27	27.6	65.3
	Three Children	16	16.3	81.6
	Four children or more	18	18.4	100.0

continued on following page

Table 4. Continued

Factor	Subgroup	Frequency	Percent	Cumulative Percent
Ethnic Identity	Bahraini - Arab	60	61.2	61.2
	Other Arab	6	6.1	67.3
	Other Asian	29	29.6	96.9
	African	1	1.0	98.0
	European	2	2.0	100.0

4.4. Correlation Results

The Spearman's rho analysis revealed several statistically significant, though generally weak, associations between demographic and socio-economic factors and Hofstede's cultural dimensions. These results, summarized in Table 5, provide insight into how individual characteristics shape cultural orientations within Bahrain's public sector workforce (Hofstede, 1984; Hofstede & Minkov, 2010; Scutariu & Bodnărescu, 2023; Ali, 1995).

Table 5. Correlations Between Socio-Demographic Factors and Hofstede's Cultural Dimensions

Factor	Cultural Dimension(s)	Direction of Correlation	Strength (Spearman's ρ)	Significance (p)
Gender	None	–	–	–
Nationality	Individualism (IDV)	Negative	–.202	.046*
	Long-Term Orientation (LTO)	Positive	.258	.010**
Age	Long-Term Orientation (LTO)	Positive	.211	.037*
Generational Cohort	Individualism (IDV)	Positive	.214	.034*
Educational Background	Uncertainty Avoidance (UAI)	Negative	–.208	.040*
Field of Study	Indulgence (IND)	Negative	–.220	.030*
Job Category	None	–	–	–
Work Experience	None	–	–	–
Monthly Household Income	Uncertainty Avoidance (UAI)	Negative	–.316	.002**
	Indulgence (IND)	Positive	.221	.029*

continued on following page

Table 5. Continued

Factor	Cultural Dimension(s)	Direction of Correlation	Strength (Spearman's ρ)	Significance (p)
Religion	Uncertainty Avoidance (UAI)	Negative	–.283	.005**
Mother Language	Uncertainty Avoidance (UAI)	Negative	–.207	.041*
Disability	Not tested (no cases)	–	–	–
Family Status	None	–	–	–
Number of Children	None	–	–	–
Ethnic Identity	Long-Term Orientation (LTO)	Positive	.212	.036*

*Significant at the 0.05 level (two-tailed).
**Significant at the 0.01 level (two-tailed).

The analysis indicated that nationality, age, generational cohort, educational background, field of study, monthly household income, religion, mother tongue, and ethnic identity were all significantly associated with at least one cultural dimension. Specifically, nationality was negatively correlated with Individualism (rs = –.202, p = .046) but positively correlated with Long-Term Orientation (rs = .258, p = .010), while age also showed a positive correlation with Long-Term Orientation (rs = .211, p = .037). Generational cohort correlated positively with Individualism (rs = .214, p = .034), and ethnic identity with Long-Term Orientation (rs = .212, p = .036). Education and language factors both demonstrated negative correlations with Uncertainty Avoidance: educational background (rs = –.208, p = .040) and mother tongue (rs = –.207, p = .041), suggesting that higher education levels and linguistic diversity reduce reliance on rigid rules (Soares et al., 2007; Scutariu & Bodnărescu, 2023). Field of study was negatively correlated with Indulgence (rs = –.220, p = .030), and religion was negatively associated with Uncertainty Avoidance (rs = –.283, p = .005), echoing prior studies linking faith traditions to structured uncertainty management (Shahin & Wright, 2004; Hofstede, 2002). Income exerted a twofold influence, with higher monthly household income linked to lower Uncertainty Avoidance (rs = –.316, p = .002) and higher Indulgence (rs = .221, p = .029), consistent with earlier findings that economic security facilitates greater openness and gratification-seeking behaviors (De Mooij & Hofstede, 2011; Wang & Duan, 2025).

In contrast, no significant relationships were observed for gender, job category, work experience, family status, or number of children, indicating that these factors did not meaningfully shape cultural orientations within the sample. Taken together, the findings underscore that socio-demographic and economic factors exert modest but measurable influences on cultural values, with income, religion, and nationality showing the clearest associations. At the same time, the absence of relationships for other factors highlights the complexity of cultural dynamics in Bahrain's public sector workforce (Ali, 1995; Budhwar & Mellahi, 2012).

4.5. Hypothesis Testing

In addition to the correlation analysis, hypothesis testing was employed to determine whether generational cohorts exhibited statistically significant differences across Hofstede's six cultural dimensions (Table 6). Appropriate statistical procedures were applied, with one-way ANOVA used when assumptions of normality and homogeneity of variance were met, and the Kruskal–Wallis's test adopted when these assumptions were violated (Cleff, 2014; Creswell & Creswell, 2017). Although descriptive means varied across generations, for example, Baby Boomers reported higher Power Distance (M = 41.67), while Generation Y recorded the highest Indulgence (M = 65.32)—these apparent differences did not reach statistical significance. As summarized in Table X, all tests yielded non-significant results ($p > .05$), indicating that no generational cohort differences were observed across the six Hofstede cultural dimensions (PDI, IDV, MAS, UAI, LTO, IND). While the mean values suggest observable patterns, such as older cohorts tending toward slightly higher Power Distance and lower Indulgence, these trends cannot be generalized statistically. Consequently, the null hypotheses were retained for all six tests, confirming that generational cohort did not exert a proportional impact on cultural values in this sample of Bahrain's public sector workforce. This finding is consistent with prior research that has questioned the extent to which generational categories explain meaningful variation in workplace values (Costanza et al., 2012; Joshi et al., 2011; Parry, 2014).

Table 6. Hofstede Dimensions by Generation: Means, Test Statistics, and Decisions (N = 98)

Dimension	Baby Boomers (n=9)	Generation X (n=42)	Generation Y (n=47)	Total (N=98)	Test Used	Statistic	p-value	Decision
Power Distance (PDI)	M = 41.67, SD = 28.28	M = 32.86, SD = 42.56	M = 26.60, SD = 54.64	M = 30.66, SD = 47.63	ANOVA	F(2,95) = 0.451	.638	Retain H_0
Individualism (IDV)	M = −11.67, SD = 30.31	M = −10.00, SD = 43.24	M = 13.40, SD = 54.39	M = 1.07, SD = 49.10	Kruskal–Wallis	H(2) = 4.488	.106	Retain H_0
Masculinity (MAS)	M = 19.44, SD = 18.45	M = 14.17, SD = 42.38	M = 20.85, SD = 57.77	M = 17.86, SD = 48.79	Kruskal–Wallis	H(2) = 1.489	.475	Retain H_0

continued on following page

Table 6. Continued

Dimension	Baby Boomers (n=9)	Generation X (n=42)	Generation Y (n=47)	Total (N=98)	Test Used	Statistic	p-value	Decision
Uncertainty Avoidance (UAI)	M = –42.22, SD = 43.95	M = –30.00, SD = 47.60	M = –16.91, SD = 59.48	M = –24.85, SD = 53.52	ANOVA	F(2,95) = 1.190	.309	Retain H_0
Long-Term Orientation (LTO)	M = –6.67, SD = 24.11	M = –18.21, SD = 45.48	M = –31.17, SD = 46.17	M = –23.37, SD = 44.72	ANOVA	F(2,95) = 1.643	.199	Retain H_0
Indulgence (IND)	M = 47.78, SD = 42.29	M = 63.33, SD = 59.69	M = 65.32, SD = 55.01	M = 62.86, SD = 55.79	ANOVA	F(2,95) = 0.371	.691	Retain H_0

These findings demonstrate that, although mean scores varied across generational cohorts, cultural values within the Bahraini public sector workforce do not differ significantly by age group. This result stands in contrast to strands of Hofstede's cultural framework and earlier research that posited generational differences as key drivers of cultural orientations (Costanza et al., 2012; Joshi et al., 2011). The absence of statistically significant effects in this context may be attributed to the homogenizing influence of organizational structures, shared institutional norms, and the broader socio-cultural environment of Bahrain, which emphasizes collective identity over generational divides (Barakat, 1993; Shahin & Wright, 2004). These findings suggest that generational distinctions, while often emphasized in global HRM discourse, may hold less relevance in societies where collectivist traditions and centralized institutional practices limit the expression of age-based cultural differences. The following Discussion chapter further situates these results within the existing literature, with particular attention to how contextual, societal, and institutional factors contribute to the stability of cultural values across generational cohorts.

4.6. Observations On Bahrain

Supplementary findings emphasized local perceptions of organizational culture. A substantial majority of participants concurred that religion (64.3%), historical legacy (65.3%), and language (62.2%) are essential influences on Arab culture. Regarding public sector performance, 60.2% thought that Bahraini public enterprises are in the early stages of adopting contemporary management principles. Furthermore, 63.3% reported an absence of explicit promotion and incentive criteria, while 52% believed that professional advancement is more contingent upon personal loyalty than talent. Notably, just 23% perceived that natives oppose oversight by expats, indicating a certain level of receptiveness to multicultural leadership.

5. DISCUSSION

The findings of this study present a nuanced portrait of Bahrain's public sector culture, where traditional values coexist with emerging modern management principles. The quantitative analysis revealed that nationality and religion are the most influential predictors of cultural values, while differences in generational cohorts are statistically insignificant. This challenges the widespread assumption that generational diversity is a defining driver of workplace behavior, suggesting that in Bahrain's public institutions, national identity, collective faith, and institutional norms shape cultural orientations far more profoundly than age-based distinctions.

The low Power Distance (PDI = 30) observed at Works Affairs reflects flatter hierarchies and accessible leadership—unusual within the Arab administrative model, which is traditionally associated with centralized authority (Ali, 1995). This structural openness strengthens internal trust and supports an external image of transparency and accountability. However, HR leaders must ensure that empowerment does not lead to blurred authority or weakened control. From an impression management perspective, low PDI enhances the institution's reputation as participative and citizen-oriented, provided leadership visibility remains strong.

The extremely low Individualism score (IDV = 1) indicates a deeply collectivist culture, characterized by loyalty, relationship-based trust, and a strong sense of group belonging. While this cohesion promotes stability and harmony, it also breeds risk: favouritism, personal alliances, and constrained innovation. These patterns jeopardize meritocracy and can undermine Bahrain's modernization goals. HR departments should thus prioritize merit-based promotions, clear appraisal standards, and anonymous reporting mechanisms to reconcile collectivism with fairness. At the same time, public-sector impression management should emphasize inclusiveness and unity while communicating a shift toward transparent, performance-driven governance.

The feminine orientation (MAS = 18)—emphasizing cooperation and social balance—fosters a collaborative climate aligned with public service values. However, this may dilute accountability if not reinforced by performance measures. HR strategies should maintain a balance between empathy and responsibility, ensuring that the Ministry's external image projects both compassion and professionalism.

A low Uncertainty Avoidance (UAI = –25) indicates flexibility, tolerance for ambiguity, and an innovation potential. However, this flexibility must be systematized through structured innovation policies to prevent inconsistency. In impression management terms, this adaptability projects an image of reform-readiness and administrative agility—valuable traits in a public institution transforming.

The short-term orientation (LTO = –23) reflects a preference for immediate stability over long-term planning and attachment to tradition. While this conservatism safeguards institutional continuity, it constrains innovation and responsiveness to future challenges. HR policy should therefore institutionalize foresight programs and continuous learning systems, while public communication should highlight a narrative of "modernization anchored in heritage."

Finally, high Indulgence (IND = 63) signifies openness, optimism, and emphasis on personal well-being—an image consistent with Bahrain's progressive public ethos. However, excessive indulgence risks complacency. HR managers must reinforce discipline and productivity without diminishing employee morale, ensuring that the Ministry's external reputation reflects both human-centered values and professional rigor.

The generational hypothesis yielded no statistically significant differences across Hofstede's six dimensions. This finding aligns with global meta-analyses (Costanza et al., 2012) and supports the argument that institutional culture and shared national identity neutralize age-based variations (Joshi et al., 2011). Generational diversity, while a popular theme in Western HRM, appears less relevant in Bahrain's collectivist public environment, where institutional homogenization outweighs individual cohort traits. As such, HR policies should avoid overemphasizing generational segmentation and instead focus on managing deeper, culturally rooted variables—such as nationality, religion, and education—that more directly influence organizational values and behaviors.

The figure 3 below presents the conceptual framework developed from this empirical study. It captures the interplay between Hofstede's cultural dimensions and the key moderating variables identified in the analysis, among which nationality and religion emerged as the most statistically significant factors in shaping the cultural values of the public workforce (Hofstede, 1984; Yaghi et al., 2025). In contrast, other diversity factors such as age, education, and income demonstrated varying degrees of influence (Costanza et al., 2012; Wang & Duan, 2025). This framework, therefore, provides a structured lens for understanding how cultural values in the public sector are continuously negotiated and redefined within the Bahraini context (Ali, 1995; Komisarof & Akaliyski, 2025).

Figure 3. Cultural values conceptual framework for public sector organizations

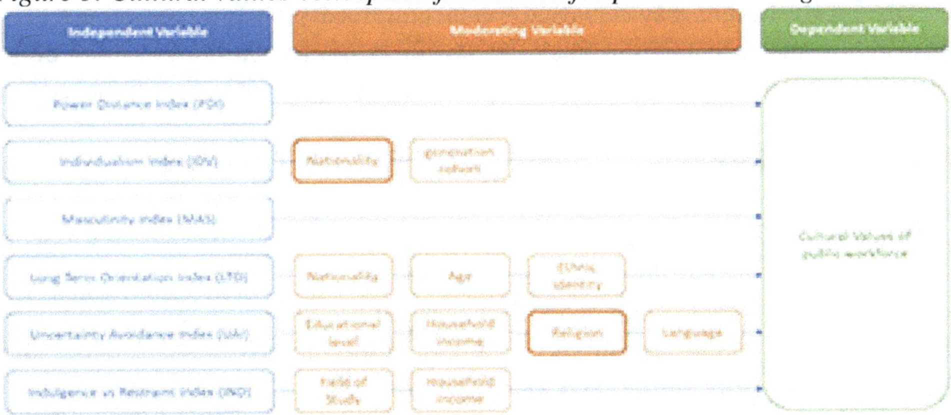

Implications for HR Policy and Institutional Image

The results of this study provide actionable insights for HR leaders seeking to translate cultural understanding into tangible organizational improvements. These implications are not only operational but also strategic, as they directly influence how public institutions manage their internal culture and external reputation.

- **Balance Collectivism and Meritocracy:** Introduce transparent, competency-based recruitment and promotion systems that preserve social harmony while rewarding performance.
- **Leverage Low Power Distance for Engagement:** Encourage participative leadership and two-way communication to enhance internal trust and public perception of accountability.
- **Institutionalize Innovation:** Transform cultural flexibility (low UAI) into structured innovation programs that support creative problem-solving within defined parameters.
- **Promote Inclusive Leadership:** Utilize intercultural training to bridge nationality- and religion-based divides, promoting unity and mutual respect within a diverse workforce.
- **Strengthen Impression Management through HRM:** Align internal HR reforms with external messaging—positioning Bahrain's public institutions as both culturally authentic and globally competent.

In essence, the results underscore that Bahrain's public sector is not generationally fragmented but culturally cohesive, grounded in collective values that simultaneously enable and constrain modernization. HR managers play a critical role in mediating this balance. By designing systems that honour cultural depth while promoting merit, transparency, and accountability, they can transform internal harmony into a credible institutional image—the very core of impression management in the public sector.

Study Limitations and Directions for Future Research

Although this research has successfully achieved its objectives and developed a conceptual framework illustrating the impact of diversity factors on the cultural values of public servants in the workplace, several limitations should be acknowledged. Recognizing these constraints is important for interpreting the findings and identifying avenues for further investigation (Creswell & Creswell, 2017).

First, the survey was conducted within a single public organization, with a relatively small sample size (N = 98). Consequently, the findings should be interpreted with caution, as they may not be fully generalizable to the entire public sector workforce in the Kingdom of Bahrain. Replicating the study across multiple organizations and with larger samples would enhance external validity (Berman et al., 2016; Scutariu & Bodnărescu, 2023).

Second, the analysis of generational differences was limited to three cohorts—Baby Boomers, Generation X, and Generation Y. These categories, while commonly used in both scholarly and practitioner literature, are not universally recognized and may oversimplify the complexity of age-related diversity (Deal, 2007; Joshi et al., 2011). Future studies may consider alternative or locally relevant classifications to capture generational dynamics more accurately (Costanza et al., 2012; Wang & Duan, 2025).

Third, data obtained from the Baby Boomer cohort was notably smaller than for other generations, reflecting the younger demographic profile of Works Affairs employees. This imbalance may have constrained the ability to draw robust conclusions about this group's cultural values. Subsequent research could aim to balance generational representation or focus on comparative analyses across sectors with different age structures (Neo et al., 2024).

Fourth, the disability factor was excluded from the analysis, as none of the respondents reported any form of disability. This omission limits the scope of the diversity dimensions considered in the study. Future research should actively include disability-related variables where possible, as this remains a critical dimension of workforce diversity (Shahin & Wright, 2004; Budhwar & Mellahi, 2012).

Fifth, the calculation of constant values c(x) for the Uncertainty Avoidance Index (UAI) and Long-Term Orientation (LTO) dimensions could not be completed. This was due to the absence of a common or base country to serve as a benchmark for distinguishing between the old and new datasets. Addressing this methodological challenge in future research would improve the accuracy of cross-cultural comparisons (Hofstede, 1984; Hofstede & Minkov, 2010; Zheng et al., 2025).

Finally, several sensitive or difficult-to-measure diversity factors—including sexual orientation, military experience, personal perceptions, and political beliefs—were excluded. While understandable, these omissions mean that the framework presented here does not capture the full spectrum of potential influences on cultural values. Future studies may explore these dimensions through carefully designed methodologies that ensure confidentiality and ethical sensitivity (Komisarof & Akaliyski, 2025; Bolzonella, 2024; Darul Wiyono et al., 2024).

In light of these limitations, future research should broaden the scope of inquiry by incorporating larger and more diverse samples, refining generational classifications, and addressing neglected diversity variables. Such efforts will strengthen the understanding of how multiple factors interact to shape cultural values and impression management in the Bahraini public sector and beyond (Ali, 1995; Yaghi et al., 2025).

CONCLUSION

Cultural diversity exerts a dual influence on organizational life. On the positive side, it can enhance job satisfaction, stimulate creativity, foster innovation, and improve staff retention (Budhwar & Mellahi, 2012; Costanza et al., 2012). Conversely, it can also generate barriers, miscommunication, and conflicting behaviors (Shahin & Wright, 2004). Understanding this balance is crucial for public sector organizations seeking to harness the benefits of diversity while minimizing its challenges (Ali, 1995; Barakat, 1993).

This study aimed to assist human resource managers in the Bahraini public sector in identifying the key factors influencing employees' cultural values. The study aimed to offer insights into the design of policies and programs that enhance the positive aspects of cultural diversity and support the attainment of institutional goals (Berman et al., 2016).

This study utilized Hofstede's cultural dimensions, a prominent framework in cross-cultural research (Hofstede, 1984; Hofstede, 2002; Hofstede & Minkov, 2010). The Value Survey Module (VSM) was converted into a digital format (Hofstede & Minkov, 2013) utilizing Microsoft Forms and was administered in February 2021 to a representative sample of Works Affairs employees. From a total of 1,080 staff members, 98 valid responses were obtained and analyzed utilizing SPSS statistical software (Cleff, 2014).

The findings revealed that nine out of the fifteen diversity factors analyzed exhibited either positive or negative correlations with Hofstede's cultural dimensions. The factors included nationality, generational cohort, age, ethnic identity, field of study, education level, religion, household income, and language. Further statistical analysis indicated that only nationality and religion significantly influenced cultural values (Neo et al., 2024; Yaghi et al., 2025). In contrast, the generational cohort factor—commonly believed to have a significant impact—was determined to have minimal to no substantial effect (Wang & Duan, 2025). This study advises HR managers to refrain from using generational stereotypes and to concentrate on the more significant factors outlined in the conceptual framework (Joshi et al., 2011).

The study was conducted rigorously and credibly; however, its limitations should be acknowledged. The study focused on one public organization and involved a limited sample size (N = 98), which limits the applicability of the results to the broader Bahraini public sector. This study establishes a significant basis for comprehending cultural diversity within the GCC context (Al-Rasheed, 2001; Scutariu & Bodnărescu, 2023). This document functions as a preliminary manuscript and resource for HR practitioners and researchers examining the influence of cultural values on workplace dynamics within public institutions (Mentzer, 2023).

Future research may extend these findings by exploring the identified diversity factors in more detail, broadening the study to include other public organizations with larger and more representative samples, or assessing the applicability of the conceptual framework in various contexts (Bolzonella, 2024). Furthermore, the use of qualitative approaches can provide deeper insights and may reveal new aspects of cultural diversity that quantitative methods may overlook (Creswell & Creswell, 2017). This research will enhance academic knowledge and offer practical insights for policymakers and HR managers addressing the challenges of cultural diversity in the public sector (Darul Wiyono et al., 2024).

The findings emphasize that cultural values significantly influence employee self-presentation and interpretation of others in the workplace. Understanding diversity presents both a challenge for human resource management and a critical aspect of impression management, influencing individual interactions, collaboration, and trust-building within the Bahraini public sector (Komisarof & Akaliyski, 2025; Zheng et al., 2025).

REFERENCES

Ailon, G. (2008). Mirror, mirror on the wall: Culture's consequences in a value test of its own design. *Academy of Management Review*, *33*(4), 885–904. DOI: 10.5465/amr.2008.34421995

Al-Rasheed, A. M. (2001). Features of traditional Arab management and organization in the Jordan business environment. *Journal of Transnational Management Development*, *6*(1), 53–68.

Ali, A. (1995). Cultural discontinuity and Arab management thought. *International Studies of Management & Organization*, *25*(3), 7–30. DOI: 10.1080/00208825.1995.11656657

Barakat, H. (1993). *The Arab world: Society, culture, and state*. University of California Press. DOI: 10.1525/9780520914421

Berman, E. M., Bowman, J. S., West, J. P., & Van Wart, M. R. (2016). *Human resource management in public service: Paradoxes, processes, and problems* (5th ed.). SAGE.

Bolzonella, F. (2024). *Evaluating through culture: Rethinking Hofstede's framework in policy analysis*. European Evaluation Journal.

Boxall, P. (1994). Placing HR strategy at the heart of business success. *Personnel Management*, *26*(7), 32–35.

Boyle, G. J. (1991). Does item homogeneity indicate internal consistency or item redundancy in psychometric scales? *Personality and Individual Differences*, *12*(3), 291–294. DOI: 10.1016/0191-8869(91)90115-R

Budhwar, P., & Mellahi, K. (2012). Human resource management in the Middle East. In Brewster, C., & Mayrhofer, W. (Eds.), *Handbook of research on comparative human resource management* (pp. 504–523). Edward Elgar Publishing., DOI: 10.4337/9780857938718.00029

Cleff, T. (2014). *Exploratory data analysis in business and economics: An introduction using SPSS, Stata, and Excel*. Springer. DOI: 10.1007/978-3-319-01517-0

Costanza, D. P., Badger, J. M., Fraser, R. L., Severt, J. B., & Gade, P. A. (2012). Generational differences in work-related attitudes: A meta-analysis. *Journal of Business and Psychology*, *27*(4), 375–394. DOI: 10.1007/s10869-012-9259-4

Creswell, J. W., & Creswell, J. D. (2017). *Research design: Qualitative, quantitative, and mixed methods approaches* (5th ed.). SAGE Publications.

Cronbach, L. J. (1951). Coefficient alpha and the internal structure of tests. *Psychometrika, 16*(3), 297–334. DOI: 10.1007/BF02310555

d'Iribarne, P. (2009). National cultures and organizations in search of a theory: An interpretative approach. *International Journal of Cross Cultural Management, 9*(3), 309–321. DOI: 10.1177/1470595809346601

Deal, J. J. (2007). *Retiring the generation gap: How employees young and old can find common ground.* John Wiley & Sons.

Goffman, E. (1990). *The presentation of self in everyday life*. Penguin. (Original work published 1959)

Hofstede, G. (1984). *Culture's consequences: International differences in work-related values* (2nd ed.). SAGE.

Hofstede, G. (2002). Dimensions do not exist: A reply to Brendan McSweeney. *Journal of Technological Advancements, 55*(11), 1355–1361. DOI: 10.1177/0018726702055011921

Hofstede, G., & Minkov, M. (2010). *Cultures and organizations: Software of the mind* (3rd ed.). McGraw-Hill.

Hofstede, G., & Minkov, M. (2013). *Values survey module 2013 manual*. GeertHofstede.com. https://geerthofstede.com/research-and-vsm/

Jackson, T. (2020). Towards a framework for understanding cross-cultural management learning and education. *International Journal of Management Reviews, 22*(3), 279–297. DOI: 10.1111/ijmr.12234

Jehn, K. A., Northcraft, G. B., & Neale, M. A. (1999). Why differences make a difference: A field study of diversity, conflict, and performance in workgroups. *Administrative Science Quarterly, 44*(4), 741–763. DOI: 10.2307/2667054

Joshi, A., Dencker, J. C., & Franz, G. (2011). Generations in organizations. *Research in Organizational Behavior, 31*, 177–205. DOI: 10.1016/j.riob.2011.10.002

Komisarof, A., & Akaliyski, P. (2025). New developments in Hofstede's individualism–collectivism: A guide for scholars, educators, trainers, and other practitioners. *International Journal of Intercultural Relations, 107*, 102200. Advance online publication. DOI: 10.1016/j.ijintrel.2025.102200

Loden, M., & Rosener, J. B. (1991). *Workforce America! Managing employee diversity as a vital resource*. McGraw-Hill.

McSweeney, B. (2002). Hofstede's model of national cultural differences and their consequences: A triumph of faith—A failure of analysis. *Human Relations*, *55*(1), 89–118. DOI: 10.1177/0018726702551004

Mentzer, M. S. (2023). Public sector corruption among the United States: Exploring the impact of cultural values. *Business & Professional Ethics Journal*, *42*(2), 251–266. DOI: 10.5840/bpej2023620143

Neo, S., Bertram, I., Szydlowski, G., Bouwman, R., de Boer, N., Grimmelikhuijsen, S., Charbonneau, É., Moon, M. J., & Tummers, L. (2024). Working 9 to 5? A cross-national analysis of public sector worker stereotypes. *Public Management Review*, *26*(7), 2064–2093. DOI: 10.1080/14719037.2023.2254306

Parry, E. (2014). *Generational diversity at work: New research perspectives*. Routledge.

Pettigrew, A. M. (1979). On studying organizational cultures. *Administrative Science Quarterly*, *24*(4), 570–581. DOI: 10.2307/2392363

Roberge, M.-É., & Van Dick, R. (2010). Recognizing the benefits of diversity: When and how does diversity increase group performance? *Human Resource Management Review*, *20*(4), 295–308. DOI: 10.1016/j.hrmr.2009.09.002

Saxena, A. (2014). Workforce diversity: A key to improve productivity. *Procedia Economics and Finance*, *11*, 76–85. DOI: 10.1016/S2212-5671(14)00178-6

Scutariu, P., & Bodnărescu, A. (2023). A micro-research on Hofstede's cultural dimensions in local public administration. *European Journal of Law and Public Administration*, *10*(1), 57–68. DOI: 10.18662/eljpa/10.1/195

Shahin, A. I., & Wright, P. L. (2004). Leadership in the context of culture: An Egyptian perspective. *Leadership and Organization Development Journal*, *25*(6), 499–511. DOI: 10.1108/01437730410556743

Soares, A. M., Farhangmehr, M., & Shoham, A. (2007). Hofstede's dimensions of culture in international marketing studies. *Journal of Business Research*, *60*(3), 277–284. DOI: 10.1016/j.jbusres.2006.10.018

Triandis, H. C. (1988). Collectivism vs. individualism: A reconceptualization of a basic concept in cross-cultural social psychology. In Verma, G. K., & Bagley, C. (Eds.), *Cross-cultural studies of personality, attitudes and cognition* (pp. 60–95). Palgrave Macmillan., DOI: 10.1007/978-1-349-08120-2_3

Wang, L., & Duan, X. (2025). Generational diversity and team innovation: The roles of conflict and shared leadership. *Frontiers in Psychology*, *15*, 1501633. Advance online publication. DOI: 10.3389/fpsyg.2024.1501633

Webber, S. S., & Donahue, L. M. (2001). Impact of highly and less job-related diversity on work group cohesion and performance: A meta-analysis. *Journal of Management*, *27*(2), 141–162. DOI: 10.1177/014920630102700202

Wiese, S. A., Lehmann, J., & Beckmann, M. (2024). Organizational culture and the usage of Industry 4.0 technologies: Evidence from Swiss businesses [Preprint]. *arXiv*. https://arxiv.org/abs/2412.12752

Wiyono, D., Tanjung, R., Setiadi, H., Marini, S., & Sugiarto, Y. (2024). Organizational transformation: The impact of servant leadership on work ethic culture with burnout as a mediating factor in the hospitality industry. *arXiv*. https://arxiv.org/abs/2407.01533

Yadav, S., & Lenka, U. (2020). Workforce diversity: From a literature review to future research agenda. *Journal of Indian Business Research*, *12*(4), 577–603. DOI: 10.1108/JIBR-08-2019-0243

Yaghi, A., Yaghi, M., & Yaghi, I. (2025). Impact of national culture on the transfer of leadership training: The role of Hofstede's cultural dimensions. *International Journal of Training and Development*, *29*(2), 95–107. DOI: 10.1111/ijtd.12346

Zheng, F., Zhao, C., Yasmin, F., & Sokolová, M. (2025). Hofstede's cultural dimensions and proactive behavior as antecedents of entrepreneurial innovativeness. *Acta Psychologica*, *256*, 105034. Advance online publication. DOI: 10.1016/j.actpsy.2025.104948

Chapter 5

Family and Consumer Sciences Education as a Vehicle for Impression Management

Julian Thomas Costa
https://orcid.org/0009-0001-9739-7870
Pace University, USA

ABSTRACT

This chapter examines the role of Family and Consumer Sciences (FCS) education in the shaping and management of personal image across personal, professional, and digital contexts. At its core, FCS (also known to many as "home economics") is an interdisciplinary field that prepares individuals to lead effective lives through knowledge of personal and family skills, housing, clothing, nutrition, human development, and interpersonal communication. However, its role in impression management and image formation, while implicit in many of its subdisciplines, is often under-theorized in mainstream academic discourse. This chapter seeks to bring this to the forefront of scholarship by making a case for FCS as a vital contributor to the intellectual understanding of personal image management.

INTRODUCTION

Throughout the twentieth and twenty-first centuries, the attainment of practical skills and the ability to manage one's personal affairs effectively have contributed to the perception of possessing *cultural capital.* An individual's competencies, and the manner in which they present themselves in social settings, can elicit trust,

DOI: 10.4018/979-8-3373-5519-1.ch005

respect, and even admiration. Within the formative years of schooling, one setting for cultivating such qualities is the family and consumer sciences classroom, which is sometimes referred to as home economics. Family and consumer sciences (FCS) is an interdisciplinary field centered on life skills and personal effectiveness. The International Federation for Home Economics (IFHE) defines the discipline as the original field of research on the economic, social, and ecological aspects of everyday living. This perspective underscores the discipline's foundational role in addressing practical household concerns through a multidisciplinary approach that combines research, education, and advocacy (International Federation for Home Economics, n.d.). As FCS professor Sharleen L. Kato (2008) observed, Family and Consumer Sciences builds upon the foundational human needs of food, clothing, shelter, and relationships, emphasizing the interdependence between individual well-being and social context. Within these everyday domains, the enactment of self: how one dresses, eats, designs one's home, and relates to others constitutes an ongoing performance that communicates identity and values. Thus, FCS provides a natural arena for examining impression management as both a personal and social process. For many students, it represents the only opportunity to gain pragmatic training in areas such as clothing care, nutrition, interpersonal interaction, and caregiving. Despite the far-reaching impact of FCS education, its implicit role in shaping impression management remains largely overlooked in academic discourse.

The IFHE Position Statement: *Home Economics in the 21st Century* expands this definition, situating the profession within the human sciences and emphasizing its interdisciplinary and transdisciplinary nature. It identifies Home Economics as a field committed to "achieving optimal and sustainable living for individuals, families, and communities," and recognizes that the capacities and choices of individuals extend from the household to the "glocal" sphere (IFHE, 2008). This broader framing underscores that FCS is not confined to domestic skills, but rather serves as a catalyst for empowerment, ethical awareness, and transformative practice, which are core dimensions also embedded in impression management.

It is important to recognize that impression management is not static; it evolves over time as individuals encounter new social, professional, and cultural environments. The foundational skills learned in FCS classrooms during formative years provide the groundwork for ongoing self-presentation, which adapts to career trajectories, social roles, and digital landscapes. For example, a student who learns conflict resolution and interpersonal awareness in high school may later refine these skills to navigate workplace negotiations, professional networking, or leadership responsibilities. By emphasizing this temporal dimension, FCS education highlights the long-term applicability of its lessons, demonstrating how early skill acquisition can shape lifelong patterns of ethical and strategic impression management.

Family and Consumer Sciences (FCS) is guided by a clear mission: to provide leadership and support for professionals whose work assists individuals, families, and communities in making informed decisions about their well-being, relationships, and resources to achieve optimal quality of life (American Association of Family and Consumer Sciences [AAFCS], 2007, as cited in Kato, 2008, p. 52). Within this mission, domains such as apparel design, nutrition, housing, and interpersonal relationships are not simply technical skills. They become tools for enhancing identity, self-concept, and social competence. From this perspective, FCS education naturally intersects with the study of impression management, offering students structured opportunities to develop both personal and social efficacy.

The purpose of this chapter is to position FCS education as a key contributor to the intellectual understanding of personal image management. Specifically, it will examine how FCS aligns with the conceptual framework: the "ABCDE" of impression management, namely, Appearance, Behavior, Communication, Digital presence, and Emotional balance. While I concur with this pragmatic framing, I extend this view by arguing that FCS also cultivates students' awareness of self-presentation and social perception, which are central elements of impression management. This chapter seeks to bring this overlooked dynamic to the forefront of scholarship by making a case for FCS as a vital contributor to the intellectual understanding of personal image management. This view of FCS as both a preventative and restorative practice is echoed by long-time educators Melinda Swafford and Elizabeth Ramsey, who note in their 2023 book, *Family and Consumer Sciences: Preventative and Restorative Education*, that "FCS educators help individuals and families identify practices of interactions that strengthen family relationships and identify how to use resources to meet needs during everyday life and during times of stress" (Swafford & Ramsey, 2023, p. xvii). Though elements of impression management are implicit in many FCS subdisciplines, they have received limited attention in mainstream academic discourse.

Family and Consumer Sciences has long been shaped by both social expectations and professional innovation, a duality explored in historical and contemporary accounts of the field. Stage and Vincenti (1997) trace the gendered roots of home economics, revealing how early practitioners, predominantly women, negotiated societal expectations while striving to establish a legitimate professional identity. In doing so, they navigated the tension between domestic labor and intellectual rigor, creating a space in which women could exercise expertise, leadership, and influence. This history illuminates the ways in which FCS has always been intertwined with notions of personal image and societal perception, as practitioners modeled both competence and social responsibility in their work.

Nichols (2015) builds on this historical foundation by examining how home economics has adapted to modern challenges, emphasizing resourcefulness, innovation, and responsiveness to change. She portrays FCS not as a static discipline but as a field attuned to societal shifts, technological advances, and evolving family structures. Modern practitioners, according to Nichols, cultivate skills that extend beyond the home, preparing individuals to navigate professional environments, manage personal resources, and make informed decisions that enhance well-being. This perspective complements contemporary FCS goals of fostering resilience, critical thinking, and effective interpersonal communication, highlighting the continuity between past and present approaches to personal and family development.

Both Stage and Nichols underscore the dual focus of FCS: preparing individuals to meet practical needs while promoting broader social competence. Stage's analysis of gender roles demonstrates how early home economists challenged and redefined cultural norms, while Nichols illustrates the profession's capacity for innovation in response to changing societal demands. Together, these accounts offer insight into how FCS equips individuals to cultivate not only technical and domestic skills but also the self-awareness, adaptability, and social acuity that underpin effective personal image and interpersonal engagement.

Although LEAD FCS standards provide structured outcomes for education in the United States, the historical and contemporary perspectives offered by Stage and Nichols suggest that the value of FCS extends beyond prescribed competencies. The profession's emphasis on ethical decision-making, resourcefulness, and socially responsible behavior aligns with the broader goals of fostering holistic development, emotional intelligence, and personal effectiveness. The evolution of FCS reflects a consistent commitment to preparing individuals for meaningful participation in family, community, and professional contexts, bridging historical traditions with contemporary relevance.

THEORETICAL FOUNDATION

The concept of impression management is often associated with the work of sociologist Erving Goffman, whose seminal text *The Presentation of Self in Everyday Life* (1959) presented the dramaturgical model of social interaction. As Goffman explains, individuals engage in a constant "performance" of self, and whether consciously or unconsciously, they manage the impressions they make on others. Goffman's frequent metaphor of everyday life as theater, where people are actors navigating frontstage and backstage behaviors, provides a useful lens for understanding the ways individuals curate appearance, mannerisms, and communication to align with social expectations and cultural norms.

Impression management, according to Goffman, is not merely superficial but a fundamental concept of social cohesion. In a myriad of social situations, people must interpret social cues and modify their behaviors in response to them in order to function within various social contexts. Subsequent scholars have expanded on this foundation, exploring impression management in relation to identity performance, social stratification, and digital life. For instance, contemporary theorists in image studies and media theory have pointed to the increasing complexity of self-presentation in a digital age, where social media platforms require constant negotiation between authenticity and curation (Hogan, 2010; Marwick & Boyd, 2011).

Connections can also be made between impression management and various sociological constructs such as cultural capital (Bourdieu, 1984), emotional labor (Hochschild, 1983), and symbolic interactionism, all of which highlight the ways in which social actors present and manage facets of identity to achieve desired outcomes. In particular, cultural capital, which is the non-financial social assets that promote social mobility, can be developed through coursework in Family and Consumer Sciences (FCS) education where such competencies are often taught. Among these are communication styles, aesthetic choices, and behavioral norms, each of which influences social perception and individual positioning within social hierarchies.

Though it has maintained a longstanding presence in sociological literature, impression management has seldom been explicitly connected to FCS education. Yet the curriculum of FCS, which is historically known for its focus on practical life skills, provides a structured setting in which students can develop and refine the very competencies that Goffman and others describe as central to self-presentation. FCS classrooms offer both the content knowledge and the experiential learning necessary to foster nuanced self-awareness and interpersonal acumen. Such empowerment is gained through explicit instruction as well as gaining a sense of pride through lessons in apparel selection, meal planning, family dynamics, or professional etiquette. These elements not only serve practical purposes but also function as tools for constructing and negotiating identity in various social arenas. In this way, FCS education can be seen as a vehicle for developing "applied impression management," or, the practical enactment of theoretical principles through everyday decisions and interactions. It occupies a unique position at the crossroads of personal development, social performance, and cultural literacy, offering a rich, yet underexplored, context for impression management theory to be made manifest in educational practice.

At the institutional level, these applied dimensions of self-presentation are reinforced by international policy frameworks that define the purpose and scope of Family and Consumer Sciences. The interdisciplinary and applied character of FCS aligns with the International Federation for Home Economics (2008) position paper, *Home Economics in the 21st Century*'s emphasis on synthesizing knowledge across domains to "enhance wellbeing and advocate for individuals, families, and communities." Impression management, viewed through this lens, becomes not only an individual skill set but a socially transformative practice. When FCS instruction integrates aesthetic, behavioral, communicative, and emotional competencies, it advances what IFHE identifies as the profession's ethical imperative: to empower learners toward reflective, responsible, and sustainable living.

THE ABCDE FRAMEWORK: MAPPING IMPRESSION MANAGEMENT IN FCS EDUCATION

Although not part of Goffman's original conceptualization of impression management, the "ABCDE" orientation offers a pragmatic and systematic way to apply impression management theory across multiple contexts.

Figure 1. A visual representation of the ABCDE Model of Impression Management.

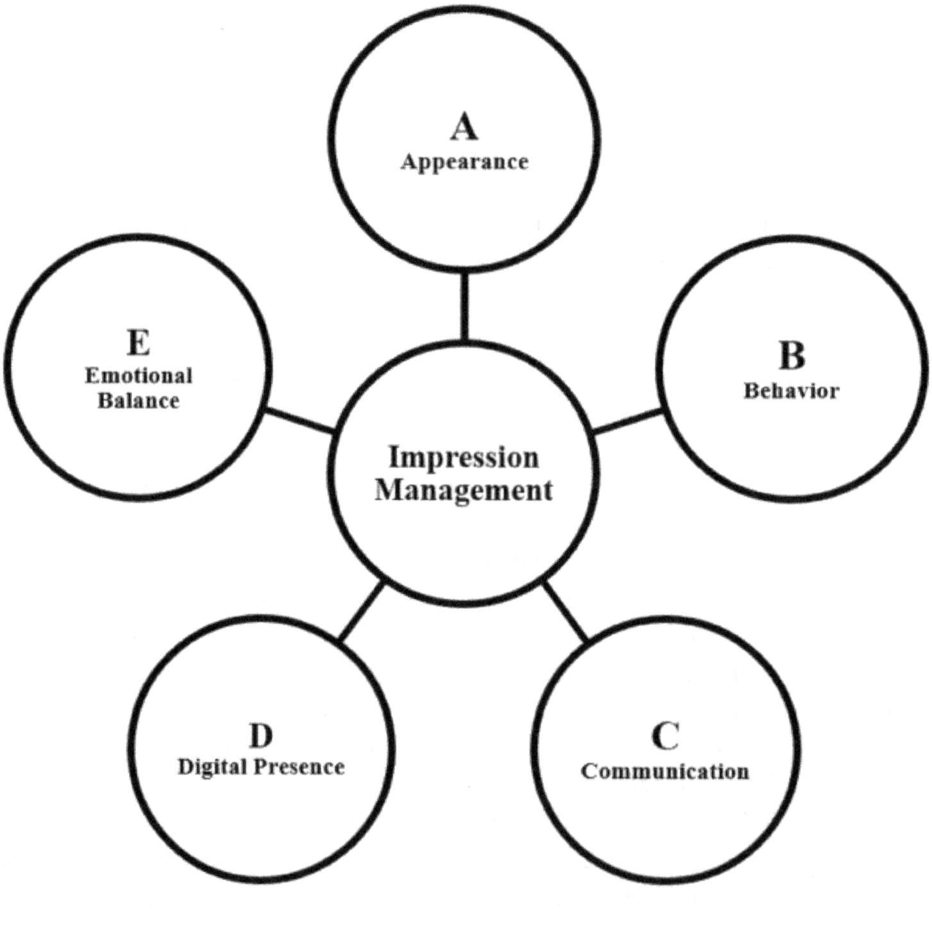

Within the field of Family and Consumer Sciences (FCS), this framework can be used to illuminate the disciplinary connections between personal presentation, social adaptation, and cultural communication.

The "A" of impression management stands for appearance. Personal grooming and attire function as powerful forms of nonverbal communication (Hybels & Weaver, 2005), signaling aspects of one's self-concept, social awareness, desired status, and aesthetic preferences. Whether an individual is dressed casually or in formal attire, clothing communicates important messages about identity and belonging across cultural contexts (Kaiser, 2012). FCS courses underscore this connection through lessons in design, aesthetics, textiles, and apparel construction. From exploring the theoretical implications of color symbolism (Entwistle, 2015) to learning practical skills such as sewing or garment care, students are encouraged to view clothing as both a personal resource and a communicative tool. Clothing, accessories, and body adornment, as Kato (2008) notes, are more than functional necessities. They are semiotic cues that reveal cultural identity, gender norms, and social status (p. 48). Kato (2008) emphasizes that when apparel design concepts are taught within FCS, clothing is more than a material good; it is an artifact of life that can enhance the quality of life for individuals, families, and communities (p. 52). Clothing thus functions as a social, emotional, and physical tool, supporting self-concept and facilitating intentional impression management. In the context of the ABCDE model, attire becomes a deliberate vehicle through which students learn to express identity, convey competence, and navigate social expectations. Therefore, the "appearance" dimension of impression management aligns closely with FCS's enduring concern for how individuals use dress and design to communicate belonging and personal agency.

Through this instruction, several core messages emerge. First, clothing is an asset that requires knowledge and care to maintain. Second, appearance communicates identity and influences social perception, whether intentionally or unintentionally. Third, individuals can adapt strategically to diverse social contexts by making thoughtful appearance-related choices, thereby demonstrating both self-awareness and social competence, key dimensions of effective impression management.

Social competence extends beyond physical appearance to encompass behavior, the "B" of impression management. The actions, habits, and social norms that govern how individuals conduct themselves in shared spaces contribute significantly to how identity is perceived and evaluated by others (Argyle, 1988; Goffman, 1959). Behavior is both contextually shaped and adaptable, requiring individuals to modify their conduct in response to differing social expectations and environments. This dimension of impression management is deeply embedded in Family and Consumer Sciences (FCS) curricula, particularly in topics such as etiquette, manners, conflict resolution, and family relationships. Relationships have always been central to FCS inquiry. Kato (2008) describes the modern family as a "psychological family," characterized by emotional bonds and expressive relationships (p. 48). Impression management, in this context, extends beyond self-presentation to include the maintenance of family identity and shared reputation within the community. Instruction in child development and family dynamics often incorporates behavioral modeling and reinforcement, helping students understand how values and habits form through interaction and observation (Berns, 2021). FCS classrooms provide structured opportunities for learners to practice appropriate behaviors across a range of interpersonal contexts, from the dinner table to the workplace to the family unit. The LEADFCS Parenting Standards (15.1.3) further affirm that parenting and interpersonal modeling influence not only individual development but also social norms and community well-being. By analyzing how nurturing practices and discipline styles shape social outcomes, FCS learners recognize behavior as both personally enacted and socially transmitted.

Importantly, the teaching of behavior in FCS extends far beyond the "do's and don'ts" traditionally associated with moral or disciplinary instruction. It is a values-based enterprise that fosters students' understanding of civility, empathy, reliability, and time management, which are traits that not only influence immediate impressions but also contribute to long-term character formation and social adaptability (Halpern & Donaghey, 2018). Through this behavioral lens, FCS education positions impression management as an ethically grounded process of learning how to engage with others respectfully, responsibly, and with cultural awareness.

Engagement with others, through verbal, nonverbal, or mediated channels, falls under the broad umbrella of communication, the "C" of impression management and one of its most foundational tools. Within Family and Consumer Sciences (FCS), communication skills are embedded throughout the curriculum, appearing in interpersonal relationship units, family dynamics modules, and career readiness instruction (Stewart & Logan, 2018). Some programs also offer a stand-alone communication course or incorporate public speaking and presentation assignments as experiential learning opportunities for students to develop and demonstrate interpersonal competence.

Although communication is frequently addressed in language arts or speech curricula, FCS courses often take a more contextual and relational approach, emphasizing communication as a lived, interpersonal process rather than a purely linguistic skill. In the FCS classroom, students are exposed to models of effective communication that include active listening, tone and emotion awareness, conflict mediation, and in more comprehensive programs, assertiveness training (Hybels & Weaver, 2005; Pearson et al., 2017). Such instruction fosters the ability to engage meaningfully in diverse relationships and to understand communication as a dynamic exchange that shapes both personal and social identity. These communication goals mirror

LEADFCS competencies such as applying communication strategies that promote emotional well-being among family members (15.2.2). Integrating such standards ensures that communication education in FCS remains evidence-based, relational, and developmentally responsive across the lifespan.

Importantly, communication skills in FCS are not taught in isolation, but as part of a broader system of relational competence. Effective communication requires the ability to interpret situations, read nonverbal cues, and consider contextual subtexts that may influence expression and perception (Burgoon, Guerrero, & Floyd, 2016). Culture, social setting, and medium, whether face-to-face or digital, each affect how messages are constructed and understood (Hall, 1976). FCS education thus prepares students to navigate these nuances with sensitivity, fostering not only practical communication skills but also intercultural awareness and emotional intelligence, both of which are essential to effective impression management.

In the twenty-first century, individuals must manage their impressions not only in face-to-face or proxemic social contexts but also in virtual environments. How one presents themselves online—often referred to as their digital footprint—and the choices they make in language, imagery, and engagement practices all influence how they are perceived by others (boyd d., 2014; Leaver, Highfield, & Abidin, 2020). Digital presence, the "D" of impression management, has therefore become an essential extension of self-presentation in contemporary life. Although Goffman's (1959) work on impression management predates social media, his dramaturgical model remains instructive for understanding how individuals perform identity through digital platforms such as Instagram, LinkedIn, and TikTok (Hogan, 2010). FCS education has increasingly recognized the importance of preparing students to navigate these online spaces responsibly. Topics such as digital citizenship, media literacy, and online safety have become integral to modern curricula (Ribble & Miller, 2013). Instruction in these areas equips students to construct a positive and ethical digital footprint, develop discernment in information sharing, and understand the long-term implications of their online behaviors.

These lessons are not limited to technical skill development. Through discussions and activities addressing privacy settings, cyberbullying, digital branding, and responsible content creation, students learn that their online actions carry real-world social consequences (Livingstone, 2014). Such instruction aligns with the broader educational goal of cultivating ethical, reflective participants in both physical and digital communities—individuals who can balance authenticity, accountability, and awareness in their self-presentation across multiple domains of life.

Consider how these skills manifest in specific scenarios. A student trained in digital citizenship might curate a LinkedIn profile to highlight leadership experiences from school clubs or community service, demonstrating both professionalism and ethical awareness. Gender-inclusive lessons ensure that students of all identities feel empowered to take on roles traditionally associated with a particular gender, such as project leadership or culinary mastery. Similarly, cultural competencies learned through FCS activities can help students navigate international internships, cross-cultural collaborations, or volunteering in diverse communities. These examples illustrate how the ABCDE dimensions translate directly into real-world impressions that influence professional, civic, and organizational success.

The last letter in the model, "E," refers to emotional balance, which is of utmost importance when attempting to form a positive impression on others. Whereas appearance, behavior, communication, and digital presence are externally observable, emotional balance reflects an individual's internal ability to regulate affect, maintain composure, and respond appropriately to social cues. Goffman (1967) explored this dimension through his discussion of embarrassment and composure within Interaction Ritual, noting that successful social performance often depends on one's capacity to manage emotion in ways that sustain both personal dignity and the "face" of others. In this sense, emotional regulation functions as a form of impression management that protects the continuity and civility of interaction.

Within Family and Consumer Sciences (FCS) education, emotional balance is nurtured through both content knowledge and interpersonal practice. Lessons in family dynamics, child development, and conflict resolution teach students to recognize emotions as integral to human relationships and to manage them with empathy and self-control. Whether navigating disagreements during a group project, managing stress in caregiving simulations, or handling frustration when a cooking experiment goes awry, learners are guided to view emotion not as a disruption but as a communicative signal requiring thoughtful response. These experiences align with Goffman's (1963) notion of situational propriety: understanding when and how certain emotional expressions are acceptable within given social contexts.

Goffman (2009) later elaborated on these dynamics in his essay *Remedial Work*, emphasizing the social processes through which individuals repair disrupted impressions and restore equilibrium after a transgression or mistake. Such "remedial interchanges," which include apologies, justifications, and requests for forgiveness, serve as essential mechanisms for sustaining civility and reaffirming mutual respect. In the context of FCS education, students learn similar restorative practices when resolving interpersonal conflict, acknowledging errors, or negotiating responsibility in collaborative environments. By teaching the art of social repair alongside emotional control, FCS instruction transforms impression management from mere composure into a practice of relational accountability, where emotional balance becomes the foundation for ethical and enduring human connection.

Developing emotional balance is closely linked to the cultivation of emotional intelligence, a competency that supports employability, leadership, and interpersonal success. FCS educators emphasize self-awareness, active listening, and perspective-taking as foundational elements of emotional maturity. These aims are also reflected in the LEADFCS national content standards, which highlight the importance of communication strategies that promote emotional well-being within families (Standard 15.2.2). By encouraging learners to apply nurturing and emotionally intelligent communication practices, FCS instruction reinforces both interpersonal stability and family cohesion as foundations for overall well-being. These skills enable students to maintain poise under pressure, express empathy across cultural and relational boundaries, and engage ethically with others both in person and online. As such, emotional balance serves as the unifying thread of impression management, bridging the inner life of the self with the outer dynamics of social perception.

Within the ABCDE framework, students learn to navigate the interplay between personal presentation and social perception, developing abilities that extend beyond individual competence to interpersonal understanding and adaptability. Beyond technical skills, FCS emphasizes unifying themes that cut across its specializations, including communication, critical thinking, appreciation for human diversity, global thinking, and moral, ethical, and spiritual development (Baugher et al., 2003; Kato, 2008, p. 53). These integrative themes complement the ABCDE dimensions by encouraging students not only to manage impressions effectively but also to reflect on the social, ethical, and intercultural consequences of their actions. By grounding impression management in these principles, FCS provides a holistic educational space where self-presentation is inseparable from ethical reasoning, civic awareness, and cultural literacy, reinforcing the discipline's role in cultivating well-rounded, socially responsible individuals, which is a purpose made tangible through the five dimensions of the ABCDE framework.

In addition to interpersonal and ethical competencies, FCS instruction grounds impression management in the essential human needs of food, clothing, shelter, and relationships (Kato, 2008, pp. 47–48). Food, beyond its biological necessity, reflects cultural norms, social practices, and even ethical considerations, allowing students to understand how dietary choices can signal identity and values within diverse communities. Clothing functions as both protection and a social tool, conveying personal identity, cultural affiliation, and social status, and offering tangible opportunities for students to practice self-presentation thoughtfully. Shelter and interior spaces similarly communicate values, priorities, and lifestyle, illustrating how the environments we inhabit affect social perception. Finally, relationships, which are the psychological and social bonds within families and communities, underscore the relational dimension of impression management, highlighting the ways interpersonal interactions shape both self-concept and public perception. By connecting the ABCDE dimensions to these fundamental areas of human need, FCS provides students with a holistic understanding of how daily choices, behaviors, and environments contribute to the impressions they make and interpret.

The five dimensions--Appearance, Behavior, Communication, Digital presence, and Emotional balance--illustrate the holistic nature of impression management as cultivated through Family and Consumer Sciences education. Each element represents a distinct yet interrelated domain of self-presentation, blending the tangible with the psychological, and the personal with the social. Through FCS instruction, students learn not only how to look appropriate and act responsibly but also how to communicate effectively, navigate digital spaces with integrity, and regulate their emotions with composure and empathy. In synthesizing these capacities, the FCS classroom becomes a site where theory and practice intersect, and where Goffman's insights into everyday performance find applied expression in students' lived experiences. The ABCDE model thus encapsulates the discipline's enduring mission: to prepare individuals who are competent, self-aware, and socially attuned across the many stages and settings of contemporary life.

SKILLS AS HUMAN CAPITAL

Having established the connections between appearance, behavior, communication, digital presence, and emotional balance as dimensions of impression management, it becomes important to consider how these competencies contribute to broader forms of social and economic value. Within the Family and Consumer Sciences (FCS) curriculum, these interpersonal and self-presentational capacities function as a form of human capital—skills and behaviors that enhance employability, social mobility, and civic participation. Drawing on Goffman's (1967) concepts of deference and demeanor, as well as his discussion of face engagements (1963), this section explores how FCS education cultivates the social competencies that underpin economic and relational success.

Building upon the ABCDE framework, these competencies also serve as tools for identity rehearsal and social capital formation, providing students with the skills necessary to navigate and succeed in various social and professional contexts. Pin and Turndorf (2009) highlight the importance of educational settings as arenas for identity rehearsal, where individuals can experiment with social roles, receive feedback, and internalize norms in a low-stakes environment. Within FCS classrooms, this process is deliberate: students practice managing impressions, adapting behavior to varying social contexts, and navigating relational dynamics that mirror the wider social world.

The developmental orientation of Family and Consumer Sciences aligns closely with national standards emphasizing the interconnected nature of physical, emotional, social, moral, and cognitive growth (LEADFCS, 2018, Standard 12.1.1–12.1.2). These dimensions of human development are cultivated through the everyday practices of

FCS education, which include reflection, collaboration, and applied problem-solving, which foster not only technical proficiency but also self-regulation, empathy, and moral reasoning. Students learn to interpret and respond to the emotional and social cues of others, an essential aspect of what Goffman (1967) described as maintaining face and sustaining mutual respect in interaction.

Moreover, FCS education situates development within the broader social and technological environments that shape identity. Consistent with Standard 12.2.2, instruction acknowledges that social media, economic pressures, and cultural expectations influence how individuals present themselves and negotiate belonging. By examining these influences in the classroom and through experiential learning, FCS encourages learners to critically assess external forces while cultivating internal resources such as confidence, adaptability, and relational awareness.

Family and Consumer Sciences education, however, extends beyond traditional classrooms into a broad spectrum of community, professional, and nonformal learning contexts. Across diverse international and cultural settings, FCS content is adapted to meet the practical needs of individuals and families, while simultaneously fostering social competencies and relational awareness. Nonformal contexts, including community workshops, vocational training programs, professional development initiatives, and outreach projects, provide learners with opportunities to apply theoretical knowledge in realistic scenarios, observe experienced practitioners, and experiment with social roles in ways that reinforce identity rehearsal and skill acquisition. In the United States, much of this effort is led by extension education, which developed from the land-grant college system established by the Morrill Act of 1862, although comparable outreach programs exist worldwide under different models.

These varied contexts share several core elements: understanding learners' needs, designing relevant and interactive learning experiences, facilitating meaningful engagement, and evaluating outcomes (Hitch & Youatt, 2002). By encountering a range of interpersonal and cultural situations, learners refine their ability to navigate social norms, interpret cues, and respond adaptively. For example, participants in a community-based nutrition program may practice planning meals for families with differing cultural traditions, while students engaged in workplace or volunteer placements learn to manage collaboration, follow hierarchical structures, and negotiate responsibilities. Each of these experiences reinforces both technical proficiency and the subtle interpersonal competencies that constitute human and social capital.

Importantly, the international scope of FCS education demonstrates that the cultivation of social and relational skills is not tied to a specific pedagogical model or cultural context. Whether delivered through school-based instruction, extension programs, professional workshops, or online platforms, FCS provides structured opportunities for learners to practice responsible decision-making, communication, collaboration, and leadership. Although the LEADFCS standards are specific to the

United States, their emphasis on emotional well-being, communication competence, and social responsibility parallels international frameworks in home economics education that stress holistic human development (Åberg-Bengtsson, 2009; IFHE, n.d.). These repeated, contextually rich experiences ensure that skills developed in the classroom are transferable to professional, civic, and personal domains, thereby bridging the gap between formal education and real-world social engagement. Through deliberate scaffolding of nonformal and cross-cultural learning opportunities, FCS education fosters adaptive judgment, interpersonal acumen, and ethical awareness—competencies that support employability, civic participation, and the creation of meaningful social networks.

As explained by educators Elizabeth Hitch and June Pierce Youatt (2002), family and consumer sciences content is communicated in a variety of settings—classrooms, human services, community outreach programs, and business contexts—yet all share the need to understand learners, develop instructional plans, engage in interaction, and evaluate outcomes (2002, p. 5).

Goffman's (1971) concept of "remedial work" further elucidates this process. Remedial work involves the perpetrator of an untoward act engaging in "damage limitation" to reframe the behavior as acceptable. In FCS education, students engage in remedial work through group projects, collaborative cooking, and caregiving simulations, allowing them to negotiate errors, adjust behaviors, and restore social equilibrium. This reinforces both ethical and social competencies, enabling students to navigate complex social interactions with confidence.

Through repeated engagement with practical tasks, students develop not only technical skills but also a repertoire of behavioral strategies, relational cues, and communication approaches. FCS classrooms thus serve as rehearsal spaces where identity, social competence, and self-presentation are continuously negotiated and refined. These competencies become instruments through which students experiment with social identities, receive feedback, and internalize the dynamics of respect, credibility, and relational influence. The ability to manage impressions effectively cultivates social capital: the trust, reciprocity, and recognition that facilitate collaboration, leadership, and professional advancement.

Education in FCS, whether explicitly or implicitly, teaches lessons in responsibility. The term responsibility, derived from the Latin *respondere* ("to respond"), underscores one's ability to act reliably and with awareness of others' needs. In Goffman's (1967) terms, responsible behavior reflects demeanor, the presentation of self as trustworthy and self-controlled, and deference, the acknowledgment of others' expectations and rights within social encounters. Caring for a child, handling potentially dangerous utensils, or managing personal finances demands attentiveness, foresight, and relational awareness. These competencies translate directly into the social currencies Goffman identified as foundational to human interaction, positioning responsibility as a bridge between personal character and social capital.

Beyond personal reliability, FCS education develops "interactional capital," the ability to interpret and adapt to the expectations of others in shared environments. Goffman (1963) described such adaptability as the effective "allocation of involvement," whereby individuals regulate attention, posture, and participation according to situational demands. Similarly, Goffman's (1969) notion of strategic interaction illuminates how individuals assess social situations, anticipate responses, and present themselves to achieve favorable outcomes. FCS activities such as collaborative cooking, event planning, or caregiving simulations provide low-stakes arenas to rehearse these skills. Through such experiential learning, students acquire not only technical knowledge but also the embodied judgment that supports credibility, teamwork, and leadership—traits that carry economic value and form the social fabric of responsible leadership.

Being competent involves having the knowledge, skills, and attitudes to perform effectively (Spencer & Spencer, 1993). In social and professional contexts, competence requires navigating the subtleties of human interaction. Goffman (1981) highlighted the importance of response cries and other verbal and nonverbal cues in signaling attentiveness and social alignment. Within FCS classrooms, students practice these cues when collaborating on tasks such as meal preparation, project planning, or caregiving simulations. Goffman's (1963) exploration of unforced interaction and allocation of involvement provides a framework for understanding how students monitor attention in groups, recognize social obligations, and adjust participation. These exercises cultivate "applied competence": the ability to perform technical skills while managing impressions, maintaining group harmony, and responding appropriately to others.

Maturity in impression management involves integrating self-awareness, social perceptiveness, and emotional regulation, all central to FCS education. Drawing on Goffman's (1967) concepts of deference, demeanor, embarrassment, and alienation, students are guided to anticipate social consequences and navigate potentially awkward interactions. Lessons in professional etiquette, family dynamics, or peer collaboration provide structured opportunities to recover from minor social missteps, thereby developing adaptive judgment. Behavior in Public Places (Goffman, 1963) emphasizes maintaining boundaries, managing mutual involvement, and interpreting situational norms, all of which FCS students practice in both formal and informal learning contexts. Through repeated exposure, students cultivate emotional resilience and practical acumen, strengthening their human capital for diverse social and professional settings.

Taken together, lessons in responsibility, interactional competence, applied skill, and adaptive judgment illustrate how FCS education cultivates a multifaceted form of human capital. Students emerge not only with practical knowledge in areas such as nutrition, caregiving, and personal finance but also with social and emotional capacities necessary to navigate complex interpersonal landscapes. Drawing on Goffman's (1963, 1967, 1969, 1981) insights, it is clear that the FCS classroom provides structured opportunities to practice deference, demeanor, strategic interaction, response management, and situational awareness—skills that translate into employability, civic participation, and relational success. Thus, FCS education bridges personal development and social utility, demonstrating that cultivating self-presentation and relational acumen is a core component of preparing students for life's practical, social, and economic demands.

LEADERSHIP AND ORGANIZATIONAL APPLICATIONS

Beyond individual development, the competencies cultivated through Family and Consumer Sciences (FCS) education have relevance in professional, leadership, and organizational contexts. Skills in appearance, behavior, communication, digital presence, and emotional balance translate directly into effective leadership and civic engagement. For instance, a student who has developed social awareness and adaptive behavior through collaborative FCS activities, such as event planning or group culinary projects, can leverage those skills to manage teams, communicate with diverse stakeholders, and build trust in professional settings.

In organizational contexts, FCS-derived competencies function as "applied social capital," enabling leaders to influence perception, navigate office politics, and model ethical standards. Communication skills, honed in classroom simulations, become critical for managing meetings, public presentations, and cross-departmental collaboration. Similarly, emotional balance, which is cultivated through conflict resolution or caregiving simulations, supports resilience and composure under pressure, both of which are hallmarks of effective leadership. These transferable skills extend into civic and political arenas as well. Leaders, social entrepreneurs, and public officials benefit from the ability to project competence, empathy, and credibility, which are all qualities nurtured in FCS education. By situating impression management within organizational and leadership contexts, FCS demonstrates its broader societal value, preparing learners for roles that extend far beyond the classroom into community engagement, professional environments, and public service.

IMPRESSION MANAGEMENT AND LEADERSHIP IN EDUCATIONAL AND COMMUNITY CONTEXTS

Leadership involves far more than positional authority; it is also an act of social performance. In both educational and community contexts, leaders must continuously manage impressions through their demeanor, communication, and decision-making processes. Family and Consumer Sciences (FCS) education provides a foundation for understanding how these impressions are constructed, perceived, and sustained over time. By developing competencies in the ABCDE framework, students cultivate the skills that enable them to project credibility, empathy, and ethical integrity, qualities central to effective leadership (Goleman, 1998).

Within educational institutions, for example, teachers and administrators engage in impression management daily. The tone of an email, the consistency of classroom expectations, and the handling of conflict all shape perceptions of fairness and professionalism. FCS educators, who are trained to balance interpersonal awareness with organizational goals, model leadership that integrates self-presentation with service. Their ability to read social contexts and respond with composure exemplifies what Gardner and Avolio (1998) describe as the "dramaturgical" dimension of leadership, which is the conscious alignment of one's public image with authentic moral intent.

Similarly, in community organizations, the impression a leader conveys can determine credibility, trust, and engagement. Nonprofit directors, civic organizers, and extension educators often rely on emotional intelligence and relational transparency to motivate collective action. Here, impression management is not manipulative but communicative as it allows leaders to express shared values, signal reliability, and foster social cohesion. By teaching students to navigate such interactions with awareness and authenticity, FCS education contributes to the cultivation of leaders who can balance image with substance, ensuring that public perception reinforces rather than undermines ethical purpose.

CONTEXTUAL VARIABILITY

While FCS education develops broadly transferable competencies, the enactment of these skills is always contingent upon context. What counts as appropriate, respectful, or effective self-presentation depends on the situation and audience. Goffman's (1963, 1967, 1981) examinations of situational propriety, embarrassment, and conversational response provide a nuanced lens for understanding how impression management shifts across interpersonal and institutional settings. This section considers how FCS instruction helps learners interpret these contextual cues and adjust their verbal, behavioral, and emotional expressions accordingly.

Extending this discussion, Goffman's (1974) *Frame Analysis* offers a powerful conceptual tool for explaining how individuals interpret and organize experience. Frames are the cognitive and social structures that define "what is going on" in any given situation, guiding both expression and interpretation. Misalignment of frames can lead to misunderstanding or social friction—phenomena familiar to both educators and students. FCS instruction trains learners to identify and adapt to shifting frames, whether they are moving between family and workplace roles, navigating formal and informal communication, or interpreting tone and meaning in digital environments. By cultivating this frame awareness, FCS education enhances not only social adaptability but also interpretive intelligence, or, the ability to read situations and align one's behavior accordingly.

The meaning of a particular action or display can vary widely depending on social norms, gender roles, and socioeconomic class. For example, sewing a garment may signal diligence and skill in one context, while in another, it may be interpreted as a display of domesticity or adherence to traditional gender expectations. Similarly, preparing a meal for peers may communicate hospitality and competence in a family setting but could be read as performative or even competitive in a professional or formal social environment. By engaging in these activities under guided instruction, students learn to anticipate how audiences may interpret their actions and to modulate behavior, tone, and nonverbal cues accordingly (Goffman, 1963, 1967).

This context-dependence underscores the flexibility and fluidity of impression management in daily FCS practice. Students practice shifting their demeanor, deference, and conversational engagement to suit different settings, whether collaborating on a group project, interacting with teachers, or participating in community service. FCS classrooms thus serve as microcosms of broader social life, providing low-stakes opportunities to rehearse adaptive strategies, recognize social boundaries, and interpret the subtleties of cultural and institutional expectations. In doing so, learners acquire a form of social literacy that allows them to navigate diverse interpersonal landscapes with awareness, tact, and strategic sensitivity (Goffman, 1963, 1969, 1981).

DIGITAL IMPRESSION MANAGEMENT

The fluidity of self-presentation becomes even more complex in virtual environments, where digital interfaces mediate visibility, authenticity, and control. Building on Goffman's (1969) framework on strategic interaction, this section examines how the dramaturgical model extends into digital spaces, where users actively curate identity through calculated acts of display, concealment, and response. Within FCS education, lessons on digital citizenship and media literacy enable students to navigate this strategic terrain ethically and effectively.

In the twenty-first century, impression management extends beyond face-to-face interactions to encompass digital environments, where choices in language, imagery, and engagement shape others' perceptions. Just as context influences interpretation in physical settings, the norms and expectations of online spaces, such as social media platforms, professional networks, and email communication, dictate the appropriate presentation of self. Goffman's (1963, 1967, 1981) concepts of demeanor, deference, and strategic interaction remain instructive for understanding how individuals perform identity in digital contexts, highlighting the continuity between offline and online impression management.

Within FCS education, digital literacy has become an essential component of self-presentation. Students are introduced not only to broad concepts of responsible online behavior but also to specific skills such as email literacy, digital etiquette, and professional correspondence. Crafting clear, polite, and purposeful emails requires attention to tone, formatting, and audience expectations are elements that parallel traditional principles of civility, situational awareness, and strategic interaction (Goffman, 1969). For instance, the same message might be interpreted differently depending on whether it is sent to a peer, teacher, or potential employer, reinforcing the importance of context-sensitive communication in digital spaces.

Beyond email, FCS curricula often address social media engagement, digital branding, and online collaboration. Students learn to manage their digital footprints, balancing authenticity with professionalism, and to anticipate how posts, comments, and shared content will be interpreted by diverse audiences (boyd, 2014; Leaver, Highfield, & Abidin, 2020). By translating the principles of appearance, behavior, and communication into the digital sphere, learners develop a nuanced understanding of impression management that spans both physical and virtual arenas. In doing so, FCS education equips students with the technical, social, and ethical competencies needed to navigate digital interactions with confidence, discernment, and strategic awareness.

GENDER AND IMPRESSION MANAGEMENT

Family and Consumer Sciences (FCS) education has long been intertwined with gendered expectations, a legacy that continues to influence the field's approach to appearance, behavior, and communication. Historically, FCS was rooted in preparing women for roles as wives and mothers, emphasizing domestic skills as essential components of femininity. This gendered foundation has shaped the norms and standards taught within the discipline, often reinforcing traditional gender roles. As noted by Swafford and Ramsey (2023), "The field's history of opening career opportunities for women and responding to domestic and social issues" reflects both empowerment and constraint, as it navigated societal expectations of women's roles both inside and outside the home. Historical analyses of home economics highlight the central role of women in establishing and shaping the profession. Stage and Vincenti (1997) document how early home economists navigated societal expectations of women while promoting scientific approaches to household management and education. This legacy underscores how gender has historically influenced both the content and delivery of FCS education. Contemporary FCS standards, particularly those analyzing the influences of gender, culture, and social context on human development (e.g., LEAD FCS Standard 12.2.3), reflect a continuation of this awareness, emphasizing equitable development opportunities, critical engagement with social norms, and the promotion of inclusive practices across the life span.

In recent decades, there has been a concerted effort within FCS to become more inclusive and equitable for all genders. This shift involves challenging traditional gender norms and creating curricula that welcome diverse gender identities. Educators are increasingly incorporating discussions on gender fluidity, non-binary identities, and the deconstruction of stereotypical gender roles into their teaching practices. This evolution aims to foster an environment where all students can engage with FCS content without the constraints of outdated gender expectations.

Despite these efforts, tensions persist around gender expectations within FCS education. Some students and educators continue to grapple with the field's historical associations with femininity, which can influence perceptions of the discipline's relevance and appeal. These tensions are particularly evident in enrollment patterns, where FCS courses are often still perceived as more suited for women, potentially deterring male students from participating. Educators navigate these challenges by emphasizing the universal applicability of FCS skills, such as financial literacy, nutrition, and interpersonal communication, and by actively promoting the field as valuable for all students, regardless of gender.

Students' gender identities also play a significant role in their engagement with FCS content. For instance, male students might feel societal pressure to conform to traditional masculine norms, which can affect their willingness to participate in activities traditionally associated with femininity, such as cooking or sewing. Conversely, female students may encounter expectations to excel in domestic tasks, which can influence their confidence and interest in these areas. Educators are increasingly aware of these dynamics and strive to create inclusive learning environments that validate all students' experiences and identities, encouraging them to explore and develop a broad range of skills.

CROSS-CULTURAL AND GLOBAL PERSPECTIVES

Beyond gender, impression management is profoundly influenced by cultural frameworks that dictate the rhythms and rules of social exchange. Drawing on Goffman's (1963, 1967) insights into the variability of public behavior and ritualized interaction, this section situates Family and Consumer Sciences (FCS) education within a global context. Kato (2008) reminds us that even the most basic needs--food, clothing, and shelter--are culturally mediated, shaped by values and beliefs about what is appropriate, desirable, or taboo. Such variation illustrates how impression management occurs not only through interpersonal interaction but also through the visible and material symbols of daily life: the foods we serve, the homes we inhabit, and the aesthetic choices we make. By emphasizing intercultural awareness and adaptability, FCS instruction prepares students to navigate diverse norms of deference, expression, and emotional display across cultural settings.

Cultural context shapes not only *what* is communicated but *how* impressions are formed and interpreted. As Goffman (1967) observed, acts of deference and demeanor vary across societies, reflecting differing hierarchies of respect, politeness, and relational distance. What is considered confident self-presentation in one culture may be perceived as arrogance in another, while displays of humility or indirect communication may be interpreted as deference or uncertainty depending on the setting. Goffman's (1963) work on stigma further clarifies how context mediates the moral evaluation of behavior. Traits or actions that elicit approval in one environment may generate discomfort or exclusion in another, revealing how impression management is not only a matter of individual control but also of social perception. Within FCS, this awareness is critical: educators help students navigate differing expectations of gender, class, and culture, while encouraging respect for identities that have been historically stigmatized or marginalized. Through this lens, impression management becomes a practice of social inclusion—an effort to ensure that all participants can engage with dignity, regardless of how their self-presentation might be read through dominant cultural frames. FCS education encourages students to recognize these variations, promoting sensitivity to cross-cultural differences in dress, body language, verbal expression, and social etiquette.

CULTURE, GENDER, AND RELIGIOUS DIMENSIONS

While culture shapes norms of self-presentation, gender and religion similarly influence impression management. FCS education acknowledges that expectations related to masculinity, femininity, and non-binary identities can shape participation in activities such as cooking, sewing, or leadership simulations. Educators increasingly work to create inclusive curricula that challenge traditional gender norms and support diverse identities, ensuring that all students can develop competencies without restriction.

Religious beliefs and practices also intersect with impression management, influencing dress codes, dietary choices, communication styles, and interpersonal etiquette. For example, students from faith-based communities may manage impressions in ways that honor religious observances while navigating secular environments. By discussing these dimensions explicitly, FCS education encourages learners to understand and respect the moral, ethical, and social frameworks that guide behavior across different communities, preparing students for engagement in both multicultural and faith-sensitive professional, civic, and organizational contexts.

Ethical and religious dimensions of impression management remind us that personal image is inseparable from moral accountability. In many faith traditions, outward demeanor is seen as a reflection of inward character, as well as a visible testimony of values such as humility, compassion, and stewardship. For instance, modesty in dress, honesty in communication, and empathy in service are not only cultural expectations but also ethical imperatives that shape how individuals are perceived within their communities. FCS education, which emphasizes responsible decision-making and respect for human dignity, naturally aligns with these principles. Lessons addressing professionalism, consumer choices, and social responsibility encourage students to consider how everyday actions such as what they wear, how they speak, how they care for others communicate ethical commitments as much as personal style.

In faith-based educational settings, these discussions become even more pronounced. Teachers may integrate ethical frameworks grounded in religious teachings into lessons on nutrition, consumer behavior, or digital presence, encouraging students to see impression management as a form of moral communication rather than superficial performance. For example, a lesson on sustainable fashion may explore not only aesthetic and economic concerns but also ethical production practices and moral accountability to workers and the environment (Treviño & Nelson, 2021). Similarly, instruction on online communication may incorporate reflection on truthfulness, respect, and empathy as components of digital ethics. Through these approaches, FCS instruction models integrity-based impression management where congruence between values and behavior becomes the measure of an individual's true image. In doing so, it highlights that cultivating a positive impression is not about self-promotion but about aligning self-presentation with ethical and spiritual integrity.

Even within a globally shared framework of human needs (food, clothing, shelter, and relationships), the ways these needs are enacted and expressed carry culturally specific meanings. For instance, in Japanese home economics education (*kateika*), emphasis is placed on *reigi* (etiquette) and discipline as markers of personal responsibility and respect for collective harmony (Muta, 2008; Shibata, 2019). Lessons in manners, orderliness, and precision mirror Goffman's (1967) notion of "deference rituals," in which emotional restraint and attentiveness to others sustain social cohesion. By contrast, Scandinavian models of FCS, particularly in Finland, Norway, and Sweden, tend to integrate sustainability, equality, and ecological awareness into household management and self-presentation (Åberg-Bengtsson, 2009; Palojoki, 2017). Here, social responsibility and environmental consciousness become extensions of moral and aesthetic impression management, aligning with contemporary values of global citizenship. These examples, while brief, illustrate how culturally grounded interpretations of everyday behavior enrich the broader pedagogical goals of FCS without diverting from its universal human focus.

In an increasingly interconnected world, the ability to adjust one's communicative and behavioral style to different cultural expectations has become a vital form of global competence. Topics such as international cuisine, textile traditions, family structures, and hospitality customs offer rich opportunities for students to explore how cultural norms shape daily practices and interpersonal interactions. Through experiential learning, such as preparing foods from multiple regions or examining dress and design across cultures, students gain both practical skills and an appreciation for cultural diversity. This not only broadens their aesthetic and ethical awareness but also enhances their ability to engage respectfully in multicultural environments, a critical aspect of twenty-first-century impression management.

Furthermore, FCS educators increasingly address global supply chains and the ethical implications underlying consumption and production, helping students link personal choices to broader systems of labor, sustainability, and cultural exchange (McGregor, 2018). These discussions foster what could be termed *global impression literacy*: an awareness of how everyday actions and appearances reflect broader values of equity, sustainability, and cultural respect. FCS, therefore, moves beyond domestic or national boundaries to cultivate citizens capable of presenting themselves and acting responsibly within a global community.

Ultimately, these cross-cultural examples demonstrate that while the outward forms of impression management differ across societies, the underlying human endeavor, to present oneself with integrity, competence, and consideration, remains consistent. Whether expressed through the Japanese emphasis on etiquette and collective harmony or the Scandinavian integration of sustainability and equity, the principles guiding self-presentation reflect shared aspirations for respect, responsibility, and social connection. By helping students interpret and adapt to such cultural variations, FCS education not only cultivates practical and ethical versatility but also underscores the universality of impression management as a social process. This global orientation situates FCS as a bridge between individual practice and collective understanding: an educational space where cultural specificity meets the broader human pursuit of meaningful and mindful interaction

These dimensions of human capital, contextual variability, digital presence, gender, and culture illustrate the multifaceted nature of impression management as cultivated through Family and Consumer Sciences education. Across each domain, FCS serves not only as a site of practical skill development but also as a laboratory for social understanding, where students learn how identity is constructed, interpreted, and negotiated in diverse contexts. By bridging theory and practice, FCS educators enable learners to see that impression management is not mere performance but a lifelong process of ethical self-presentation, cultural fluency, and relational responsibility. In doing so, the FCS discipline affirms its enduring relevance as both a personal and civic enterprise, one that equips individuals to participate thoughtfully and authentically in an interconnected world.

CONCLUSION

Impressions are not formed in isolation. They are cultivated through a series of visible and invisible actions that occur throughout one's life. These include choices in personal grooming and attire, verbal and nonverbal communication, digital presence, emotional self-regulation, and perceived competence in tasks such as cooking, caregiving, and household management. Family and Consumer Sciences (FCS) education addresses these domains in both theoretical and applied ways, equipping students with the knowledge and habits of mind needed to navigate social perception with intentionality and confidence. By fostering self-awareness, practical competence, and social adaptability, FCS becomes a vital context for developing impression management, one that merits greater recognition within both educational practice and scholarly discourse.

The conceptual framework of the ABCDE model—Appearance, Behavior, Communication, Digital presence, and Emotional balance—offers a conceptual framework for examining how FCS instruction translates Goffman's (1959, 1963, 1967, 1969, 1981) dramaturgical theories of self-presentation into lived experience. Within this framework, students not only learn to shape impressions but also to interpret and respond to the social cues of others across diverse settings. This dynamic interplay between theory and practice positions FCS as a uniquely holistic educational space in which technical skill development and sociocultural understanding converge.

Impression management within FCS also extends beyond the individual to encompass community engagement and global citizenship. As learners grapple with issues of equity, sustainability, and cultural respect, they recognize that self-presentation and the ways one consumes, communicates, and relates, carries ethical weight that reverberates across social and cultural boundaries. In this sense, FCS contributes to the cultivation of both personal integrity and collective responsibility, preparing individuals to participate thoughtfully and inclusively in an increasingly interconnected world. As Kato (2008) articulated, the foundations of FCS rest upon meeting essential human needs and understanding how individuals and families express identity through their material and relational worlds. Viewed through the lens of impression management, these everyday acts become vehicles for self-presentation and social connection, thereby confirming FCS's enduring role in cultivating both the art and ethics of living well.

As global societies become increasingly interconnected, the ability to manage impressions across cultural, organizational, and digital boundaries is a vital 21st-century skill. The Family and Consumer Sciences (FCS) framework provides a robust foundation for this endeavor, offering practical tools and ethical guidance applicable to diverse audiences. Policymakers can draw on FCS principles to design community programs that promote emotional intelligence, cultural awareness, and leadership development. Business leaders and nonprofit managers can apply the ABCDE model to professional training programs that enhance employee communication, customer relations, and organizational image. Educators can adapt these principles to digital learning environments, helping students understand how virtual behaviors reflect identity and ethics.

For researchers, the juncture of impression management and FCS presents a promising avenue for interdisciplinary inquiry. Future studies could examine how FCS-based instruction influences professional advancement, civic participation, or global citizenship. Cross-cultural comparisons could also reveal how impression management principles manifest differently across gendered, religious, or socioeconomic contexts. By continuing to explore these applications, scholars and practitioners can ensure that FCS education remains at the forefront of preparing individuals for authentic, responsible participation in personal, professional, and civic life.

The principles of impression management cultivated through FCS education have implications beyond the classroom. Policy makers, civic leaders, and organizational managers can leverage these insights to support training programs that emphasize ethical self-presentation, cultural literacy, and emotional intelligence. Communities and NGOs may also integrate FCS-informed curricula to strengthen leadership capacity and social cohesion among diverse populations.

Future research could explore the measurable impact of FCS education on professional success, civic engagement, and political leadership. Quantitative and qualitative assessments, ranging from observational studies of communication behaviors to longitudinal tracking of career outcomes, can help identify how early-life training in impression management influences adaptive behavior in adulthood. By articulating these applications, FCS positions itself as a foundational contributor to social science research, extending the relevance of its lessons to all walks of life.

Ultimately, viewing FCS through the lens of impression management underscores the discipline's enduring relevance. Far from being a static or antiquated subject, it emerges as a dynamic site of social learning that integrates self-knowledge, interpersonal skill, and cultural literacy. As education continues to evolve alongside technological, cultural, and economic shifts, the principles embedded in FCS remind us that the art of living well is inseparable from the art of relating well. In nurturing both competence and character, FCS education sustains its role as a cornerstone of human development and a catalyst for authentic, adaptive, and ethical self-presentation.

REFERENCES

Åberg-Bengtsson, L. (2009). Home economics education in the Nordic countries: Trends and traditions. *Scandinavian Journal of Educational Research, 53*(5), 449–465.

Argyle, M. (1988). *Bodily communication* (2nd ed.). Methuen.

Baugher, S. L., Anderson, C. L., Green, K. B., Nickols, S. Y., Shane, J., Jolly, L., & Miles, J. (2003). *Body of knowledge of family and consumer sciences.* American Association of Family and Consumer Sciences.

Berns, R. M. (2021). *Child, family, school, community: Socialization and support* (11th ed.). Cengage Learning.

Bourdieu, P. (1984). *Distinction: A social critique of the judgement of taste* (R. Nice, Trans.). Harvard University Press. (Original work published 1979).

Boyd, d. (2014). *It's complicated: The social lives of networked teens.* Yale University Press.

Burgoon, J. K., Guerrero, L. K., & Floyd, K. (2016). *Nonverbal communication* (2nd ed.). Routledge. DOI: 10.4324/9781315663425

Entwistle, J. (2015). *The fashioned body: Fashion, dress and modern social theory* (2nd ed.). Polity Press.

Gardner, W. L., & Avolio, B. J. (1998). The charismatic relationship: A dramaturgical perspective. *Academy of Management Review, 23*(1), 32–58. DOI: 10.2307/259098

Goffman, E. (1959). *The presentation of self in everyday life.* Doubleday Anchor.

Goffman, E. (1963). *Behavior in public places: Notes on the social organization of gatherings.* Macmillan Publishing Co.

Goffman, E. (1963). *Stigma: Notes on the management of spoiled identity.* Prentice-Hall.

Goffman, E. (1967). *Interaction ritual: Essays in face-to-face behavior.* Aldine.

Goffman, E. (1969). *Strategic interaction.* University of Pennsylvania Press.

Goffman, E. (1971). *Relations in public: Microstudies of the public order.* Basic Books.

Goffman, E. (1974). *Frame analysis: An essay on the organization of experience.* Harvard University Press.

Goffman, E. (1981). *Forms of talk*. University of Pennsylvania Press.

Goleman, D. (1998). *Working with emotional intelligence*. Bantam Books.

Hall, E. T. (1976). *Beyond culture*. Anchor Books.

Halpern, C., & Donaghey, J. (2018). *Social and emotional learning in action: Experiential activities to teach empathy, decision-making, and interpersonal skills*. Routledge.

Hitch, E. J., & Youatt, J. P. (2002). *Communicating family and consumer sciences: A guidebook for professionals*. Goodheart-Willcox.

Hogan, B. (2010). The presentation of self in the age of social media: Distinguishing performances and exhibitions online. *Bulletin of Science, Technology & Society, 30*(6), 377–386. DOI: 10.1177/0270467610385893

Hybels, S., & Weaver, R. L. (2005). *Communicating effectively* (7th ed.). McGraw-Hill.

International Federation for Home Economics. (2008). *Home economics in the 21st century: IFHE position statement.* https://www.ifhe.org/fileadmin/user_upload/e_ifhe/policy/IFHE_Position_Statement_2008.pdf

International Federation for Home Economics. (n.d.). *About home economics.* https://www.ifhe.org/about-us/about-home/economics

Kaiser, S. B. (2012). *Fashion and cultural studies*. Berg Publishers.

Kato, S. L. (2008). *Foundations of family and consumer sciences: Careers serving individuals, families, and communities*. Goodheart-Willcox.

Leaver, T., Highfield, T., & Abidin, C. (2020). *Instagram: Visual social media cultures*. Polity Press.

Livingstone, S. (2014). Developing social media literacy: How children learn to interpret risky opportunities on social network sites. *Communications, 39*(3), 283–303. DOI: 10.1515/commun-2014-0113

Marwick, A. E., & boyd, . (2011). I tweet honestly, I tweet passionately: Twitter users, context collapse, and the imagined audience. *New Media & Society, 13*(1), 114–133. DOI: 10.1177/1461444810365313

McGregor, S. L. T. (2018). Understanding consumers' moral responsibility for sustainable consumption. *International Journal of Consumer Studies, 42*(6), 588–597.

Muta, K. (2008). Reform of Japanese home economics education and gender equality. *Gender and Education, 20*(6), 627–642.

Nichols, S. (2015). *Remaking home economics: Resourcefulness and innovation in changing times*. University of Minnesota Press.

Palojoki, P. (2017). Sustainability and food education in the Finnish home economics curriculum. *International Journal of Home Economics, 10*(1), 56–67.

Pearson, J. C., Nelson, P. E., Titsworth, S. B., & Hosek, A. M. (2017). *Human communication* (6th ed.). McGraw-Hill Education.

Pin, R., & Turndorf, H. (2009). Identity rehearsal in educational settings. *Journal of Educational Psychology, 101*(2), 345–356. DOI: 10.1037/a0014567

Ribble, M., & Miller, T. N. (2013). Educational leadership in an online world: Connecting students to technology responsibly, safely, and ethically. *Phi Delta Kappan, 94*(5), 41–44. DOI: 10.1177/003172171309400509

Shibata, M. (2019). Home economics in Japan: Citizenship, gender, and sustainability. *Journal of Family and Consumer Sciences Education, 37*(2), 15–27.

Spencer, L., & Spencer, S. M. (1993). *Competence at work: Models for superior performance*. Wiley.

Stage, S., & Vincenti, V. B. (Eds.). (1997). *Rethinking home economics: Women and the history of a profession*. Cornell University Press. DOI: 10.7591/9781501729942

Stewart, M. C., & Logan, R. (2018). *Social and professional skills for teens*. Goodheart-Willcox.

Swafford, M., & Ramsey, E. (2023). *Family and consumer sciences: Preventative and restorative education*. Cognella Academic Publishing.

Treviño, L. K., & Nelson, K. A. (2021). *Managing business ethics: Straight talk about how to do it right* (8th ed.). Wiley.

U.S. Congress. (1862). *Morrill Act of 1862, ch. 130, 12 Stat. 503*. https://www.ourdocuments.gov/doc.php?flash=false&doc=32

Chapter 6

From Flexing to Shaming: The Morality of Displaying Suspicious Wealth

Ikbal Maulana
https://orcid.org/0000-0002-3727-3809
National Research and Innovation Agency (BRIN), Indonesia

Purwadi Purwadi
https://orcid.org/0000-0001-7985-0398
National Research and Innovation Agency (BRIN), Indonesia

Perdhani Yunia Putri
https://orcid.org/0009-0009-5561-7191
National Research and Innovation Agency (BRIN), Indonesia

Imelda Imelda
https://orcid.org/0000-0003-2258-9488
National Research and Innovation Agency (BRIN), Indonesia

Musfiah Saidah
Syarif Hidayatullah Jakarta Islamic State University, Indonesia

ABSTRACT

Social media has normalized narcissistic forms of self-presentation, where users emulate celebrity-like practices such as exaggerated self-display and the flaunting of excessive wealth. However, public outrage arose when a young social media user displayed luxury goods believed to be beyond the means of his father, a government employee. This case triggered a wave of crowdsourced surveillance and digital vigilantism, as users searched for and exposed other officials and their family members who similarly showcased their wealth. Using corpus-assisted discourse studies

DOI: 10.4018/979-8-3373-5519-1.ch006

(CADS) on 44,445 comments from 575 YouTube videos, this study maps users' reactions to understand their sentiments, perceptions, and expectations regarding corruption and law enforcement. The findings reveal the power of collective online investigations in uncovering perceived corruption and compelling moral compliance and institutional responses, as well as generating public shaming toward those who commit moral transgressions.

INTRODUCTION

Possessions have long been regarded as an important component of one's sense of self. Many people base their self-worth on what they own (Ferraro et al., 2011); possessions may not only represent personal achievement gained through hard work but also signify social status. Thus, displaying them becomes a part of self-presentation (Belk, 1988). Possessions can function as signifiers that communicate more powerfully than words, since it constitutes visible evidence of one's social position or achievement.

People who purchase luxury brands may seek to heighten their feelings of accomplishment—a sense of a successful self rather than a display of arrogance—but they may be perceived by others as signaling arrogance rather than achievement (McFerran et al., 2014). Displaying wealth excessively—beyond what others typically do—can be perceived as an act of ostentation and may undermine cooperation (Srna et al., 2022). In Indonesia, where modesty and social harmony are highly valued, overt self-promotion or narcissistic behavior is traditionally regarded as inappropriate. Within such a context, standing out from the crowd by flaunting one's wealth is generally frowned upon, as consideration for others' feelings serves as a key social regulator of individual behavior. Yet, in the digital sphere, social media has begun to erode these traditional norms, encouraging more individualistic and performative expressions of identity.

Social media has seduced users to be narcissistic (Maulana, 2018; Murray, 2015). A popular saying once circulated among Indonesian social media users: "It's better to be narcissistic than to feel inferior." The phrase indicates an emerging norm of accepting exaggerated self-presentation while suppressing negative self-evaluation, thereby preserving or enhancing self-esteem (Andreassen et al., 2017). Moreover, the shift toward narcissism or conspicuous consumption on social media is often subtle, occurring gradually and collectively, so that individuals do not feel they are committing a moral transgression. This transformation reflects a seamless integration of cultural forces: the public sharing of digital documentation, a microcelebrity culture that encourages attractive self-presentation, and the normalization of wealth display (A. E. Marwick, 2015).

Many aspire to emulate the celebrities they worship and perceive social media as a space where such aspirations are attainable. As Marwick and Boyd (2011) note, there is no clear boundary between ordinary users, microcelebrities, and established celebrities; popularity exists along a continuum of visibility. Consequently, social media users tend to be more tolerant of behaviors that mimic celebrity culture, including displays of wealth through showing off expensive goods or vehicles, or by vacationing in distant, exotic destinations. Moreover, while self-presentation can extend to the vast and indefinite reach of a social network, it can also originate from the most private, hidden spaces—such as an individual's room—where the user is physically invisible to others, making social control difficult to enforce. Moreover, interaction without bodily presence frees social media users from social systems that "express and are expressed in the routines of daily social life, mediating the physical and sensory properties of the human body (Giddens, 1984, p. 36).

Social media provides users with flexibility in self-presentation. It can both conceal and expose them to a wider public. It enables users to construct a persona that differs from their offline or analogue identity. Social media and its accompanying digital technologies offer limitless tools for enhancing self-presentation (Shulman, 2022). Various free or low-cost tools are available that allow even non–tech-savvy individuals to engineer their digital appearance, enabling greater control over their online identity (Sheth & Solomon, 2014). Since most social media interactions are asynchronous (not in real time), users can carefully select the best photographs or videos of themselves, allowing them to present the most attractive, idealized, or successful version of the self (Maulana, 2018; Taylor & Strutton, 2016).

However, presenting oneself on digital platforms is not without challenges. Under the audience's gaze, social media users gain popularity but are also subjected to surveillance (Sullivan, 2013). The pressure of impression management is heightened on social media, where one's actions are constantly monitored by many. As Goffman (Goffman, 1956) asserts, individuals observe how others respond to them and adjust their behavior accordingly. Maintaining a particular public image therefore requires careful self-presentation to preserve or enhance one's personal branding (Duffy & Chan, 2019).

DIGITAL SOCIAL IDENTITY: FROM POSSESSION TO MORALITY

In front of an audience or within their social circles, individuals perform particular personas (Goffman, 1956). These personas may differ significantly from the norm or resemble those around them. Regardless of how far they diverge from their peers, people still need to belong to certain groups because belonging makes social life easier. To signal this belonging, they adopt specific group characteristics (de Oliveira Leite et al., 2021). These characteristics may be visible—such as the clothes or accessories they wear, the goods they display, or the cars they drive—but they can also be less visible, including behaviors, norms, moral values, and even political preferences.

The identity of individuals has long been understood as encompassing everything they possess—from their bodies and abilities to their spouses, children, and material belongings (Belk, 1988). What people possess serves as an indicator of their identity, status, or social class. However, possessions are also one of the means through which people manage impressions before others, alongside verbal and non-verbal communication (Goffman, 1956). Possession display, as a form of self-presentation, can be used either to assert equality with one's audience or to emphasize distinction from them (Bourdieu, 1984).

Becoming a micro-celebrity is a form of self-presentation, an ongoing process rather than a fixed state (Mortensen & Kristensen, 2020). Even before gaining a large audience, some social media users strive to emulate the behavior of celebrities. For those who are not yet popular, the easiest way—if they already have the wealth—is to showcase expensive products or displays of affluence. In an unequal society, showing wealth becomes an easy way to signal that one belongs to a distinct class—a special minority rather than the common people (Bourdieu, 1984).

Digital technology has also intensified consumerism. Through online shopping, the market now operates without limits of time or space, penetrating even the private lives of Internet users. With the use of big data and advanced analytics, online consumers have become subjects of constant surveillance, allowing marketing to be tailored to individual preferences (Maulana, 2019; Zuboff, 2015). The competition to appear attractive on social media, along with mutual envy among users, has further fueled conspicuous consumption, as displaying oneself wearing or owning branded products has become a form of status signaling (Taylor, 2020; Taylor & Strutton, 2016). Consumption can serve as a means of self-definition and self-expression, as people often select products and brands that reflect their identities and convey who they are (Schau & Gilly, 2003). Audiences, in turn, often enjoy seeing others showcase their wealth—some may feel envy and be encouraged to imitate them, while others may simply admire such displays or treat them as a form of escapism from their own problems.

While possessions have become increasingly salient markers of identity on social media, people also consciously or unconsciously hold intangible characteristics, including moral identity, which is central to their self-concept (de Oliveira Leite et al., 2021). Through upbringing and social interaction, individuals develop moral virtues—which are socially constructed—and refine their moral intuitions. These moral characteristics create a readiness to feel flashes of approval or disapproval toward other people's behaviors (Haidt & Joseph, 2004). On social media, the increasingly prominent phenomenon of cancel culture is often triggered by the perception that someone has committed a moral transgression—by saying or doing something considered wrong (Greig & Hogg, 2025).

FROM CELEBRIFICATION TO SCANDAL

In co-present interactions, individuals inhabit multiple social spheres that shape their behavior. Within intimate spheres, such as among family members and close friends, they tend to be more relaxed and express themselves with greater spontaneity. In contrast, in more public or formal settings—what Goffman (1956) refers to as the "frontstage"—individuals engage in impression management, consciously performing roles that align with the expectations and norms of the social context.

In offline social life, events pass and fade, leaving traces only in the memories of those who witnessed them—memories that inevitably weaken over time. Social media, however, has made the "frontstage" of social life more enduring, as performances are now recorded and preserved on digital platforms. When something is online or shared on social media, it becomes—or will eventually become—part of the frontstage. On these platforms, the separation between different social spheres effectively disappears. What users intend to show to certain audiences can easily leak or spread to others they do not personally know. Distinctions in social behavior that are clearly maintained across different settings in offline interactions can no longer function effectively in digital environments (A. E. Marwick & boyd, 2011).

There is no longer a closed social sphere in which only a small number of people interact and know what has been talked about. In any social media interaction, therefore, users must anticipate a wider audience than those they personally know. While people generally tolerate the weaknesses or imperfections of their close friends, they tend to deliberately perform a particular persona in front of strangers—one that may sometimes diverge from their actual selves (Shulman, 2022).

Social media may seduce users into becoming celebrities at various levels of popularity. They are not merely the audience of other celebrities or microcelebrities; they deliberately perform in front of the camera with full awareness that their images will be viewed by others. There is also a growing tendency for users to compare themselves with their idealized selves and to strive to present those idealized versions to others (Gran, 2025). Social media can also intensify unhealthy envy among users, as people compare their real lives to the idealized images others share—and those others are often doing the same in return (Taylor, 2020). People may perceive popularity on social media as being objectified, since it is represented through quantifiable metrics such as the number of friends, followers, views, likes, and other forms of engagement (Brubaker, 2020). The tendency to compare oneself with others is further intensified by visual displays on social media. Since much of this comparison involves visual displays of wealth—where expensive or luxury goods are showcased—social media users may experience a sense of relative deprivation (Yan et al., 2025).

The road to fame can be slippery. Just as top celebrities may stumble into scandals that end their careers, the same can happen to microcelebrities. Before the rise of social media, investigative and tabloid journalism were the primary forces in defining what counted as scandalous, publicly exposing violations of moral and legal norms and prompting reactions on behalf of the public (Kristensen & Jerslev, 2025). On social media, it is the public, not the platform, that determines when an event becomes a scandal (Pozner & Hannigan, 2023). However, the public is not a fixed entity; it is an open-ended network of strangers who recognize one another as spectators of the same thing (Starr, 2021). On social media, the boundaries between the media, the public, and the subjects of scandals are no longer as distinct as they were in traditional media. Today, every social media user is part of the media ecosystem, even if they differ in their levels of popularity. As a result, when they transgress moral values, their actions can be portrayed as scandalous by other users (Trottier, 2018). Social media also enables users to monitor one another out of personal curiosity (Sullivan, 2013), but when moral transgressions occur, they may actively participate in enforcing social punishment (Aitchison & Meckled-Garcia, 2021).

The cases featured in the YouTube videos whose comments form the dataset examined in this chapter revolve around social media users—either government officials, state employees, or their family members—who display signs of wealth online. Public enthusiasm for exposing such individuals was initially sparked by a case involving a young man whose sadistic physical assault provoked widespread outrage. He tortured his victim so brutally and so relentlessly—even after the victim was already helpless—that the victim eventually fell into a coma and remained unconscious for an extended period.

What intensified public anger even further was something that had previously appeared ordinary: the perpetrator maintained a social media account, like many young Indonesians, and frequently posted photos with vehicles that most Indonesians would consider expensive, even though such items are not uncommon among wealthier users. The issue, however, was that he was the son of a low-level tax office official, raising questions about how he could possess such costly vehicles. Therefore, public suspicion—and in many cases full certainty—quickly emerged that such wealth could only have been obtained through corrupt practices. This anger also motivated many users to hunt for other social media accounts engaging in *flexing*. When those individuals were identified as government officials, state employees, or their family members, users exposed them, made their posts go viral, and turned them into targets of public shaming.

While in politics—particularly in the past—a political scandal was a social construct formed through the agreement among the public, the media, and the elites that a transgression had occurred (Warner, 2023). In the scandals discussed in this chapter, elites were not involved in defining what was considered scandalous. It was the public who felt betrayed by those at the center of the scandal. Only later did elites—particularly the heads of the institutions where the suspects worked—respond by issuing statements that aligned with public sentiment.

Corruption has been widely recognized as a transgression of public norms and a betrayal of the public interest and trust (Chang & Chu, 2006; de Oliveira Leite et al., 2021). Therefore, it immediately triggered public outrage, leading users to begin a kind of witch hunt—searching for displays of wealth by the children or wives of government officials, as well as by the officials themselves. Social media has proven to be an effective platform for collective digital vigilantism, facilitating the crowdsourcing of surveillance practices toward anyone who attracts a significant amount of suspicion (Cheong & Gong, 2010; Trottier, 2017). Through mutual information sharing, the identities of some social media users—previously known only within relatively small networks—became widely recognized and were even reported in mainstream media. Within a few weeks, triggered by anger toward the young man involved in the case, social media users uncovered several individuals who had made inappropriate displays of wealth, with assets appearing far beyond what their official salaries could justify. As a result, many began to suspect that their wealth had come from illegitimate sources, possibly through corrupt practices. By exposing these individuals and making the cases go viral, social media users expected legal action to be taken against them. When such efforts failed, the exposure functioned as a form of online public shaming, serving to socially punish those perceived as violating moral norms (Aitchison & Meckled-Garcia, 2021).

On social media, many users have generally been tolerant of displays of wealth, even though such displays are costly signals that not everyone can afford to make (Cannon & Rucker, 2019; Han et al., 2010). Many view them as a form of entertainment to be enjoyed. However, when they discover that those flaunting their wealth are government officials or their family members, it feels as though they have been betrayed. In a country where many people still struggle to find and keep jobs, and where luxury brands remain out of reach for most, learning that some government officials and their families have violated public trust provokes anger and fuels public outrage. Even when their possessions are obtained through legitimate means, people may still perceive them as unethical, given that much of society continues to live below a decent economic standard (Huigen, 2025).

METHODOLOGY

Data

This article examines a dataset containing 44,445 comments from 575 YouTube videos retrieved through Google Search using the following search phrases:

- pejabat fleksing OR flexing site:.youtube.com
- pejabat pamer kekayaan site:.youtube.com
- pejabat pamer harta site:.youtube.com
- pejabat pamer mewah site:.youtube.com

First, the links were collected using the above search phrases. The keywords used were *pejabat* (official), *pamer* (display), *fleksing* or *flexing* (displaying wealth), *harta* (wealth), and *mewah* (luxury). The results of the search were a collection of URLs or links. Using a Python script, metadata was scraped from the YouTube server through the Application Programming Interface (API). From the description fields of the metadata, YouTube video IDs were further filtered to ensure that only relevant links were retained, as some irrelevant YouTube videos not containing information about government officials (or their families) displaying wealth or luxury were also included.

Data Analysis

The data analysis was assisted by **KeyText** (Maulana, 2025), a software tool that provides features for detecting similar words using a word-embedding algorithm (Mikolov et al., 2013), as well as keyword-in-context (KWIC) or concordance. KeyText was also used to generate lists of n-grams from the dataset. To identify the main topics, the top 30 most frequent n-grams were grouped into similar themes. The relationships among these themes were then explored using the KWIC feature, focusing on words that were part of the n-grams or semantically related words identified through word embedding.

DATA AND FINDINGS

The dataset contains responses from YouTube commenters regarding the news on the revelation of government officials or their families displaying wealth. Figure 1 shows the number of comments over time for each month. The number of comments suddenly peaked in February 2023 and increases drastically in the following month.

Prior to February 2023, there has been YouTube videos on government officials displaying wealth, but did not go viral, not attract public attention.

The case that occurred in February 2023 began with an emotional complaint made by a young woman to her then-boyfriend, who later became the perpetrator, about her former boyfriend—the victim. The victim, who was 17 years old, was subsequently subjected to a severe assault by the 20-year-old perpetrator. During the attack, the perpetrator continued to torture the victim even after he was helpless. What sparked public outrage was that the perpetrator recorded the assault on video and circulated it online, showing him saying that he did not care if the victim died and uttering other sadistic remarks.

What sparked public outrage was that the perpetrator seemed unbothered about sharing the video with his friends (Noviansah, 2023), which was later leaked and went viral on social media, as if he was unconcerned that his act of torturing another person could lead to imprisonment. What also drew public attention was that he had arrived at the scene driving a Rubicon—an expensive car for most Indonesians. To make matters worse, it was later revealed that he was the son of a government official working at the tax office. The public perceived that such a car was far beyond what a government employee could afford, leading to suspicions that it had been obtained through illegitimate or corrupt practices.

Figure 1. Distribution of YouTube comments (2021–2025) on videos related to displays of wealth by government officials or their family members

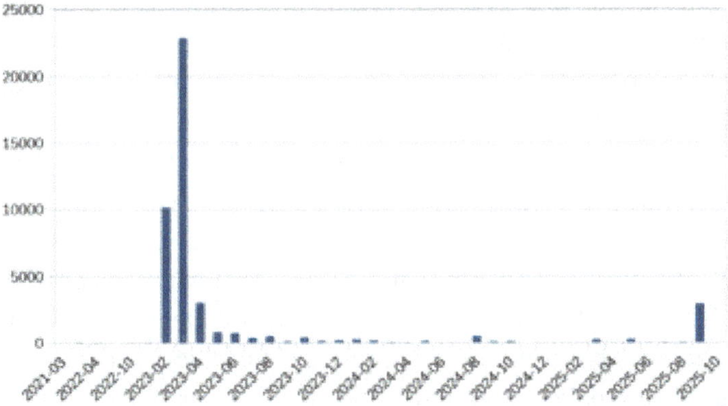

Figure 1 shows that in February, YouTube comments related to the event reached more than ten thousand. In the following months, the number of comments more than doubled. While many comments still referred to the initial case, new cases were also uncovered by social media users. They engaged in crowd-searching to identify either the children of government officials or the officials themselves who excessively displayed their wealth. Consequently, by March 2023, several such individuals had been identified through their own social media posts, and soon these cases were also reported by mainstream media.

Soon, the social media posts of a regent's daughter—revealing her and the regent's luxurious lifestyle—were identified and made viral by other users. While regents often come from wealthy families even before entering politics, their displays of wealth, though considered unethical, are less surprising. What drew greater public attention were government employees who were not expected to afford luxury goods yet openly displayed them. For example, social media users discovered a prison warden flaunting luxury items such as a Harley-Davidson motorcycle, cash, a dirt bike, and even a swimming pool allegedly located in his home. Another government employee was targeted by the Corruption Eradication Commission (KPK) after his wife and children frequently flaunted luxury handbags on social media. Several more cases were uncovered by social media users, including a customs official who frequently showcased his wealth and was subsequently investigated by the KPK, and another who was investigated for the ostentatious behavior of his wife and children.

Unigrams

Table 1 presents the 30 most frequent keywords (unigrams) found in YouTube comments. The analyzed videos were selected using the search phrases "pejabat flexing" (government official flexing), "pejabat pamer kekayaan" (official showing off wealth), "pejabat pamer harta" (official displaying wealth), and "pejabat pamer mewah" (official showing off luxury). Hence, it is unsurprising that the most frequent keywords include "pejabat" (official), "pamer" (show off), and "harta" (wealth). Interestingly, the keyword "pajak" (tax) appears as the second most frequent term, alongside "rakyat" (people), "uang" (money), "korupsi" (corruption), "negara" (state), "anak" (child), and "Indonesia", which all rank within the top ten.

Given that the case which triggered public outrage involved the son of a tax office official, it is understandable that "pajak" (tax) and "anak" (child) emerged as prominent keywords. Many commenters associated the purchase of luxury goods with "uang" (money) believed to be the proceeds of "korupsi" (corruption). Such suspicions stem from the perception that the "gaji" (salary) of government employees is insufficient to afford the luxury items flaunted on social media, either by the officials themselves or by their family members. Consequently, these officials were seen as betraying the "rakyat" (people), and many commenters demanded that they be "dihukum mati" (sentenced to death).

Table 1. List of 30 most frequent keywords/unigram

No	Unigram	Translation	Frequency
1	pejabat	official	7536
2	pajak	tax	7046
3	rakyat	people / citizens	6600
4	pamer	show off / display	4442
5	harta	wealth / assets	4338
6	uang	money	4099
7	korupsi	corruption	4080
8	negara	state / country	3411
9	anak	child	3198
10	indonesia	Indonesia	2979
11	kaya	rich/wealthy	2823
12	bayar	pay	2659
13	hasil	result / outcome / earnings	2152
14	koruptor	corruptor / corrupt official	2136
15	kpk	Corruption Eradication Commission	2072
16	duit	money	1897
17	punya	have / own	1872
18	hidup	life/live	1852
19	mati	die/dead	1590
20	hukum	law	1501
21	pasti	certain / surely	1485
22	biar	let / allow	1473
23	baru	new	1412
24	gaji	salary	1383
25	kekayaan	wealth / prosperity	1366
26	tau	know	1301
27	makan	eat	1254
28	korup	corrupt (adjective)	1201
29	negeri	country	1171
30	miskin	poor	1152

Trigrams

The list of trigrams in Table 2 reveals clearer topics in the YouTube comments dataset. By capturing longer word sequences, trigrams provide richer contextual cues that help identify more specific themes and relationships between concepts. In this dataset, trigrams often reflect evaluative or moral expressions, allowing for a deeper understanding of how commenters articulate their criticism, moral judgment, and collective sentiment toward government officials and their families. This list of trigrams is grouped into seven thematic categories.

Table 2. List of the most frequent trigrams

No	NGram	Translation	Frequency
1	malas bayar pajak	reluctant to pay taxes	127
2	duit bapaknya halal	is his father's money legitimate?	113
3	makan uang haram	living off illicit money	113
4	stop bayar pajak	stop paying taxes	101
5	suka pamer harta	likes to show off wealth	100
6	anak orang kaya	rich person's child	98
7	pajak dan beacukai	tax and customs office	97
8	taat bayar pajak	obedient in paying taxes	92
9	maling uang rakyat	steal people's money	82
10	gaya hidup mewah	luxurious lifestyle	75
11	oknum pejabat koruptor	corrupt official	75
12	pejabat yang suka	official who likes	69
13	rakyat bayar pajak	people pay taxes	69
14	makan uang rakyat	take people's money	69
15	pejabat pamer harta	official showing off wealth	66
16	uang pajak rakyat	people's tax money	64
17	pejabat yang pamer	official who shows off	61
18	anak pejabat pajak	tax official's child	60
19	pakai uang rakyat	use people's money	54
20	harta hasil korupsi	wealth from corruption	54
21	uang hasil korupsi	money from corruption	54
22	maling duit rakyat	thief of people's money	53
23	hukum mati koruptor	sentence corruptors to death	52
24	pejabat di negeri	officials in this country	51

continued on following page

Table 2. Continued

No	NGram	Translation	Frequency
25	usah bayar pajak	don't bother paying taxes	50
26	pamer di medsos	show off on social media	48
27	pejabat di indonesia	officials in Indonesia	48
28	pejabat yang korupsi	officials who commit corruption	44
29	pamer harta hasil	showing off wealth from	44
30	mati bagi koruptor	death for corruptors	43

1. Wealth Display and Lifestyle Critique

The first group of trigrams includes *suka pamer harta* (likes to show off wealth), *gaya hidup mewah* (luxurious lifestyle), and *pamer di medsos* (showing off on social media), as well as an apparently incomplete phrase, *pamer harta hasil* (showing off wealth from…), which upon examination is most often followed by *korupsi* (corruption). On social media, the act of *pamer* (showing off) is generally perceived as normal. One of the motivations for being on social media is self-presentation before an audience, including the display of what users possess (Belk, 2013; A. E. Marwick, 2015; Sheldon & Bryant, 2016).

For government officials, state employees, and their families, however, showing off excessive wealth is seen as less acceptable. It becomes even more unacceptable when the wealth displayed is perceived to exceed what they could legitimately afford. In such cases, suspicion that their wealth is illicit spreads easily among the public.

2. Corruption and Illicit Money

Corruption is inherently difficult to measure, especially when the public perceives law enforcement against it as weak. Consequently, indicators of corruption often depend on public perceptions, which are susceptible to bias and may not correspond to the actual extent of corrupt practices (de Oliveira Leite et al., 2021). The trigrams in this group therefore reflect public anger in situations where corruption cannot be precisely identified.

Public anger at those who display wealth believed to be obtained illicitly is evident in the trigrams produced by the commenters. They are accused of *makan uang haram* (living off illicit money) or *maling uang rakyat* (stealing people's money). Their wealth is described as *uang hasil korupsi* (money from corruption). These trigrams express strong moral and religious condemnation of corrupt practices. The frequent use of *haram* (forbidden) and *halal* (permitted) frames corruption not only as a legal violation but also as a profound moral sin. Commenters often accuse officials of *makan uang rakyat* (literally "eating people's money"), implying both theft and desecration of public resources. These expressions construct corruption as an immoral act against both society and God, situating economic crime within a broader moral discourse.

3. Corrupt Officials and Accountability

This group, which includes trigrams such as *oknum pejabat koruptor* (corrupt official individuals), *pejabat di Indonesia* (officials in Indonesia), and *pejabat yang korupsi* (officials who commit corruption), reflects the public's deep distrust of state officials. The use of the word *oknum* in *oknum pejabat koruptor* was originally intended to indicate that such corrupt officials are exceptions rather than the norm—only a few individuals deviating from otherwise honest institutions. The term *oknum* is commonly used by the press or government to soften the issue and suggest that corruption is not systemic. However, an examination of the concordance (keyword-in-context) in the dataset reveals public frustration with this framing. Many commenters argue that there are *"banyak banget oknum"* (so many exceptions) or *"terlalu banyak oknum"* (too many exceptions), implying that the term has lost its meaning—because if there are too many, then it is no longer an exception. As *oknum* becomes meaningless, commenters frequently generalize corruption to the entire political class, implying that being a *pejabat* (official) is synonymous with being corrupt. These expressions reveal a pervasive cynicism toward government institutions, where accountability is perceived as absent and moral decay as systemic.

4. Institutional Focus

This group includes only one trigram, namely *pajak dan bea cukai* (tax and customs offices), which identifies the institutional context most frequently associated with corruption in the discussion. Despite consisting of only one trigram, it ranks as the seventh most frequent, with a frequency of 97. Although the individuals displaying wealth are not exclusively officials from these institutions or their families, the public already harbors negative sentiment toward them. The Directorate General of Taxes (*Ditjen Pajak*) and the Directorate General of Customs (*Bea Cukai*) have become focal points of collective criticism because commenters perceive these institutions as both the gatekeepers of public funds and the sites where corruption thrives. This institutional distrust illustrates how outrage over individual cases extends to the state apparatus itself, which is viewed as structurally complicit in corruption.

5. Nepotism and Privilege

This group, consisting of *anak pejabat pajak* (tax official's child) and *anak orang kaya* (rich person's child), highlights public resentment toward hereditary privilege. Commenters often refer to the children of officials as visible symbols of corruption, whose displays of luxury on social media expose their families' illicit wealth. The trigram *anak orang kaya* (rich person's child) was particularly common when the case first broke on social media, before the public learned that the perpetrator was the son of a tax official. This early reaction reveals public prejudice toward those who appear far wealthier than average citizens. However, public anger escalated sharply after it was revealed that he was the son of a low-ranking government official—someone who, based on his salary, would not reasonably be able to afford such expensive vehicles.

6. Tax Morality and Resistance

This group contains trigrams such as *malas bayar pajak* (reluctant to pay taxes), *stop bayar pajak* (stop paying taxes), and *usah bayar pajak* (don't bother paying taxes). These phrases represent public frustration toward the government's misuse of tax funds. Many commenters express symbolic resistance by rejecting the moral obligation to pay taxes, arguing that their money would only be stolen by corrupt officials. Conversely, other trigrams like *taat bayar pajak* (obedient in paying taxes) and *rakyat bayar pajak* (people pay taxes) are used to contrast the integrity of ordinary citizens with the moral failure of the state employees. Together, they reflect the erosion of public trust in taxation as a social contract between citizens and the government.

7. Capital Punishment and Retribution

Trigrams such as *hukum mati koruptor* (sentence corruptors to death) and *mati bagi koruptor* (death for corruptors) signify extreme public anger and disillusionment with the state's inability to curb corruption. The call for capital punishment emerges as a form of moral retribution and symbolic justice. For many commenters, legal penalties such as imprisonment are seen as insufficient, and only death can restore moral balance. These expressions dramatize the scale of outrage and reveal how corruption is framed not just as a crime but as a moral betrayal of the nation deserving ultimate punishment.

Taken together, these seven themes reveal how public discourse around officials' and their families' displays of wealth extends far beyond individual acts of ostentation. The comments reflect a broader moral and political anxiety about inequality, corruption, and the erosion of public trust in state institutions. Expressions of outrage link personal misconduct to systemic failure—turning specific cases of *flexing* into symbols of institutional decay. The focus on wealth, family privilege, and the misuse of tax money underscores how conspicuous consumption by those tied to public office violates deeply held notions of fairness and accountability. Ultimately, these online reactions illustrate a form of digital moral economy, where social media users collectively police moral boundaries and call for justice in the face of perceived corruption and privilege.

Based on the seven themes identified above, the conceptual map in Figure 2 was created, with labels simplified for clarity and conciseness. The node "People" was added because most of the other nodes are related to it. It is the people who pay taxes, but they are also the ones who suffer from corruption. Moreover, wealth display is perceived as an immoral behavior that demonstrates a lack of sympathy toward the feelings of ordinary citizens.

Figure 2. Conceptual mapping of wealth display revealing corruption practices and triggering public distrust

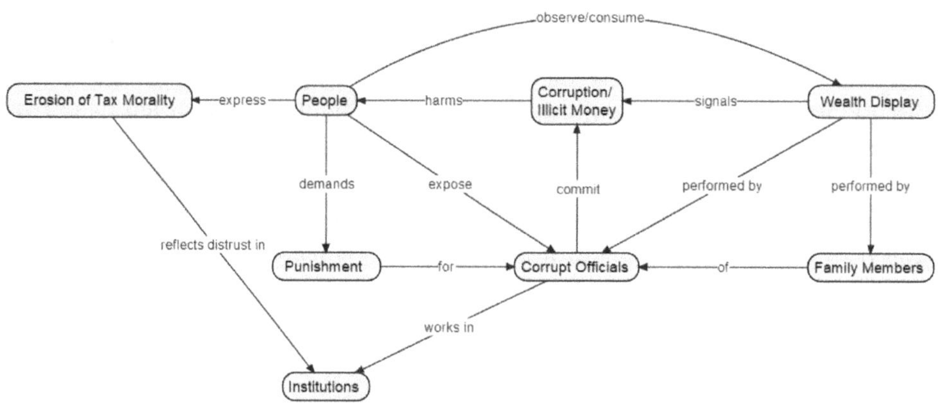

DISCUSSION

The dataset contains comments on YouTube videos featuring government officials (or their family members) who show off their wealth. Hence, as anticipated, *pejabat* (officials), *pajak* (tax), *rakyat* (people/citizens), *pamer* (show off/display), and *harta* (wealth/assets) are the top five unigrams/keywords, as shown in Table 1.

As will be shown in this and the following sections, these terms frequently co-occur and are closely connected across a large number of comments.

Wealth Display Implies Corruption

What triggers public outrage is the perception that the wealth displayed by the family members—wives or children—of government officials, or by the officials themselves, can only come from corruption. The public may exaggerate these accusations, assuming that all such displays by officials' wives or children are funded by their husbands' or fathers' illicit money, dismissing the possibility that they may have earned their own income. However, seeing the response from the institutions where these officials work—by strongly reprimanding them, or at least by not strongly denying the allegations—the public tends to view their suspicions as justified. In a society that is still developing its democracy and lacks openness, various interpretations can emerge. People may rely on moral intuition rather than examining facts and reasoning about them (Haidt, 2001), especially since such facts are often unavailable.

Table 3. Examples of comments perceiving wealth displays as derived from illicit money or corruption.

No	Comment	Translation
1	"ya kalau gaya hidup mewah anak dan keluarganya melebihi gajinya...sangat mungkin korupsi!"	"Well, if the luxurious lifestyle of an official's children and family exceeds their salary... it's very likely corruption!"
2	"kaya hasil korupsi, logika saja hitung gaji perbulan berapa "	"Rich from corruption — just use logic, calculate how much their monthly salary is "
3	"kalau ada asn lihat saja dari segi kemewahannya apabila gaji dan kekayaanya tidak sesuai gaji asn. bisa diselidiki dari mana mereka mendapatkan uang untuk gaya hidup yang melebihi gaji asn. jangan lupa istri cerminan suami."	"If you see a civil servant, just look at their level of luxury — if their wealth doesn't match their salary, it should be investigated where they get the money to live beyond their means. Don't forget, a wife is a reflection of her husband."
4	"kita pura-pura terkejut berjamaah, padahal sudah rahasia umum, pns pejabat rata-rata kekayaannya nggak sesuai gaji"	"Let's all pretend to be shocked together, even though it's an open secret that most civil servants and officials have wealth that doesn't match their salaries."

The first three comments in the above Table 3 reflect public reasoning that when government officials or their family members display wealth or assets far beyond their salaries, such wealth must have come from illicit sources. This is a simple yet difficult-to-deny reasoning. The fourth comment points to the perceived long-standing open secret that the wealth of government employees and officials often exceeds their official earnings. Thus, the accusation is not new; people have long been aware of it through word-of-mouth. However, on social media, it appears that people now have what they consider hard evidence of corruption (even if indirect), as they can see the displays of wealth made by the accused.

The Immoral Act of Wealth Display

Prior to the *Mario Dandy* case—the son of a tax official who assaulted another youth—social media users seemed encouraged to show off, including by displaying their wealth. Such behavior was part of the pursuit of *micro-celebrity* status, as emulating celebrities on digital platforms had become normalized (Mohamad, 2021). However, when the individuals flaunting their wealth were the children or wives of government officials or employees, their displays were suddenly perceived as immoral. The framing of such behavior as immoral requires sufficient media attention (Starr, 2021); while in the past this depended on traditional media corporations, on social media the public can now mobilize their own form of collective coverage. Nonetheless, this depends on whether the issue in question is widely perceived as a transgression of shared public norms.

Displaying legitimate wealth in the media, including on social media, is generally considered acceptable and is even a common feature in mainstream media coverage of celebrities. However, when wealth is perceived as illegitimate—implying that it is not genuinely earned—it tends to provoke public anger, as illustrated by the first comment in Table 4. In a context where many citizens struggle to pay taxes, corruption is frequently equated with the act of robbing or stealing from the people. Even, the first comment warns that the public may grow angry and protest against officials and their families who flaunt wealth stolen from the people's money.

Table 4. Examples of comments where the display of wealth co-occurs with the term rakyat (people).

No	Comment	Translation
1	"sebentar lagi bakal demo nie rakyat indonesia karena selalu disuguhi tontonan pejabat dan keluarganya yang pamer harta hasil jarahan uang rakyat"	"Soon there will probably be a protest by the Indonesian people, because they keep being shown scenes of officials and their families showing off wealth stolen from the people's money."
2	"ngeri ..memang mental pejabat kita...pamer gaya hidup mewah dari hasil korupsi..sementara rakyat susah setengah mati bayar pajak "	"Terrifying… that's really the mentality of our officials—showing off a luxurious lifestyle from the proceeds of corruption, while the people struggle desperately to pay taxes. "
3	"orang kaya baru suka pamer harta kekayaan yang diperoleh dari merampok uang rakyat."	"Newly rich people like to show off the wealth they obtained by stealing the people's money."

Furthermore, the perceived immorality of displaying wealth or a luxurious lifestyle is reinforced when it is contrasted with the hardships faced by ordinary citizens. As a developing country, Indonesia still has many people living below the poverty line, working hard merely to maintain a modest life. Therefore, displaying wealth—especially when it is seen as belonging to the people—is regarded as immoral. Table 5 contrasts comments that criticize displays of wealth or luxury with the struggles of ordinary citizens.

Table 5. Contrasting the luxurious lifestyles of government officials' families with the hardships of ordinary citizens

No	Comment	Translation
1	"emak-emak pamer harta hasil korupsi suaminya yang koruptor, ruarrr biasa, saat masyarakat sulit dapat kerja, itulah emak-emak yang woiii..."	"A woman showing off the wealth gained from her corrupt husband—how extraordinary! At a time when people are struggling to find jobs, that's the kind of woman who, wow..."
2	"bangga nya aku jadi anak pejabat korupsi.. hidup mewah tanpa kerja keras... enak kali hidupmu tanpa kerja keras.. orang lain banting tulang sampai sakit, belum tentu seperti hidup kau bajingan"	"I'm so proud to be the child of a corrupt official... living a luxurious life without hard work. Must be nice to live so easily without effort... while others work themselves to exhaustion, even to illness, and still can't live like you, you bastard."
3	"rakyat masih banyak yang hidup susah dan miskin tapi para pejabat dan istri dan anak" nya pada hidup mewah dan glamour"	"Many citizens are still living in hardship and poverty, while officials and their wives and children live in luxury and glamour."

Wealth Display Gives Opportunity to Corruption Eradication

Corruption has long been regarded by the public as a serious problem, yet people often feel helpless in confronting it. Although electoral democracy has been regularly practiced through elections every five years, ensuring government accountability—and especially bureaucratic accountability—remains a challenge. What makes corruption particularly troubling is that the perceived perpetrators no longer seem to hide what they have gained illegitimately; their wealth is visible for all to see.

The public believes that corruption is massive, as reflected in the frequent use of the phrases *bukan rahasia* ("not a secret") and *rahasia umum* ("open secret")—two expressions that reveal how corruption is perceived as a normal yet unacceptable part of everyday life. The phrase *bukan rahasia* implies that the public already knows about such practices because they have become common and frequently encountered. In contrast, *rahasia umum* conveys that although everyone is aware of these practices, they cannot be openly discussed in formal settings. Officially or legally, it is as if the problem does not exist.

By using a window span of five, the collocates of *bukan rahasia* ("not a secret") were extracted using KeyText. There are 91 YouTube comments containing *bukan rahasia*, and the resulting collocates are listed in Table 6. The collocates include *pejabat* (official), *pegawai* (employee), and *negeri* (state), which can be combined into *pegawai negeri* (civil servant), also known as *aparat sipil negara* (ASN). Two institutions are frequently perceived as *sarang* (nests) of corrupt officials or civil servants due to the large circulation of money within them—namely, the tax office and the customs office. The outcome of corruption, of course, is *harta* (wealth).

Table 6. The top ten collocates of bukan rahasia ("not a secret")

No	Collocate (Indonesian Word)	English Translation	Frequency
1	umum	public	36
2	pajak	tax	19
3	pejabat	official	17
4	beacukai	customs	13
5	pegawai	employee	9
6	negeri	state / civil (depending on context, often *civil servant*)	5
7	asn	civil servant (Aparatur Sipil Negara)	4
8	harta	wealth / assets	4
9	sarang	nest / hub (metaphorically, "hotbed")	3
10	perpajakan	taxation	3

The phrase *bukan rahasia* ("not a secret") is expanded into the three-word phrase *sudah bukan rahasia* ("no longer a secret"), which is more common in everyday conversation. The latter phrase appears in 34 comments, three of which are shown in Table 7. The first comment refers to accusations that certain individuals (*oknum*, a term used to avoid generalizing) in the customs office have abused their positions. The second comment suggests that those who were caught were merely unlucky, implying that others are doing the same—since it is no longer a secret. The third comment states that corruption and abuse of power among government employees have long been known, as reflected in their wealth. What is needed, the commenter argues, is not more discussion but more serious law enforcement.

Table 7. Comments containing sudah bukan rahasia ("no longer a secret")

No	Comment	Translation
1	"... **sudah bukan rahasia** lagi bahwa oknum beacukai punya potensi menyalahgunakan jabatannya......karena berkaitan dengan keluar masuknya barang di wilayah"	"... it's **no longer a secret** that certain individuals in the customs office have the potential to abuse their positions... since their work is related to the flow of goods in and out of the country."
2	"yang ini lagi apes saja bro...yang lain masih ada.... **sudah bukan rahasia** lagi"	"This one just got unlucky, bro... there are still many others out there... it's **no longer a secret**."
3	"semua asn di semua intansi yang punya jabatan kayaknya sih dari dahulu kala pasti kaya-kaya **sudah bukan rahasia** di negeri ini, kalau mau bahas sekarang mah sudah basi, sekarang mah mestinya perubahan hukum"	"All civil servants in every institution who hold positions have probably been rich since long ago—it's **no longer a secret** in this country. Talking about it now is already old news; what we really need now is legal reform."

The top ten collocates of *rahasia umum* ("open secret") are shown in Table 8. The list is similar to that in Table 6 but includes three institutions frequently mentioned: the tax office, the customs office, and the National Land Agency (BPN). An interesting collocate is *basah* (literally "wet"), referring to workplaces where, despite comparable official salaries, opportunities to gain illicit income through bribery are much greater. While corruption may occur in any institution, these three are perceived as offering the most lucrative opportunities. They also attract greater public resentment because their corrupt practices directly affect citizens, unlike those who embezzle government funds through budget manipulation or markups, whose excessive wealth still provokes disapproval but feels less immediate.

Table 8. The top ten collocates of rahasia umum ("open secret")

No	Word	Translation	Frequency
1	pejabat	official	32
2	pajak	tax	25
3	kaya	rich	14
4	beacukai	customs	12
5	pegawai	employee	9
6	gaya	style	7
7	indonesia	Indonesia	7
8	negara	state / country	7
9	basah	Is an adjective commonly combined with *lahan* (field); *lahan basah* literally means "wet field," but figuratively refers to a "lucrative post" or "a position offering opportunities for illicit gain."	6
10	bpn	National Land Agency	5

The first comment in Table 9 implies the meaning of *rahasia umum* ("open secret"). People are not surprised that officials are rich—they already know—but it remains questionable because their wealth does not match their official salaries. As stated in the second comment, it only became a public fuss after an actual case emerged. While an open secret cannot be openly discussed, people are also not supposed to show their surprise; yet, the cases in the dataset seem to provide an opportunity for them to express it.

Table 9. Comments containing rahasia umum ("open secret")

No	Comment	Translation
1	"nggak kaget kalau para pejabat kaya.sudah menjadi rahasia umum .walaupun penuh dengan tanda tanya. "	"Not surprised that officials are rich. It's already an open secret, although it's still full of question marks. "
2	"sudah jadi rahasia umum gaya mewah para aparatur negara, rame baru ada kasus saja.."	"The luxurious lifestyle of state officials has long been an open secret; it became a fuss after a case emerged."
3	"sudah jadi rahasia umum jika beacukai dan perpajakan adalah lahan basah sarang koruptor, biarpun waktu dilantik mereka disumpah di bawah kitab suci tetap saja lihat yang merah-merah langsung khilaf"	"It has long been an open secret that customs and taxation offices are lucrative breeding grounds for corrupt officials. Even though they take an oath on the holy book when inaugurated, they still lose their integrity the moment they see red-colored bills."

The popularity of the phrases *bukan rahasia* ("not a secret") and *rahasia umum* ("open secret") indicates the ineffectiveness of law enforcement in addressing financial corruption. However, the current public uproar over the display of wealth by government officials and their families opens an opportunity for stronger anti-corruption efforts. The anger expressed on social media also reflects the public's impatience with corruption and their support for more decisive law enforcement.

The tendency of officials and their family members to flaunt their wealth or luxurious lifestyle paradoxically facilitates law enforcement efforts, as suggested by the comments in Table 10. Such public displays make it easier for authorities and citizens alike to identify possible cases of corruption.

Table 10. Comments indicating opportunities for the eradication of corruption

No	Comment	Translation
	"di indonesia sebenarnya gampang menangkap koruptor karena mereka memamerkan seusatu yang tidak harus dipamerkan. dan itu menjadi kecurigaan yang mudah diusut wkwkwk"	"In Indonesia, it's actually easy to catch corrupt officials because they often show off things they shouldn't. That makes suspicion easy to investigate, haha."
	"banyakin deh anak pejabat korupsi yang suka pamer harta biar gampang keciduk wkwkwk"	"Let there be more corrupt officials' children who like to show off their wealth—so it'll be easier to catch them, haha."
	"orang-orang yang kaya harus pamer di medsos apalagi asn biar terbongkar semua asal usul harta mereka"	"Rich people should show off on social media—especially civil servants—so that the sources of their wealth can all be exposed."
	"gara-gara mario_dandy kena semua sekarang pegawai yang hdupnya hedon2 .. tangkap semua pegawai yang hdupnya tidak sesuai dengan gaji"	"Because of Mario Dandy, now all the officials living a hedonistic lifestyle are getting caught up in it. Arrest all officials whose lifestyles don't match their salaries."

The phenomenon also reflects a form of *digital vigilance* or *participatory surveillance*, in which ordinary citizens actively monitor the online behavior of public officials and their families. Through social media, citizens collectively participate in identifying inconsistencies between officials' public display of wealth and their legitimate income, thereby reinforcing informal mechanisms of accountability.

An important aspect of public surveillance is making cases go viral—echoing the sentiment often expressed by social media users, including in this dataset: *"No viral, no justice."* Virality has become the only perceived way to achieve justice or to prompt investigations. This also reflects the public's deep distrust in law enforcement, as expressed in the following comments:

"selama penegak hukum yang terkait bisa disumpel..nggak beres nih membasmi tikus-tikus comberan..   *"*

"As long as the law enforcers involved can be bribed, there's no way to get rid of these sewer rats (corrupt people).   *"*

Wealth display among certain officials or civil servants and their families has long been apparent, but internal disciplinary mechanisms within their institutions—as well as law enforcement—are widely perceived as ineffective. These institutions tend to wait for external pressure before taking action. Since social media encourages users to publish personal details and makes it easy for others to find them, interpersonal surveillance becomes easier, turning social media into a significant force for enforcing moral compliance (Trottier, 2017). However, social media is also vulnerable to the spread of misinformation and disinformation.

Table 11 shows comments illustrating how the virality generated by users' surveillance ultimately forces institutions to take action against those who engage in wealth display. Only after cases involving their staff or officials went viral did the top management of government institutions take action to investigate their subordinates. This prompted the public to question why authorities waited until an issue became viral before summoning those involved, as reflected in the first and second comments in Table 11. Consequently, the public emphasized the need to keep such cases viral to ensure that justice is upheld, as expressed in the third comment.

Table 11. Comments indicating the need of virality to pressure disciplinary and law enforcement

No	Comment	Translation
1	"sudah viral saja lu baru benah benah diri ...kemarin-kemarin kemana saja lu para pejabat malu ya sama masyarakat. "	"Only after it's gone viral do you start cleaning up... where were you all this time, you officials? Feeling ashamed now in front of the public, huh?"
2	"kenapa nggak dari dulu dipanggil, nunggu viral dulu???"	"Why weren't they summoned earlier? Did they have to wait until it went viral???"
3	"viralkan terus, agar tidak ada permainan hukum"	"Keep making it go viral, so there won't be any legal maneuvering."

Since government institutions appeared more concerned with avoiding public embarrassment than with enforcing norms or regulations to ensure clean governance—as evidenced by their appeals to civil servants and officials not to display their wealth—many members of the public responded with cynicism. One commenter expressed this sentiment sarcastically:

"korupsi/pencucian uang itu boleh-boleh saja, sah-sah saja..yang tidak boleh di republik ini adalah pamer-pamer."

"Corruption or money laundering is perfectly acceptable; what is not permitted in this republic is showing off."

While the public was not satisfied with the legal actions taken against corruption, by uncovering and making such cases go viral, they engaged in online public shaming that forced the officials or their family members to feel ashamed and close or lock their social media accounts to avoid further backlash. However, since public trust in law enforcement was already weak, many suspected that what happened was merely an attempt to stop displaying wealth, not to stop corruption itself. One comment reflects this sentiment:

"flexing istri-istri pejabat hidup mewah dan hedon, sekarang pejabat-pejabat tiarap dan memarahi istrinya,, , korupsi ya lanjut.... "
"Officials' wives who used to flaunt their luxury and hedonistic lifestyles—now the officials are hiding and scolding their wives, but the corruption continues... "

CONCLUSION

Social media has normalized narcissistic behaviors among its users, including flaunting wealth. Many people either enjoy watching others' wealth displays or participate in displaying their own. However, even though morality seems absent in most wealth displays, once it becomes publicly known that the sources of such wealth are illicit, moral outrage emerges. Many social media users not only express their anger toward those whose wealth is accused of being suspicious, but also engage in digital vigilantism—collectively searching for other social media users who display suspiciously illicit wealth and making them targets of online public shaming.

Due to its nature and weak institutional accountability, public accusations of corruption are often made without legal or formal evidence. These moral judgments rely on perception, which may be biased but are not entirely without reasoning. For many people, government officials or employees with publicly known salaries cannot reasonably afford the level of wealth they or their families display. Through this simple reasoning, what they showcase is often perceived as far exceeding their legitimate income, leading to the assumption that their wealth comes from illicit sources.

People have come to realize that social pressure can compel law enforcement to act. This phenomenon is often summarized in the phrase "no viral, no justice." The public exposures shown in the dataset prompted law enforcers to take action, and the associated institutions began internal examinations of those made viral by the public. However, the public remains dissatisfied. Legal or disciplinary actions seem to occur only after cases go viral, while similar cases that fail to attract online attention are often ignored. Thus, despite public expectations for stronger anti-corruption enforcement, what has emerged instead is a form of online public shaming—a collective effort to impose moral accountability when formal institutions fail to function effectively.

REFERENCES

Aitchison, G., & Meckled-Garcia, S. (2021). Against Online Public Shaming: Ethical Problems with Mass Social Media. [JSTOR.]. *Social Theory and Practice*, *47*(1), 1–31. DOI: 10.5840/soctheorpract20201117109

Andreassen, C. S., Pallesen, S., & Griffiths, M. D. (2017). The relationship between addictive use of social media, narcissism, and self-esteem: Findings from a large national survey. *Addictive Behaviors*, *64*, 287–293. DOI: 10.1016/j.addbeh.2016.03.006

Belk, R. W. (1988). Possessions and the Extended Self. [JSTOR.]. *The Journal of Consumer Research*, *15*(2), 139–168. DOI: 10.1086/209154

Belk, R. W. (2013). Extended Self in a Digital World. *Journal of Consumer Research*, *40*(3), 477–500. JSTOR. DOI: 10.1086/671052

Bourdieu, P. (1984). *DIstInctIon: A Social Critique of the Judgement of Taste* (R. Nice, Trans.). Harvard University Press.

Brubaker, R. (2020). Digital hyperconnectivity and the self. *Theory and Society*, *49*(5), 771–801. DOI: 10.1007/s11186-020-09405-1

Cannon, C., & Rucker, D. D. (2019). The Dark Side of Luxury: Social Costs of Luxury Consumption. *Personality and Social Psychology Bulletin*, *45*(5), 767–779. DOI: 10.1177/0146167218796790

Chang, E. C. C., & Chu, Y. (2006). Corruption and Trust: Exceptionalism in Asian Democracies? *The Journal of Politics*, *68*(2), 259–271. JSTOR. DOI: 10.1111/j.1468-2508.2006.00404.x

Cheong, P. H., & Gong, J. (2010). Cyber vigilantism, transmedia collective intelligence, and civic participation. *Chinese Journal of Communication*, *3*(4), 471–487. DOI: 10.1080/17544750.2010.516580

de Oliveira Leite, R., Dias, R., & Mendes, L. (2021). Morality and Perception of Corruption. *Latin American Business Review*, *22*(2), 163–188. DOI: 10.1080/10978526.2020.1777558

Duffy, B. E., & Chan, N. K. (2019). "You never really know who's looking": Imagined surveillance across social media platforms. *New Media & Society*, *21*(1), 119–138. DOI: 10.1177/1461444818791318

Ferraro, R., Escalas, J. E., & Bettman, J. R. (2011). Our possessions, our selves: Domains of self-worth and the possession–self link. *Journal of Consumer Psychology*, *21*(2), 169–177. DOI: 10.1016/j.jcps.2010.08.007

Giddens, A. (1984). *The Constitution of Society—Outline of the Theory of Structuration*. Polity Press.

Goffman, E. (1956). *The Presentation of Self in Everyday Life*. University of Edinburgh Social Sciences Research Center.

Gran, A.-B. (2025). Performing not-not-me in SoMe: A new theatrical typology of self-presentation online. *Social Media + Society*, *11*(1), 20563051251315256. DOI: 10.1177/20563051251315256

Greig, M. A., & Hogg, R. C. (2025). 'Unfollow Them!': The Role of Morality- and Emotion-Related Factors in the Cancelling Process. *Human Behavior and Emerging Technologies*, *2025*(1), 7144903. DOI: 10.1155/hbe2/7144903

Haidt, J. (2001). The emotional dog and its rational tail: A social intuitionist approach to moral judgment. *Psychological Review, 108*(4), 814–834. *Scopus*. Advance online publication. DOI: 10.1037/0033-295X.108.4.814

Haidt, J., & Joseph, C. (2004). Intuitive ethics: How innately prepared intuitions generate culturally variable virtues. *Daedalus, 133*(4), 55–65. *Scopus*. Advance online publication. DOI: 10.1162/0011526042365555

Han, Y. J., Nunes, J. C., & Drèze, X. (2010). Signaling Status with Luxury Goods: The Role of Brand Prominence. *Journal of Marketing*, *74*(4), 15–30. DOI: 10.1509/jmkg.74.4.015

Huigen, B. (2025). Vulgar things: Moral dilemmas of luxury consumption in an unequal society. *Journal of Consumer Culture, 14695405251376100*(4), 385–404. Advance online publication. DOI: 10.1177/14695405251376100

Kristensen, N. N., & Jerslev, A. (2025). When influencer logic and news media logic converge in the scandalisation of an influencer: The exposure of literary critic and influencer Katherine Diez's plagiarism. *Nordic Journal of Media Studies*, *7*(1), 93–111. DOI: 10.2478/njms-2025-0006

Marwick, A., & boyd, . (2011). To See and Be Seen: Celebrity Practice on Twitter. *Convergence (London), 17*(2), 139–158. DOI: 10.1177/1354856510394539

Marwick, A. E. (2015). Instafame: Luxury selfies in the attention economy. *Public Culture, 27*(1), 137–160. *Scopus*. Advance online publication. DOI: 10.1215/08992363-2798379

Marwick, A. E., & boyd, . (2011). I tweet honestly, I tweet passionately: Twitter users, context collapse, and the imagined audience. *New Media & Society*, *13*(1), 114–133. DOI: 10.1177/1461444810365313

Maulana, I. (2018). Spontaneous taking and posting selfie: Reclaiming the lost trust. In *Selfies as a mode of social media and work space research* (pp. 28–50). IGI Global. DOI: 10.4018/978-1-5225-3373-3.ch002

Maulana, I. (2019). Big Brothers Are Seducing You: Consumerism, Surveillance, and the Agency of Consumers. In Ozgen, O. (Ed.), *Handbook of Research on Consumption, Media, and Popular Culture in the Global Age* (pp. 57–75). IGI Global. DOI: 10.4018/978-1-5225-8491-9.ch004

Maulana, I. (2025). *KeyText* (Version 0.16) [Computer software]. https://github.com/ikbaloss/KeyText

McFerran, B., Aquino, K., & Tracy, J. L. (2014). Evidence for two facets of pride in consumption: Findings from luxury brands. *Journal of Consumer Psychology*, *24*(4), 455–471. DOI: 10.1016/j.jcps.2014.03.004

Mikolov, T., Chen, K., Corrado, G., & Dean, J. (2013). *Efficient estimation of word representations in vector space*. 1st International Conference on Learning Representations, ICLR 2013 - Workshop Track Proceedings. Scopus. https://www.scopus.com/inward/record.uri?eid=2-s2.0-85083951332&partnerID=40&md5=20428820e8b09cdfb5078ea812a71f2d

Mohamad, S. M. (2021). Micro-celebrity practices in Muslim-majority states in Southeast Asia. *Popular Communication*, *19*(3), 235–249. DOI: 10.1080/15405702.2021.1913492

Mortensen, M., & Kristensen, N. N. (2020). De-celebrification: Beyond the scandalous. *Celebrity Studies*, *11*(1), 89–100. DOI: 10.1080/19392397.2020.1704385

Murray, D. C. (2015). Notes to self: The visual culture of selfies in the age of social media. *Consumption Markets & Culture*, *18*(6), 490–516. DOI: 10.1080/10253866.2015.1052967

Noviansah, W. (2023, March 17). *Mario Dandy Ternyata Sebar Foto dan Video Saat Aniaya David* [News website]. detikNews; detikNews / detikcom. https://news.detik.com/berita/d-6624495/mario-dandy-ternyata-sebar-foto-dan-video-saat-aniaya-david

Pozner, J.-E., & Hannigan, T. R. (2023). How Relational Publics Become Scandal Audiences: Values and the construction of scandal. *Organization Theory*, *4*(3), 26317877231204085. DOI: 10.1177/26317877231204085

Schau, H. J., & Gilly, M. C. (2003). We Are What We Post? Self-Presentation in Personal Web Space. *Journal of Consumer Research, 30*(3), 385–404. JSTOR. DOI: 10.1086/378616

Sheldon, P., & Bryant, K. (2016). Instagram: Motives for its use and relationship to narcissism and contextual age. *Computers in Human Behavior, 58*, 89–97. DOI: 10.1016/j.chb.2015.12.059

Sheth, J. N., & Solomon, M. R. (2014). Extending the Extended Self in a Digital World. *Journal of Marketing Theory and Practice, 22*(2), 123–132. DOI: 10.2753/MTP1069-6679220201

Shulman, D. (2022). Self-presentation: Impression management in the digital age. In Jacobsen, M. H., & Smith, G. (Eds.), *The Routledge international handbook of Goffman studies* (pp. 26–37). Routledge. DOI: 10.4324/9781003160861-4

Srna, S., Barasch, A., & Small, D. A. (2022). On the Value of Modesty: How Signals of Status Undermine Cooperation. *Journal of Personality and Social Psychology, 123*(4), 676–692. *Scopus*. Advance online publication. DOI: 10.1037/pspa0000303

Starr, P. (2021). The Relational Public. *Sociological Theory, 39*(2), 57–80. DOI: 10.1177/07352751211004660

Sullivan, J. L. (2013). Media Audiences: Effects, Users, Institutions, and Power. *Sage (Atlanta, Ga.)*.

Taylor, D. G. (2020). Putting the "self" in selfies: How narcissism, envy and self-promotion motivate sharing of travel photos through social media. *Journal of Travel & Tourism Marketing, 37*(1), 64–77. DOI: 10.1080/10548408.2020.1711847

Taylor, D. G., & Strutton, D. (2016). Does Facebook usage lead to conspicuous consumption? *Journal of Research in Interactive Marketing, 10*(3), 231–248. DOI: 10.1108/JRIM-01-2015-0009

Trottier, D. (2017). Digital Vigilantism as Weaponisation of Visibility. *Philosophy & Technology, 30*(1), 55–72. DOI: 10.1007/s13347-016-0216-4

Trottier, D. (2018). Scandal mining: Political nobodies and remediated visibility. *Media, Culture and Society, 40*(6), 893–908. *Scopus*. Advance online publication. DOI: 10.1177/0163443717734408

Warner, S. B. (2023). Analyzing Attention to Scandal on Twitter: Elites Sell What Supporters Buy. *Political Research Quarterly, 76*(2), 841–850. DOI: 10.1177/10659129221114145

Yan, X., Fu, Y., Yang, F., & Han, Y. (2025). They Shouldn't Be Richer Than Me: How Visual Wealth Exposure on Social Media Increases Relative Deprivation. *Cyberpsychology, 19*(2). *Cyberpsychology (Brno), 19*(2). Advance online publication. DOI: 10.5817/CP2025-2-4

Zuboff, S. (2015). Big other: Surveillance capitalism and the prospects of an information civilization. *Journal of Information Technology*, *30*(1), 75–89. DOI: 10.1057/jit.2015.5

Chapter 7
Impression and Image Management Effects on Individuals' Behaviours, Appearance, Communication, Digital Presence, and Emotional Balance

Okechukwu Ethelbert Amah
https://orcid.org/0000-0002-6574-6941
Lagos Business School, Pan Atlantic University, Nigeria

ABSTRACT

In social interaction, including the organisational environment, individuals use impression management (IM) to create the image they want others to see of themselves to obtain endorsement, which can translate to organisational rewards. This image is defined by the behaviours, communication, and other attributes that the individual presents using IM. Impression management has been presented as a multidimensional construct with many dimensions. Past studies have tried to capture the benefits and shortcomings of IM. However, the review of the past studies in this book chapter identified four areas that need to be emphasised by future IM studies to understand the construct adequately. The four areas are: the effectiveness of IM dimensions over time, the establishment of an accurate dimensionality of IM, how impression

DOI: 10.4018/979-8-3373-5519-1.ch007

management can be made effective in virtual interactions, and how to understand the double-edged nature of IM. The book chapter made some suggestions on how these areas can be included in future studies on IM.

INTRODUCTION

Impression management (IM) involves individuals' conscious and unconscious processes to shape how others perceive them within various social, professional, and digital environments. These processes influence individuals' behaviours, choices in appearance, communication patterns, and digital presence, often to gain social acceptance, advance career opportunities, or align with societal expectations. There is a close relationship between impression management and image formation. IM is the conscious or unconscious efforts, behaviors, and strategies that people use to form the image that people should have of them. Thus, IM helps individuals to form the image they want to portray to the world to enhance their acceptance. Image formation encompasses the initial creation of the image and the ongoing effort to maintain or enhance the image that has been formed (GreggU @ LighthouseOD.com). Thus, image management involves creating and managing the image a person wants to create in a social environment. Creating a positive image makes individuals more aware of the need to manage the impression they make when interacting with others deliberately. In recent years, impression management (IM) has received renewed attention among scholars (Liu *et al.*, 2019; Chen et al., 2021) because it has become a deliberate process through which individuals shape how others perceive them by controlling their presentation, behavior, and actions to gain acceptance. It is considered a conscious and subconscious process in which people attempt to influence the perceptions of others by portraying themselves in a manner that creates a good impression (Sukmayadi *et al*, 2024).

Image management is a key element in managing relationships and interactions, as it encompasses individuals' deliberate efforts to control how they are perceived through their physical appearance, grooming, attire, body language, and the environments they curate around themselves. Individuals need to be intentional about using images when communicating with their audience. Managing one's image helps to gain others' social, moral, or financial support (Rosenfeld *et al.*, 2015). In a digitally interactive environment, image and impression management are integral to daily human interaction through social networking sites.

NATURE AND BENEFITS OF IMPRESSION MANAGEMENT

Impression and image management are long-standing, pervasive phenomena that impact every aspect of human relations, from individual interactions to organizational and societal dynamics. Understanding these concepts is essential for all stakeholders to enhance personal and social relationships and positively influence others within the public sphere. This process influences individual behaviors, choice of appearance, communication styles, digital identity, and emotional balance, often to achieve social acceptance, advance one's career, and align with societal expectations. IM can be positive or negative, and can be adaptive or manipulative. Positive and adaptive IM arise when people engage in authentic and genuine behaviors devoid of deceit aimed at addressing real issues. People achieve positive IM when they build authentic personal brands by authentically communicating their values, strengths, skills, and ideas, and others perceive them as reliable, trustworthy, and credible. Apart from communicating values, Tairi (2018) and Tohme and Joseph (2020) have identified other sources of authenticity, such as mindfulness and emotional intelligence. Mindfulness increases awareness of one's present moment, feelings, and actions, which can reduce inauthentic presentation. Emotional intelligence equips individuals with the skills to regulate their own emotions and those of others, and to use adaptive rather than manipulative strategies. Positive IM offers diverse personal, social, and organizational benefits, such as career advancement, leadership opportunities, and positive workplace dynamics (Geeth *et al.*, 2024). Furthermore, it provides the benefits listed below:

- Increased individual trust and recognition.
- Improved networking and collaboration.
- Enhanced career advancement opportunities.
- Greater well-being and satisfaction at work when engaging in pro-social IM that fosters inclusion and accountability.

Negative IMs are manipulative and aimed at covering the real person behind the mask. Even if people think they are authentic, negative IM can still occur when others perceive the person as manipulative or disruptive. Hence, the content and delivery of information in IM must be analyzed to avoid misperception. The practical tools that help individuals avoid misperception are based on striking a balance between self-presentation and authenticity. Past authors (Al-Shatti & Ohana, 2021; Meyerhuber, 2019; Morrison & Bies, 1991) have identified these practices as a vehicle to avoid misperception:

- Active Listening: Paying attention to others' verbal and nonverbal cues to maintain genuine communication.
- Reflective Practices: Being mindful of word choices to ensure self-presentation is explicit and consistent with personal values and identity.
- Mindful Regulation: Stemming from self-awareness helps to overcome a lack of confidence and increases authentic expression.
- Feedback: Regular feedback from others (peers, supervisors) reinforces and contributes to a positive impression management experience.

The outcomes of negative impression management include:

- Low self-esteem and lack of trust.
- Poor interpersonal relationships.
- A manipulative image and loss of credibility over the long term.
- Damage to trust, especially when the behavior appears self-serving.

Impression management has also been linked to various organizational outcomes. For example, in a laboratory experiment, Wayne and Kacmar (1991) examined the effects of IM on two aspects of the performance management process: supervisor rating and verbal communication. The authors found a positive effect of IM on performance ratings. Impression management acts as a double-edged sword, providing a positive advantage to individuals while also leading to negative consequences. For example, while IM can lead to recognition and promotion, it can also drain personal resources and lead to negative outcomes (Bolino et al., 2016; Klotz et al., 2017; Zhao & Liden, 2011). Ni et al. (2023) found that two dimensions of IM, self-promotion and ingratiation, led to resource depletion that leads to counter-productive work behavior. However, the relationship between IM and resource depletion was moderated by emotional intelligence, such that the depleting effect is reduced at high levels of emotional intelligence. Thus, emotional intelligence helps people to use IM better, be able to control the depletion of personal resources, and avoid counter-productive behaviors. The authors highlighted that employers and employees should recognize that reliance on IM for positive organizational benefits risks losing valuable personal resources and resorting to counter-productive behaviors. Hence, this is less dangerous for employees with high emotional intelligence. This might happen when emotional intelligence plays a self-regulatory role, preventing an individual from crossing the line of decency. Table 1 captures the various characteristics of IM identified by Ni *et al.* (2023).

Table 1. Impression management and its Characteristics

Theme	Explanation	Key Findings / Relationships	Implications
Definition of Impression Management (IM)	Employees' strategic behaviors aimed at shaping others' perceptions to appear competent, likeable, or valuable to their superiors.	IM includes self-promotion (showcasing achievements) and ingratiation (using flattery and friendliness).	IM helps employees gain recognition, promotions, and positive appraisals.
Forms of IM Studied	- Manager-Targeted Self-Promotion (MTS): Highlighting personal competence before supervisors. - Manager-Targeted Ingratiation (MTI): Using flattery or agreement to gain favor.	Both MTS and MTI require emotional regulation and suppression of genuine feelings, thus consuming psychological energy.	Common but risky tactics that can yield both positive and negative effects.
Theoretical Basis	Self-Control Resource Theory: Self-regulation relies on limited internal resources depleted by continuous use.	IM acts as emotional labor that draws from self-control reserves.	When depleted, employees experience ego depletion, which weakens their ability to self-regulate.
IM as a Stressor / Resource Consumer	Employees must control their emotions to appear composed, humble, or agreeable.	Both MTS and MTI significantly deplete self-control resources.	Persistent IM can lead to emotional exhaustion and a loss of authenticity.
Negative Behavioral Outcomes	Counter-productive Work Behavior (CWB): Actions that violate organizational norms and harm others or the company.	Self-control depletion mediates the relationship between IM and CWB. Employees with self-control are more likely to lie, gossip, or waste time.	IM may indirectly lead to unethical or harmful behaviors despite positive intentions.
The "Double-Edged Sword" Effect	IM benefits reputation but harms self-regulation and ethics.	- Positive edge: Career advancement and favorable appraisals. - Negative edge: Fatigue and increased counter-productive work behaviors.	IM's value depends on the balance and sustainability of self-control resources.
Moderating Role of Emotional Intelligence (EI)	EI is the ability to understand and regulate one's own and others' emotions.	High EI reduces resource depletion and weakens the IM–CWB link. Low EI employees suffer more strain and behavioral lapses.	Developing emotional intelligence can buffer the costs of IM.
Cultural and Managerial Insight	A study conducted in China's banking sector, where hierarchy and impression management are salient.	Supervisors can misinterpret excessive self-promotion or insincere ingratiation as arrogance.	

Adapted from Ni *et al.* (2023)

Practitioners and researchers have devoted much time to understanding impression management in organizational settings (Bolino *et al.*, 2016). While extensive research has explored image and impression management within organizational contexts and social psychology, much of the literature has focused on its role in career advancement, leadership perception, and workplace interactions, often neglecting its broader impact on individuals' holistic well-being and digital behaviours. This chapter aims to research how image and impression management affect individuals' behaviours, appearance, communication, digital presence, and emotional balance. It will also explore the strategies individuals must consider in managing their image and impression. These are addressed through an extensive literature review to capture as many of the existing results as possible. Addressing these gaps is essential to address some inconsistencies about IM that are observed in the existing literature. Figure 1 below indicates the flow of the book chapter. A discussion on the dimensions of IM follows the introduction. The discussion identified the known dimensions of IM and how their outcomes can be established. Thereafter, the book chapter discussed how IM relates to various aspects of individual behaviours and IM in a virtual system. The conclusion summarises the various discussions and recommendations for future research on IM.

Figure 1. Book Chapter Outline

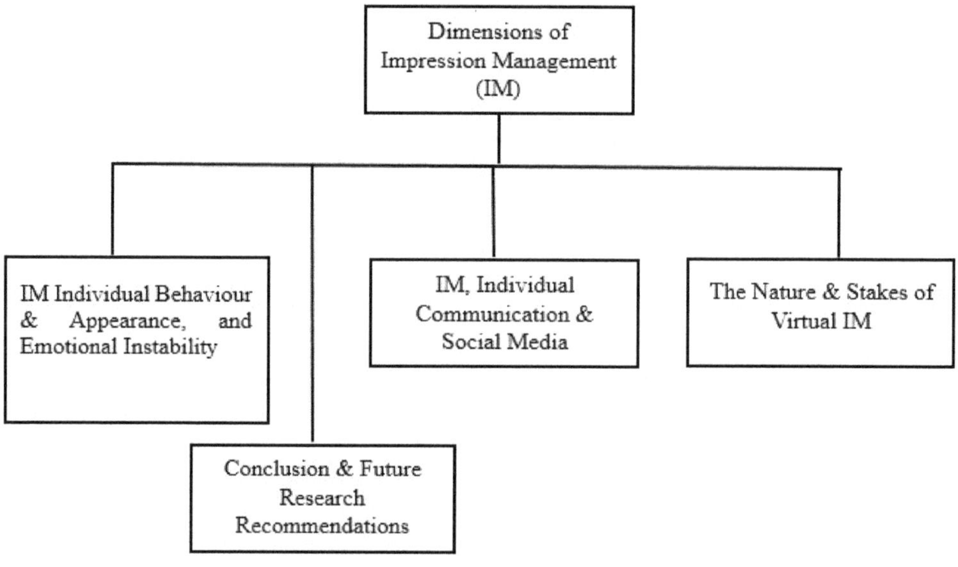

DIMENSIONS OF IMPRESSION MANAGEMENT

The most widely recommended dimensions of impression management are the strategic tactics Jones and Pittman (1982) recommended. These are ingratiation, self-promotion, exemplification, intimidation, and supplication. Many authors have empirically validated the five dimensions advocated by these authors (see Edeh *et al.*, 2023; Gadgil *et al.*, 2021; Lee, Park, & Kim, 2022). Table 2 below presents the strategic tactics, expected outcomes, and explanations.

Table 2. Dimensions of Impression Management (Adapted from Jones and Pittman, 1982).

Dimension	Goal of the Impression	Explanation
1. Ingratiation	To be seen as Likeable or Attractive	Behaving in ways that make you appealing to others, often the target of the impression. Tactics include using flattery, complimenting, agreeing with the target's opinions (opinion conformity), or doing small favors.
2. Self-Promotion	To be seen as Competent or Expert	Highlighting one's strengths, skills, abilities, and past achievements. Tactics involve describing one's accomplishments (acclaiming), taking credit for positive outcomes, and conveying a positive image of competence.
3. Exemplification	To be seen as Morally Worthy or Dedicated	Displaying behaviors that demonstrate high moral character, devotion, or dedication, often by going above and beyond. Tactics include working hard, staying late, acting as a "moral model," or making personal sacrifices to show commitment.
4. Intimidation	To be seen as Dangerous or Powerful	Attempting to control others' behavior by arousing fear or projecting an image of power and potential for harm. Tactics involve threats, aggressive behavior, or showing displeasure to establish dominance and get others to comply.
5. Supplication	To be seen as Needy or Dependent	Advertising one's weakness, limitations, or neediness to solicit help, sympathy, or leniency from others. This conveys the impression that one is incapable and, therefore, exempt from responsibility or deserving of assistance.

Many studies attempted to establish the effectiveness of these dimensions in creating a desired image (see Zhou & Xu, 2022). The results have demonstrated that the effectiveness of the dimensions is contextual, depending on the company, the cultural background of the people, and the condition of use. For example, Zhou and Xu (2022) discovered that the most commonly used dimensions are self-promotion, exemplification, and supplication. The authors categorized the dimensions as either apology or explanation. Based on this, authors such as Morrow and Yamanouchi (2020) have discovered differences in the use of these categories in English and

Japanese computer communication. Such differences have also been discovered by Lutzky (2021), Page (2014), and Xu and Yan (2020).

Apart from the categorization by Zhou and Xu (2022), there are other ways to categorize the dimensions suggested by multiple authors. For example, Leary and Kowalski (1990) considered the focus of the dimensions and suggested the assertive and defensive categories. The assertive strategies represent individuals' attempts to construct a new, positive image and include the dimensions of Ingratiation, Self-Promotion, Exemplification, and Intimidation. The defensive strategies attempt to protect or repair an already threatened or damaged image. They include ingratiation and supplication dimensions. The authors also suggested another categorization based on why people engage in impression management. Based on this, the authors identified instrumental and expressive motives. The former motive is the desire to influence others to gain specific, tangible rewards or avoid punishment. An example is when someone uses self-promotion to gain favour in an interview. The latter is the desire to define and maintain one's own identity or self-concept and have others validate that identity. For example, people can use the exemplification strategy when they genuinely want to be seen as dedicated and align the public image with the ideal self. The authors claim that the two-component model "provides coherence to the literature in the area, addresses controversial issues, and supplies a framework for future research regarding impression management" (p.1). The work of these authors is more of organizing literature on impression management and suggesting the way forward. There was no empirical study to validate their work. Despite this, considering their categorization in future research is a welcome idea worth trying.

To take advantage of the categorization process, IM study can gain a lot from the mature literature on influence tactics. Kipnis, Schmidt, and Wilkinson (1980) employed two studies and identified eight influence tactics, categorized as strong, weak, and rational. In a follow-up study by Yukl and Falbe (1990), the authors re-classified the influence tactics into hard, medium, and soft tactics. They went further to show that each category has different effects on the targets of the influence, and also performed differently depending on the direction of influence. Table 3 below shows the effects of each category based on outcome, direction, condition of use, and social acceptability.

Table 3. Outcomes of different categories of influence tactics (Adapted from Yukl & Falbe, 1990).

	Soft Tactics	Medium Tactics	Hard Tactics
Outcome	Mostly commitment	Commitment & compliance	Mostly resistance
Direction	Up, down, lateral	Laterally, down	Down
Condition of Use	When attitude change is required	Good relationship with the target	When resistance is expected
Social Acceptability	Socially acceptable	Depends on handling	Socially unacceptable

Studies in IM can borrow from the field of influence tactics by examining the performance of each strategy and categorizing it based on outcome, direction, condition of use, and acceptability. This book chapter posits that adopting this process may resolve some conflicting results in using different IM dimensions. Furthermore, it will help resolve whether IM is a multidimensional construct containing five dimensions or a third-order construct with the categorizations as second-order factors and the dimensions as first-order factors.

IMPRESSION MANAGEMENT, INDIVIDUAL BEHAVIOUR & APPEARANCE, AND EMOTIONAL INSTABILITY

Impression management involves conscious and unconscious efforts by individuals to shape how others perceive them, as well as the image created by such perception (Goffman, 1959). This section considers IM from the angle of employees and leaders to gain a comprehensive view of the effects of IM on behaviour. Behaviour is considered holistically to include performance and other forms of behaviours. For example, behaviour includes attitudes, actions, and other forms of self-expression. In modern society, people actively adjust their appearance, communication, and online presence to align with social and professional expectations (Rosenfeld et al., 2002). These adjustments are evident in dressing, body language, and speech patterns (Edeh et al., 2023). Such behaviours are driven by underlying motives to achieve acceptance and specific goals during social interactions, whether online or face-to-face (Coon et al., 2019). However, individuals ultimately cannot control how others interpret or feel about their behaviours. O'Boyle (2022) asserts that individuals in their environment are actors and performers who try to manage two types of self. These are the "front stage" and the "backstage" self. The former is the self that people want to project, which may not be authentic. However, the latter is the authentic self, which may not be what we want others to see of us. How people manage the impression of portraying the frontstage self has some behavioural consequences. When someone receives positive feedback in IM, their self-concept and self-esteem are enhanced; however, when negative feedback is received, it can negatively affect self-esteem. Whether positive or negative feedback is obtained, the whole process of IM leads to social anxiety, stress, and cognitive dissonance. Impression management may hurt life satisfaction (Wang et al., 2020).

The study by Wayne and Liden (1995) examined how subordinates' impression management behaviour influenced performance ratings, with supervisors' liking and perceived similarity mediating the relationship. Unlike previous studies, this study employed a longitudinal method to examine the development of the relationship over time. The focus of the study was the assertive IM strategies, which were categorized into supervisor-focused and self-focused IM strategies. Defensive strategies were not employed, as the focus of the study was on good performance rather than poor performance. This is a reminder that not all IM strategies are applicable in every situation. Hence, the IM strategies utilized were Ingratiation, Self-Promotion, Exemplification, and Intimidation. The theoretical basis for the hypothesized relationships was the cognitive information process, where supervisors translate their perception of subordinates' IM into an initial impression that is encoded in the way the performance rating is handled. The demographic similarity between the supervisor and the subordinate was hypothesized to contribute to the supervisor's liking and perception of similarity.

The results obtained showed that the following relationships were supported:

- Supervisor-focused impression management had a significant and positive effect on both supervisor liking and perceived similarity.
- Self-focused impression management was found to have a negative and significant effect on the supervisor's perceptions of similarity, but not on the supervisor's liking of the individual.
- Demographic similarity had a positive effect on both supervisor liking and perceived similarity.
- Supervisors' liking was not a predictor of performance rating, while perception of similarity was.
- The indirect effect of supervisor-focused IM on performance rating through perception of similarity was supported.
- Demographic similarities indirectly affect performance ratings through the perception of similarity.

The authors made valuable contributions to the understanding of the structure of IM and relationships involving the various strategies. The first is that supervisor-focused IM and demographic similarity between the supervisor and subordinate are critical in determining employees' performance ratings. At the same time, employee-focused IM was not a good predictor of performance rating and the mediator variables. The second is that the comprehensive confirmatory factor analysis challenges the existing factor structure of IM and calls for further studies to establish a factor structure that accurately captures the dynamics of the IM construct. The third is that the longitudinal survey revealed that the relationships involving IM strategies and other employee and organizational outcomes persist over time and may not be fleeting. This conclusion has been challenged by Bolino and Daniels (2014), who discovered that IM is momentary and decreases with interaction time. Another differential use of the IM strategies was established in the study by Drory and Zaidman (2007). The authors found that in a mechanistic organizational structure, employees engage in IM behaviors directed more towards supervisors and mostly involve ingratiation. In an organic structure, employees use less IM, which is directed equally to supervisors and peers, and mostly employ initiation strategies. The difference lies in that a mechanistic structure establishes authority rigidly, whereas an organic structure allows for fluid and flexible authority.

Reimann et al. (2022) examined the potential double-edged nature of IM. The research, conducted across seven experiments, challenges the traditional assumption that competence automatically breeds trust. It demonstrates that when competence is combined with impression management, it can actively reduce the trust received. The authors utilized the self-promotion and intimidation components of IM. The experiments consistently show that these tactics can substantially backfire for high-ability actors. When a high-ability actor engages in self-promotion, the increase in trust typically associated with their competence is significantly attenuated or muted. Conversely, the negative impact of self-promotion on trust is less pronounced for actors with low ability. The negative effect of impression management is explained by Attribution Theory, which suggests that competent actors are held to higher social and behavioral standards (a "liability of competence"). Self-promotion and intimidation are often viewed as deviations from the norms of modesty. For a competent actor, this deviation is seen as a violation of expectations that erodes trust. This mechanism works through the reduction of two key components of a trustee's perceived character:

- Benevolence: The perception that the trustee has the trustor's best interests at heart. Self-promotion leads to a "benevolence penalty," causing the actor to be viewed as less caring or warm.
- Integrity: The perception that the trustee is committed to an acceptable set of principles. Self-promoters are often viewed as manipulative, unsociable, or driven by ulterior motives, which can result in a low perception of their integrity.

In short, when high ability is combined with self-promotion, it decreases the trustee's perceived benevolence and integrity, reducing their trust. Since the authors used only the self-focused components of IM, can the results be generalized to supervisor-focused IM? This is an empirical question yet to be addressed by researchers.

So far, the discussion has been on the employees' behaviour due to the manager's action arising from the employees' IM. Edeh *et al.* (2023) considered how leaders' IM affects the behaviour enacted by employees, such as extra-role or discretionary behaviours. The basis of these relationships is the social influence theory (Kelman, 1958), which states that managers, as actors, set target behaviors expected from employees and use their attitudes, actions, and beliefs to influence employees to enact these target behaviors. Thus, in a social interaction, one party tries to influence the other using IM strategies. The study concluded that impression management is a crucial modern managerial skill that positively influences employees' ability to achieve organizational objectives. The authors found positive relationships between leaders' self-promotion, ingratiation, and exemplification IM strategies on employees' positive effects on coworkers, customers, and enterprise compliance. The study concluded that traditional managerial skills are no longer sufficient in contemporary service-oriented organizations due to the dynamic nature of the workplace. Impression management, therefore, is recommended as a modern leadership skill that managers and organizational leaders should adopt to boost performance and influence their subordinates toward organizational objectives. The strategies used are other-focused, and it will be interesting to examine how leaders use self-focused strategies. Can leaders use self-focused IM to elicit positive employee behaviours, or would they send a conflicting signal that elicits counter-productive behaviour? This is an empirical question requiring an empirical solution.

Another behaviour that is popularly studied in connection with impression management is attitude (Cetin, 2020). The author defined attitude as a person's "response to environmental stimuli that occurs in the mental world of the individual and turns into behaviour" (p. 82). It is an individual's general assessment about a person, subject, or object. Attitudes are crucial because they direct behaviors and are considered an important test of behaviour. The author describes two dimensions of attitude: positive and negative. The former refers to an attitude towards the environment, objects, and people that is positive, while the latter refers to a negative attitude. The study found that individuals with a positive approach utilize self-promotion by highlighting their qualities to create a positive image. Those who have a negative approach utilize intimidation to communicate with their environment fearfully or uncannily, to remain a social group member. Another interesting discovery is that people with a positive approach are not interested in intimidation. In contrast, those with a negative approach are not interested in self-promotion. This means that how people see their environment is a significant determinant of the type of IM they adopt to create the preferred image.

Image and impression management shape how individuals present themselves in social gatherings through clothing, grooming, and body language, aiming to align with desired social identities and gain acceptance (Edeh et al., 2023). Appearance often serves as the first point of judgment before verbal communication, making it a key non-verbal tool for impression management (Wang et al., 2023). In both professional and youth contexts, managing one's appearance becomes crucial for social mobility and perceived competence (Kim & Lee, 2011). Additionally, digital platforms have intensified pressures around appearance, leading individuals to engage in practices like makeup use and outfit rehearsals to align with curated online images. However, these behaviours may challenge authenticity and affect well-being (Zhang et al., 2023).

Image and impression management have a significant impact on individuals' emotional balance during face-to-face and online interactions. This occurs when the individual engages in deep acting, where the expressed emotion aligns with their heart. However, when the individual engages in surface acting, this could create emotional labour, which is detrimental to the individual's expressed behaviours (Deng *et al.*, 2020; Ni *et al.*, 2023). Thus, IM may or may not be beneficial to emotional balance, depending on the availability of self-control variables that help the individual resolve the inconsistency. During a period when individuals engage in surface acting, they utilizez self-control variables to manage the inconsistency. However, when such support is depleted, IM will become ineffective. Hence, the relationship between IM and emotional balance falls within the double-edged nature of IM.

In conclusion, the driver of how IM affects emotional balance lies in the authenticity of the presentation, as faking drains resources, while authentic alignment of behavior and beliefs promotes success. Positive feedback on curated self-presentations can boost self-esteem and perceived social support, enhancing well-being (Kim & Lee, 2011; Valkenburg et al., 2017). However, the constant effort to maintain an idealized image often creates emotional labour, stress, and anxiety, especially when individuals fear negative evaluation (Fox & Rooney, 2015; Dhir et al., 2018). Discrepancies between the authentic and presented self can lead to emotional dissonance, impacting psychological well-being (Seidman, 2013). Therefore, managing emotions effectively is essential when engaging in impression management across physical and digital environments.

IMPRESSION MANAGEMENT, INDIVIDUAL COMMUNICATION, AND SOCIAL MEDIA

Communication is central to impression management, shaping how individuals control perceptions through words, tone, and non-verbal cues across physical and digital spaces (Bolino et al., 2016). People often adjust their speech styles to appear polite, confident, or engaging, even if it requires suppressing authentic emotions, to enhance social acceptance. Effective communication is especially crucial in professional settings, where self-presentation missteps can have serious consequences, such as being perceived as less competent or ethical (Sievers et al., 2015; Macauley et al., 2021). Without effective communication, efforts at impression management would fail, as it serves as the primary channel for conveying intended images to others.

Social networking sites have become an integral part of everyday life, enabling individuals to create profiles, share content, and engage with diverse audiences (Tuten, 2023). Platforms like TikTok, Facebook, and Instagram attract high user engagement, allowing people to present themselves in ways that align with their desired image and audience expectations (Patel & Binjola, 2020). Social media facilitates effective communication, content sharing, and personal branding, making it a powerful tool for impression management (Appel *et al*., 2020). By allowing users to highlight desirable attributes while concealing others, social media offers greater control over self-presentation than face-to-face interactions. However, it also creates pressures to maintain a consistent image across platforms (Sun et al., 2021).

THE NATURE AND STAKES OF VIRTUAL IM

COVID-19 has led to an increased frequency of remote work and the number of virtual teams. The use of virtual teams has increased the complexity of IM, as communication is no longer face-to-face. In face-to-face communication, non-verbal communication is used to gauge the IM exhibited by the speaker to enhance perception by the receiver. In virtual teams, people would have to rely on other means of communication to perceive the speaker's IM. Even though much can be gained by understanding IM in virtual communication, research in this area has not kept pace with the development of virtual teams. For example, Blunden and Brodsky (2024) stated that "scholarly work has not yet sought to provide a comprehensive understanding of how people seek to—and succeed in—managing impressions via these virtual means" (p. 2198). The authors attributed this gap to the fact that research in IM in virtual teams is complex and demands a multifunctional approach that must include "management, psychology, communication, and information sciences" (p. 2198). The authors defined virtual interaction as communication through an electronic medium devoid of personal interaction. The unique features of virtual interactions make impression management behaviors more consequential, and evidence suggests that creating a positive impression (such as trust or liking) is generally more difficult virtually than in person. Key characteristics that raise the stakes of virtual IM include:

- Editability: Virtual interactions are relatively *rehearseable* or *editable* (e.g., carefully crafted emails or asynchronous video re-recording), which gives people more opportunity to manage their impressions.
- Permanence: Virtual interactions are more *permanent*, often leaving digital records that are easily searchable, retained, revisited, and shared (e.g., CC/BCC/forwarding), which raises the stakes for actors.
- Cue Constraints: Virtual interactions *shape the variety of cues* available (e.g., limiting actors to text or altering nonverbal behavior on video), which increases the likelihood of miscommunication and encourages greater effort/stress to manage impressions.

The work of Blunden and Brodsky (2024) provides a framework for understanding how individuals manage impressions in virtual work contexts. Virtual interactions, which are more editable, permanent, and often cue-constrained, make managing impressions more challenging and consequential. The review organizes virtual impression management (IM) into three categories of behavior that influence a target's perceptions of competence and warmth/affect:

- Verbal Behavior: The words used, such as self-disclosure (often increasing trust) and language mimicry (often boosting likability).
- Nonverbal Behavior: Cues beyond words, including emoticons (boosting warmth but potentially undercutting competence), text formatting, and video cues like eye contact.
- Meta Behavior: Strategies enabled by virtual affordances, such as chronemics (the time taken to reply) and messaging protocol (e.g., the use of CC/BCC).

The study concludes that these IM behaviors are crucial for shaping colleagues' impressions of intelligence, performance, trust, and authenticity in a remote work environment. These impressions of the actor across two dimensions:

- Competence-Related Impressions: Perceptions of a target's capability, such as intelligence, effort, performance, leadership ability, and competence-based trust.

- Affective-Related Impressions: Perceptions of warmth and communality, such as authenticity, warmth, likeability, intimacy, honesty, and affect-based trust.

The authors looked at two sets of theories that can be used to analyze virtual IM. The first set is fixed because the person cannot alter communication to mimic the in-person level. In contrast, the second set is not fixed, as the actor can approach in-person communication by gaining knowledge of the medium's use. The two sets of theories examined virtual communication from the perspective of the communicator, rather than the receiver. This is a significant flaw. The book chapter suggests that gaining experience in using a communication medium can enhance how the communicator conveys the message. What remains is to examine how the receiver infers meaning that affects behavior and interaction. A significant contribution from the authors is that context-based and person-based factors mediate the relationships between the virtual IM behaviours and the target impression of the actor. These factors suggest that the target's knowledge of the actor and the actor's knowledge of the communication mode influence the interpretation of IM behaviors in virtual interactions.

In virtual teams, technology made individuals' digital presence a critical aspect of impression management, often serving as employers' and collaborators' first point of contact (Van Dijck, 2013). Digital platforms enable individuals to carefully curate their online identities through images, videos, and text, allowing them to strategically shape perceptions (Ganda, 2014). Unlike spontaneous face-to-face interactions, online environments offer time and control, allowing individuals to present themselves as professional and approachable while aligning with personal and professional branding goals (Chou & Edge, 2012). As technology advances, managing one's digital presence will remain crucial for achieving both personal and professional success.

CONCLUSION

Image and impression management influence how individuals behave, appear, communicate, and present themselves, both face-to-face and online, to gain social acceptance and advance professionally. People adjust their behaviours, appearance, and communication to influence how others perceive them, while digital platforms allow for curated self-presentation and personal branding. These practices help individuals align with social and professional expectations while managing visibility in both physical and digital environments. Many studies have attempted to understand the concept of IM and its impact on key individual and organizationalz outcomes.

However, four areas that require attention are the effectiveness of IM tactics over time, the establishment of the dimensionality of the idea of IM, how impression management can be made effective in virtual interactions, and how to understand the double-edged nature of IM.

The study by Bolino and Daniels (2014) employed the dyadic theory of role emergence, establishing that IM tactics are most impactful early in the relationship (the role-taking stage) and then lose their influence as the relationship matures and impressions stabilize. Key findings from their study include the following:

- Ingratiation (e.g., flattery, favour-doing): This tactic, used to appear likeable, is expected to be positively related to supervisor ratings of likability and performance initially. However, its positive effect is hypothesized to diminish over time. Overuse might even lead to negative perceptions.
- Defensive Tactics (Apologies and Justifications): Used for damage control, these tactics are also expected to be positively related to likability and performance ratings in the early stages. Like ingratiation, this positive effect is hypothesized to weaken or become non-significant later in the relationship, as overuse can lead to long-term damage.
- Self-Promotion (e.g., highlighting accomplishments): This tactic, used to appear competent, is generally known to have a negative relationship with likability and job performance in established relationships. The study hypothesized that this negative impact would be most substantial initially and then weaken over time as performance claims are tested against actual data.

Thus, the study demonstrates that IM is crucial for new employees to establish initial positive impressions of likability and performance. However, its efficacy drops dramatically once the supervisor-subordinate relationship becomes routinized and is based more on actual performance and track record. However, a longitudinal study showed that supervisor-focused impression management has long-term effects, while self-focused IM did not.

Past studies have not resolved the issue of the dimensionality of IM. IM has been explained as a multidimensional construct and as a second-order construct, with various categorizations serving as first-order factors. The categories of IM are supervisor-focused or self-focused. The post-COVID-19 work structure has given rise to the emergence of virtual teams. Impression management has been well understood in face-to-face interactions, but its application in virtual settings remains less clear. The intersection of digital technology and IM is yet to be adequately understood. For example, when considering asynchronous and synchronous meetings involving virtual teams, the role of IM is not yet fully understood. Some authors state that when individuals increase their knowledge of digital tools, the IM improves; however, others believe there is no difference (Blunden & Brodsky, 2024). The studies need to be reviewed to determine the basis for the differences.

Impression management has always been represented as self-driven behaviour by employees or leaders. A study by de Gelder (2019) examined the possibility that organizational context could trigger employees' use of IM as a survival strategy. The research model hypothesized that IM (self-promotion, ingratiation, and exemplification) would mediate the relationship between organizational factors and stress. The organizational factors utilized included deficit-based climate, strength-based climate, and high-performance attributions. The study did not find IM playing a coping mechanism capable of reducing stress. The research concluded that while assertive IM tactics are commonly used in the workplace, there is no confirmation that employees use IM as a coping strategy triggered by organizational demands, nor can it be confirmed that IM leads to higher workplace stress. The primary practical implication is that organizations should focus on creating a strength-based climate to foster employee well-being, given the significant relationship between this IM strategy and employee well-being. Using the signalling theory, organizations use policies and procedures to signal their expectations to employees. When employees understand this signal, they place high emphasis on the organizational factor, and there is a tendency to use IM to obtain a high rating. Hence, IM can mediate the relationship between the factor and an organizational outcome. Since the organizational factors used were limited and only stress was used as the dependent variable, further studies are required to test the mediating role of IM in organizational factor and individual outcome relationships.

Many authors have established a relationship between IM and individual and organizational outcomes (see Lutzky, 2021; Page, 2014; Xu & Yan, 2020). These studies had inconsistent results, which have been attributed to many reasons. There is always a limit to which individuals can implement IM in an attempt to enhance their image among people. In such a situation, the principle of 'too-much-of-a-good-thing' (TMGT) (Kapoutsis, 2017; Treadway, 2012). TMGT occurs when valuable resources are used beyond their practical limit, such that the individual is negatively affected. IM studies can borrow from virtue ethics, where individuals self-regulate their IM so as not to get to the level of TMGT, where it becomes detrimental to the image they want to create. Amah (2022) recognized that prudence, a virtue, helped individuals self-regulate their use of political behaviour to achieve organizationall outcomes. Research in IM can benefit from including self-regulation variables to ensure that people stay within the limits of TMGT.

FUTURE RESEARCH RECOMMENDATIONS

There is no agreement yet on whether the effects of IM are short-lived or linger for a long time; hence, this issue remains unresolved. Therefore, more studies are required to establish the long-term effects of the IM strategies. Despite the number of years since IM was first introduced into organizational behaviour, its dimensionality remains unresolved. Therefore, a detailed statistical analysis is necessary to determine the optimal structure for IM. If IM is a second-order factor with the dimensions as factors, relationships with outcomes may appear differently than when it is represented as a first-order factor. There is a debate on whether the use of IM will follow the principle of TMGT and will require self-regulation to prevent moving to the negative consequences of the use of IM. The non-inclusion of this principle has been presented as a reason why studies on the relationships involving various dimensions of IM and their outcomes have been inconclusive. Thus, the book chapter recommends that future research on how IM helps people create a positive image should include self-regulatory variables as moderators of the relationship between IM and the perception of people's image. In this way, the inconclusive results obtained by past studies can be resolved.

REFERENCES

Al-Shatti, E., & Ohana, M. (2021). Impression management and career-related outcomes: A systematic literature review. *Frontiers in Psychology*, *12*, 1–12. DOI: 10.3389/fpsyg.2021.701694 PMID: 34393939

Amah, O. E. (2022). The relationship between political will and organizational, political behavior: The moderating roles of political prudence and political skill. *Journal of Business Ethics*, *176*, 341–355. DOI: 10.1007/s10551-020-04696-x

Appel, G., Grewal, L., Hadi, R., & Stephen, A T. (2020). The future of social media in marketing. *Journal of the Academy of Marketing Science*, 48, 79-95.

Blunden, H., & Brodsky, A. (2024). A review of virtual impression management behaviors and outcomes. *Journal of Management*, *50*(6), 2197–2236. DOI: 10.1177/01492063231225160

Bolino, M. C., Long, D., & Turnley, W. (2016). Impression management in organizations: Critical questions, answers, and areas of future research. *Annual Review of Organizational Psychology and Organizational Behavior*, *3*(1), 377–406. DOI: 10.1146/annurev-orgpsych-041015-062337

Cetin, O. I. (2020). Investigation of the relationship between attitude and impression management in university students. *Journal of Management* [JMML]. *Marketing and Logistics*, *7*(2), 81–90.

Chen, Y., Yang, X., Wang, L., & Zhang, X. (2021). Exploring the motivational mechanisms underlying social media use: A Self-Determination Theory approach. *Frontiers in Psychology*, *12*, 653859.

Chou, H. T. G., & Edge, N. (2012). "They are happier and having better lives than I am": The impact of using Facebook on perceptions of others' lives. *Cyberpsychology, Behavior, and Social Networking*, *15*(2), 117–12. DOI: 10.1089/cyber.2011.0324 PMID: 22165917

Coon, D., Mitterer, J. O., & Martini, T. S. (2019). *Introduction to Psychology: Gateways to Mind and Behavior* (15th ed.). Cengage Learning.

de Gelder, A. (2019). Impression management: Coping with organizational demands: A study investigating the effects of organizational climate and HR attributions on impression management behaviours and stress. http://arno.uvt.nl/show.cgi?fid=150343

Deng, H., Walter, F., & Guan, Y. (2020). Supervisor-directed emotional labor as upward influence: An emotions-as-social-information perspective. *Journal of Organizational Behavior, 41*(4), 384–402. DOI: 10.1002/job.2424

Dhir, A., Yossatorn, Y., Kaur, P., & Chen, S. (2018). Online social media fatigue and psychological well-being—A study of compulsive use, fear of missing out, fatigue, anxiety, and depression. *International Journal of Information Management, 40*, 141–152. DOI: 10.1016/j.ijinfomgt.2018.01.012

Drory, A., & Zaidman, N. (2007). Impression management behaviour: Effects of the organizational system. *Journal of Managerial Psychology, 22*(3), 290–308. DOI: 10.1108/02683940710733106

Edeh, F. O., Zayed, N. M., Darwish, S., Nitsenko, V., Hanechko, I., & Islam, K. M. A. (2023). Impression management and employee contextual performance in service organizations (enterprises). *Emerging Science Journal, 7*(2), 366–384. Advance online publication. DOI: 10.28991/ESJ-2023-07-02-05

Fox, J., & Rooney, M. C. (2015). The Dark Triad and trait self-objectification as predictors of men's use and self-presentation behaviors on social networking sites. *Personality and Individual Differences, 76*, 161–165. DOI: 10.1016/j.paid.2014.12.017

Gadgil, G., Prybutok, G., Peak, D., & Prybutok, V. (2021). Modeling the hidden mediating relationships between SNS privacy and SNS impression construction. *Computers in Human Behavior, 125*, 106941. DOI: 10.1016/j.chb.2021.106941

Ganda, M. (2014). Social media and self: Influences on the formation of identity and understanding of self through social networking sites. *University Honors Theses*, Paper 55.

Geeth, S., Chandran, J. C., & Sheethal, D. (2024). Effectiveness of impression management in improving the work experience of casual workers. *Advancing Knowledge from Multidisciplinary Perspectives in Engineering, Technology, and Management*, 70-80. https://www.rubiconpublications.com/

Goffman, E. (1959). *The presentation of self in everyday life*. Anchor.

Kapoutsis, I. (2017). Playing the political game at work: The roles of political will, political prudence and political skill. In Vigoda-Gadot, E., & Drory, A. (Eds.), *Handbook of Organizational Politics: Looking Back and to the Future* (pp. 40–58). Edward Elgar Publishing.

Kelman, H. C. (1958). Compliance, identification, and internalization three processes of attitude change. *The Journal of Conflict Resolution, 2*(1), 51–60. DOI: 10.1177/002200275800200106

Kim, J., & Lee, H. (2011). The effect of impression management on social networking site usage and social capital: Focusing on college students. *Journal of Social Media Studies*, *8*(2), 45–62.

Kipnis, D., Schmidt, S. M., & Wilkinson, I. (1980). Intraorganizational influence tactics: Explorations in getting one's way. *The Journal of Applied Psychology*, *65*(4), 440–452. DOI: 10.1037/0021-9010.65.4.440

Klotz, A. C., Bolino, M. C., Song, H., & Stornelli, J. (2017). Examining the nature, causes, and consequences of profiles of organizational citizenship behavior. *Journal of Organizational Behavior*, *39*(5), 629–647. DOI: 10.1002/job.2259

Leary, M. R., & Kowalski, R. M. (1990). Impression management: A literature review and two-component model. *Psychological Bulletin*, *107*(1), 34–47. DOI: 10.1037/0033-2909.107.1.34

Lee, J., Park, H., & Kim, S. (2022). Impression management and professional communication in workplace meetings. *International Journal of Business Communication*. Advance online publication.

Liu, F., Chow, I. H., & Huang, M. (2019). Increasing Compulsory Citizenship Behavior and Workload: Does Impression Management Matter? *Frontiers in Psychology*, *10*, 1726. Advance online publication. DOI: 10.3389/fpsyg.2019.01726 PMID: 31402890

Lutzky, U. (2021). "You keep saying you are sorry". Exploring the use of sorry in customer communication on Twitter. *Discourse, Context & Media*, *39*, 100463. DOI: 10.1016/j.dcm.2020.100463

Macauley, R., Williams, E., Reardon, R., Kind, T., & Chretien, K. C. (2021). Medical professionalism in the age of social media: A revised review of ophthalmology resident and physician use and recommendations. *Journal of Academic Ophthalmology*, *13*(1), e28–e35.

Meyerhuber, S. (2019). Active listening as a key competence in intercultural communication education- An example from an academic classroom with conceptual and theoretical embedding. *Journal of Linguistic and Intercultural Education*, *12*(2), 92–115.

Morrison, E. W., & Bies, R. J. (1991). Impression management in the feedback-seeking process: A literature review and research agenda. *Academy of Management Review*, *16*(3), 522. Advance online publication. DOI: 10.2307/258916

Morrow, P. R., & Yamanouchi, K. (2020). Online apologies to hotel guests in English and Japanese. *Discourse, Context & Media*, *34*, 100379. DOI: 10.1016/j.dcm.2020.100379

Ni, H., Li, Y., Zeng, Y., & Duan, J. (2023). The double-edged sword effect of employee impression management and counter-productive work behavior: From the perspective of self-control resource theory. *Frontiers in Psychology*, *14*, 1053784. DOI: 10.3389/fpsyg.2023.1053784 PMID: 36818121

O'Boyle, N. (2022). Performers: Goffman's Dramaturgical Perspective. In: *Communication Theory for Humans*. Palgrave Macmillan, Cham. DOI: 10.1007/978-3-031-02450-4_5

Page, R. (2014). Saying 'sorry': Corporate apologies posted on Twitter. *Journal of Pragmatics*, *62*, 30–45. DOI: 10.1016/j.pragma.2013.12.003

Patel, K., & Binjola, H. (2020). TikTok, the new alternative media for youngsters for online sharing of talent: an analytical study. Available online at. (https://papers.ssrn.com/sol3/papers.cfm?abstract_id=3600119)

Reimann, M., Huller, C., Schike, O., & Cook, K. S. (2022). Impression management attenuates the effect of ability on trust in economic exchange. *Social Science*, *119*(30), 1–9. DOI: 10.1073/pnas.2118548119 PMID: 35867823

Rosenfeld, P., Edwards, J. E., & Thomas, M. D. (2015). *Impression management*. Wiley Encyclopedia of Management.

Rosenfeld, P., Giacalone, R. A., & Riordan, C. A. (2002). Impression management: Building and enhancing reputations at work. In Giacalone, R. A., & Rosenfeld, P. (Eds.), *Impression management in the organization* (pp. 3–20). Lawrence Erlbaum Associates.

Seidman, G. (2013). Self-presentation and belonging on Facebook: How personality influences social media use and motivations. *Personality and Individual Differences*, *54*(3), 402–407. DOI: 10.1016/j.paid.2012.10.009

Sievers, S., Wodzicki, K., Aberle, I., Keckeisen, M., & Cress, U. (2015). Social cues in online communication and their effect on credibility perceptions. *Journal of Computer-Mediated Communication*, *20*(4), 434–451.

Sukmayadi, V., Darmawangsa, D., Ayub, S. H., & Fadhila, S. A. (2024). Constructing Fame: A phenomenological study of online impression management among Indonesian TikTok Celebrities. The Qualitative Report, 29(6), 1727-1741.DOI: 10.46743/2160-3715/2024.5992

Sun, Y., Fang, S., & Zhang, J. (2021). Impression management strategies on enterprise social media platforms: An affordance perspective. *International Journal of Information Management*, 60(3). ISSN 0268-4012. DOI: 10.1016/j.ijinfomgt.2021.102359

Tairi, K. (2018). Ko Wai Au (Who Am I)? Authentic Leadership and Mindfulness in Higher Education. In Lemon, N., & McDonough, S. (Eds.), *Mindfulness in the Academy*. Springer., DOI: 10.1007/978-981-13-2143-6_10

Tohme, O., & Joseph, S. (2020). Authenticity Is Correlated With Mindfulness and Emotional Intelligence. *Journal of Humanistic Psychology*, *65*(1), 139–156. DOI: 10.1177/0022167820940926

Treadway, D. C. (2012). Political will in organizations. In Ferris, G. R., & Treadway, D. C. (Eds.), *Politics in Organizations: Theory and Research Considerations* (pp. 529–554).

Tuten, T. L. (2023). *Social media marketing*. Sage Publications.

Valkenburg, P. M., Koutamanis, M., & Vossen, H. G. M. (2017). The concurrent and longitudinal relationships between adolescents' use of social network sites and their social self-esteem. *Computers in Human Behavior*, *76*, 35–41. DOI: 10.1016/j.chb.2017.07.008 PMID: 29104364

Van Dijck, J. (2013). *The Culture of Connectivity: A Critical History of Social Media*. Oxford University Press. DOI: 10.1093/acprof:oso/9780199970773.001.0001

Wang, D., Song, S., Chan, F. F. Y., & Feng, L. (2023). The impact of impression construction consumption on social identity: A study on Chinese female professionals. *Journal of Social Marketing*, *13*(2), 194–217. DOI: 10.1108/JSOCM-03-2022-0066

Wang, W., Zhou, K., Yu, Z., & Li, J. (2020). The cost of impression management to life satisfaction: Sense of control and loneliness as mediators. *Psychology Research and Behavior Management*, *13*, 407–417. DOI: 10.2147/PRBM.S238344 PMID: 32440240

Wayne, S. J., & Kacmar, K. M. (1991). The effects of impression management on the performance appraisal process. *Organizational Behavior and Human Decision Processes*, *48*(1), 70–88. DOI: 10.1016/0749-5978(91)90006-F

Wayne, S. J., & Liden, R. C. (1995). Effects of impression management on performance ratings: A longitudinal study. *Academy of Management Journal*, *38*(1), 232–260. DOI: 10.2307/256734

Xu, Z., & Yan, A. (2020). A Pragmatic Study of Image Restoration via Corporate Apology in Chinese Internet Corporations. *English Language Teaching*, *13*(6), 76. DOI: 10.5539/elt.v13n6p76

Yukl, G., & Falbe, C. M. (1990). Influence tactics and objectives in upward, downward, and lateral influence attempts. *The Journal of Applied Psychology*, *75*(2), 132–140. DOI: 10.1037/0021-9010.75.2.132

Zhang, L., Li, X., & Wang, Y. (2023). The paradox of online impression management: Effects on offline appearance anxiety and self-perception. *Journal of Consumer Psychology*. Advance online publication.

Zhao, H., & Liden, R. C. (2011). Internship: A recruitment and selection perspective. *The Journal of Applied Psychology*, *96*(1), 221–229. DOI: 10.1037/a0021295 PMID: 20954757

Zhou, K., & Xu, Z. (2022). A pragmatic study of corporate apologies for impression management: A case of the Chinese food industry. *International Journal of Linguistics*, *14*(6), 196–216. DOI: 10.5296/ijl.v14i6.20465

Chapter 8

Generative AI and the Future of Digital Impression Management: A Multidimensional Analysis

Karim Ben Yahia
https://orcid.org/0000-0001-5873-7812
College of Business Administration, University of Bahrain, Bahrain & LARIME, Tunisia

ABSTRACT

This chapter explores how generative AI (GenAI) technologies are transforming the landscape of digital impression management by reconfiguring how individuals construct, perform, and optimize their online identities. Using an interdisciplinary framework grounded in Goffman's dramaturgical theory, affordance theory, social identity theory, and emotional labor theory, the chapter introduces the ABCDE model, Appearance, Behavior, Communication, Digital Presence, and Emotional Balance, to analyze the socio-technical dimensions of AI-mediated self-presentation. Drawing on an empirical audit of 1,200 GenAI-generated professional profiles, the study reveals how algorithmic systems both enable and constrain identity expression, often reinforcing cultural, gendered, and occupational biases. The findings underscore the dual role of GenAI as both a democratizing tool and a vector of standardization, raising urgent ethical, psychological, and design challenges for equitable digital selfhood.

DOI: 10.4018/979-8-3373-5519-1.ch008

1. INTRODUCTION

In the postdigital era, the act of managing impressions, how individuals curate, construct, and communicate their identity to others, has become increasingly mediated by intelligent technologies (Wei et al. 2025). Once understood as a social performance unfolding primarily through face-to-face interaction (Goffman, 1959), impression management today occurs across platforms, timelines, and algorithms. The integration of generative artificial intelligence (GenAI), such as ChatGPT, Midjourney, Sora, and other multimodal tools, has transformed identity work into a hybrid process co-produced by human intention and machine learning (Brüns & Meißner, 2024). GenAI is not merely an accessory to self-presentation; it is a constitutive agent that shapes what forms of digital identity are possible, desirable, and visible.

This chapter explores how GenAI reconfigures digital impression management by expanding, constraining, and redistributing the labor of self-presentation. Drawing on foundational theories, including Goffman's dramaturgical model, affordance theory, social identity theory, and emotional labor theory, we argue that GenAI technologies transform impression management from a contextual social behavior into a continuous, data-driven, and algorithmically optimized performance. To structure this inquiry, we propose a five-dimensional analytical framework, Appearance, Behavior, Communication, Digital Presence, and Emotional Balance (ABCDE), to examine how GenAI affects different aspects of identity construction in online environments.

In addition to its theoretical contribution, this chapter draws on an original empirical audit of 1,200 AI-generated professional profiles to assess how GenAI tools reproduce or challenge cultural, gendered, and occupational biases in self-representation. This audit allows us to empirically test how algorithmically generated identities align with, or diverge from, dominant sociotechnical norms. The findings reveal measurable patterns of aesthetic bias, tone modulation, and visibility advantages tied to race, gender, and professional identity categories (Foka, 2024). These insights ground the theoretical arguments in concrete evidence and help illuminate the socio-technical logics embedded in synthetic identity production.

Our core claim is that GenAI reshapes not only how individuals manage impressions, but also who has access to legible, credible, and influential digital identities. While GenAI can democratize content creation and offer expressive tools to marginalized users, it can also entrench hegemonic norms, distort cultural signals, and displace authorship. Impression management in the age of GenAI is no longer about the performance of a stable self, it is about navigating an ever-evolving set of algorithmic constraints and expectations.

The chapter proceeds as follows: Section 2 outlines the four theoretical lenses that ground our analysis. Sections 3 through 7 apply the ABCDE framework to explore how GenAI transforms digital identity performance across visual, behavioral, linguistic, spatial, and emotional domains. Section 8 addresses cultural and gender dynamics, integrating the results of the profile audit. Section 9 engages with the ethical and societal implications of AI-mediated identity work, while Section 10 offers design and policy recommendations. Finally, Section 11 synthesizes the findings and reflects on the future of impression management in an AI-saturated world.

By combining conceptual depth with empirical insight, this chapter aims to contribute to a critical, interdisciplinary understanding of how GenAI is reshaping the practice, politics, and ethics of digital selfhood.

2. THEORETICAL FRAMEWORKS AND CONCEPTUAL GROUNDING

The conceptual framework presented in this chapter is anchored in four intersecting theoretical traditions: Goffman's dramaturgical theory, affordance theory, social identity theory, and emotional labor theory. Each of these frameworks contributes a vital perspective to understanding how GenAI reconfigures impression management practices in the digital age. While Goffman provides a foundation for thinking about identity as performance, affordance theory illuminates how technology mediates and constrains those performances. Social identity theory highlights the group dynamics and norm-driven aspects of digital self-presentation, and emotional labor theory foregrounds the affective costs of managing impressions in both human and AI-mediated contexts. Taken together, these lenses help us conceptualize GenAI not as a neutral tool but as a powerful agent that intervenes in the performative, technological, social, and emotional dimensions of identity.

2.1. Goffman's Dramaturgical Theory

Erving Goffman's (1959) dramaturgical model posits that everyday life is a series of performances in which individuals manage impressions by carefully curating what is shown to others (the front stage) versus what is hidden (the backstage). In this view, identity is not a fixed essence but an ongoing accomplishment produced through interactional rituals and contextual self-presentation strategies. Goffman's insights have proven especially prescient in the digital age, where online platforms serve as stages for curated performances, and where visibility, coherence, and consistency are vital to personal and professional branding.

The emergence of GenAI complicates and extends Goffman's model in at least three important ways. First, the boundaries between front stage and backstage are blurred, as AI tools often operate in both zones, generating public-facing content while also participating in private preparation processes. For example, a user may employ ChatGPT to draft LinkedIn posts (front stage) while also using it to rehearse interview responses or simulate interpersonal exchanges (backstage). Second, GenAI enables users to outsource substantial portions of their performance to algorithmic systems, raising new questions about authorship and agency. When a personal brand is largely curated by AI, who is performing, and for whom? Finally, the persistence and replicability of digital content challenge the ephemerality of Goffman's model. Unlike face-to-face performances, AI-generated impressions can be stored, shared, and algorithmically resurfaced across contexts, timelines, and audiences, what some have termed "context collapse" (Marwick & Boyd, 2011).

To address these developments, we introduce the concept of backstage algorithms, machine systems that co-construct identity performances from behind the scenes. These algorithms not only support the staging of the self but increasingly shape the scripts, aesthetics, and emotional tone of those performances. In this revised dramaturgical ecology, the human performer, the AI assistant, and the algorithmic audience (e.g., recommendation systems, engagement metrics) are entangled in a loop of co-performance (Markham, 2024). Impression management thus becomes a hybrid activity that straddles human intentionality and machine optimization, with profound implications for how we understand authenticity, identity control, and audience perception in AI-mediated environments.

2.2. Affordance Theory and the Relational Dynamics of GenAI

Affordance theory, originally developed by Gibson (1977) and later refined by Norman (1999) in the context of human-computer interaction, offers a powerful conceptual tool for analyzing the relational dynamics between users and technologies. In this framework, affordances are not intrinsic properties of an object or system, but emergent possibilities for action shaped by the interaction between user capabilities, goals, context, and the features of the technology itself. In the domain of digital impression management, affordances provide a critical vocabulary for understanding how GenAI systems enable, constrain, or redirect the strategies individuals employ to construct and perform identity online.

Generative AI platforms afford a broad range of identity-related actions: from composing coherent and context-specific text, to generating photorealistic avatars and images, to mimicking affective tone and behavioral nuances. These systems enable users to rapidly prototype and disseminate curated self-representations across platforms, LinkedIn, Instagram, TikTok, YouTube, each with distinct social norms and audience expectations. For example, ChatGPT might afford a junior professional the ability to adopt a confident, assertive tone in cover letters, while DALL·E or

MidJourney can afford artists the ability to visualize themselves through culturally resonant aesthetics they may otherwise struggle to access or express.

Yet, these affordances are asymmetrically distributed. Access to GenAI's full potential depends on a user's digital literacy, linguistic fluency, socioeconomic status, and cultural capital. An entrepreneur with media training may exploit GenAI to fine-tune their brand voice, while a user unfamiliar with prompt engineering or platform affordances may be misled or overwhelmed. Moreover, affordances can be deceptive: a tool may appear to offer freedom of expression while subtly guiding users toward standardized, platform-optimized forms of identity. As Bucher and Helmond (2018) argue, affordances are always embedded in political and economic structures that define what is "possible" or "desirable" within a given interface.

The architecture of GenAI systems often reflects the ideological values of their designers, privileging certain forms of professionalism, affect, and aesthetics over others. For instance, predictive models trained predominantly on Western corporate discourse may suggest language that conforms to white-collar, masculine-coded norms of assertiveness, ambition, or efficiency. These embedded scripts produce what we call algorithmic affordance biases, subtly steering users toward dominant identity templates (Vallor, 2024) while making alternative expressions less legible or effective within platform economies.

Additionally, GenAI introduces reflexive affordances, in which the feedback users receive, likes, shares, engagement rates, sentiment scores, influences subsequent self-presentation strategies. Users iteratively adjust their content to better align with algorithmic preferences, resulting in a co-evolution of identity and platform logic. Over time, this process can lead to performative lock-in, where individuals feel pressured to maintain a curated identity that no longer reflects their evolving self-concept but remains successful in terms of visibility and social capital.

Affordance theory thus reveals GenAI not simply as a suite of technical tools but as a socio-technical infrastructure that mediates agency, reinforces norms, and conditions identity expression. Understanding the affordances, and the limitations, of GenAI systems is essential for designing more inclusive digital environments where users are empowered to express complex, dynamic, and culturally situated identities without being reduced to algorithmic templates or marketable archetypes.

2.3. Social Identity Theory

Social Identity Theory (SIT), introduced by Tajfel and Turner (1979), provides a social-psychological framework for understanding how individuals define themselves in relation to their group memberships. According to SIT, individuals are motivated to achieve and maintain a positive self-concept by identifying with social groups that offer favorable comparisons to others. This identification with in-groups influences behavior, attitudes, and self-presentation strategies. In the context of impression management, especially in digitally mediated environments, social identity serves as both a psychological anchor and a performative resource.

Generative AI systems play a complex and sometimes contradictory role in relation to social identity. On the one hand, they afford users the ability to express affiliation with particular communities through linguistic style, visual markers, and thematic framing. AI tools can generate content that reflects the norms, jargon, or aesthetics of specific professional, cultural, or ideological groups, thereby enhancing in-group alignment. For instance, AI can help a user adopt the discourse style of a "tech-savvy entrepreneur," a "social justice advocate," or a "global executive," reinforcing social categorization and perceived credibility.

Recent research illustrates how GenAI reinforces social categorization in professional branding (Langley, 2025). For example, Hossain (2024) demonstrate that LinkedIn users increasingly employ AI-assisted summaries to signal affiliation with in-groups such as "tech entrepreneurs" or "sustainability leaders." Similarly, Popa & Chenic (2025) show that AI-generated consumer content often mirrors lifestyle communities (e.g., eco-conscious consumers, digital nomads), thereby embedding individuals within group-based identity categories that shape audience perceptions.

However, the very mechanisms that enable such alignment may also encourage conformity and discourage authentic expression (Jawad et al., 2024). When GenAI systems are trained predominantly on data reflecting dominant cultural scripts, they tend to reproduce normative expectations about how group members should appear, speak, or behave. As a result, AI-assisted impression management may inadvertently promote stereotype internalization or the suppression of marginalized identity expressions in favor of more platform-legible ones. This becomes particularly evident in professional branding scenarios where GenAI tools suggest bios, taglines, or visual templates that align with neoliberal ideals of productivity, charisma, and success.

However, these benefits come with notable risks. As van Dijck (2024) argue, platform infrastructures privilege identities that are algorithmically legible, often promoting homogeneity over diversity. This means that marginalized users may feel pressure to conform to dominant templates, such as corporate assertiveness or Western professional aesthetics, at the expense of authentic self-expression. In this sense, GenAI-assisted impression management can both strengthen in-group belonging and simultaneously erode pluralism in identity performances.

Another dimension of SIT that gains salience in the GenAI context is the process of social comparison. As users evaluate their digital personas against those of others, often enhanced by AI and algorithmically curated, they may experience pressure to emulate successful identity models, reinforcing status hierarchies within and across groups. This phenomenon can contribute to both aspiration and anxiety: while GenAI may empower users to present themselves more strategically, it may also intensify feelings of inadequacy or impostor syndrome when AI-optimized identities become the benchmark.

The dynamics of SIT are particularly visible among younger users in educational and social contexts. A recent study by Lively & Hutson (2025) shows that students use AI tools to align their online personas with aspirational peer groups, such as "future innovators" or "global citizens." While this facilitates social belonging, it also heightens comparative pressures, often leading to digital anxiety or impostor feelings when students perceive their AI-curated identities as inferior to those of their peers.

Moreover, the platform architectures in which GenAI tools are embedded often amplify these effects. Algorithms that reward homogeneity, engagement, and adherence to dominant discursive styles can distort social identity formation by promoting specific types of identity performance while penalizing others. Consequently, users may feel compelled to continuously recalibrate their self-presentation, not to reflect internal authenticity, but to maintain in-group legitimacy and algorithmic visibility.

Social Identity Theory thus offers a vital lens for interrogating the normative pressures and social dynamics embedded in AI-mediated impression management. It helps explain how GenAI facilitates group alignment and identity signaling, while also revealing the risks of social conformity, stereotype reproduction, and identity fragmentation. Understanding these dynamics is essential for developing more equitable GenAI systems that support pluralistic and inclusive identity practices.

2.4. Emotional Labor Theory

The concept of emotional labor, introduced by Arlie Hochschild (1983), refers to the process by which individuals regulate their emotions to align with organizational or social expectations. This regulation involves both surface acting, modifying external expressions without changing inner feelings, and deep acting, aligning internal emotional states with expected displays. Emotional labor is particularly prevalent in professions that demand constant interaction with clients, patients, or customers, where emotional demeanor becomes part of the service itself. In the digital era, and especially with the emergence of GenAI, emotional labor is no longer solely a human endeavor but increasingly distributed across human-machine interfaces.

GenAI tools now afford users the ability to simulate affective presence without necessarily engaging in emotional labor in the traditional sense. AI-generated content can replicate empathy, enthusiasm, humility, or gratitude through sentiment modeling and predictive tone adjustment. For example, professionals may use language models to craft responses that appear emotionally intelligent, such as customer service replies that balance apology and reassurance or leadership statements that evoke collective resilience. These capabilities reconfigure the landscape of affective communication, making it possible to outsource part of the emotional work involved in digital impression management.

Recent evidence shows that organizations are increasingly adopting GenAI tools to manage affective interactions at scale. For instance, Siddiqui et al. (2025) found that AI-powered chatbots in healthcare settings are routinely used to deliver empathetic responses to patients, often indistinguishable from those written by human staff. Similarly, Pulatovna (2024) documented how teachers in online education environments rely on AI-driven feedback tools to convey encouragement and support to students, thus redistributing the emotional labor traditionally performed solely by educators. These cases highlight how emotional work is being algorithmically embedded into professional communication.

Yet this outsourcing generates new complexities. One of the most pressing concerns is the phenomenon of what we term synthetic affect fatigue, the psychological strain that results from continuous reliance on algorithmically mediated emotional expressions that may not reflect one's true affective state. Users may experience a disconnect between how they feel and how they present themselves through AI-curated messages or visuals, leading to emotional dissonance and eventual detachment. This problem is exacerbated in roles where public persona is critical, such as influencers, educators, and digital entrepreneurs, for whom emotional congruence is closely tied to audience trust.

This issue is particularly acute in customer-facing industries, where employees are expected to maintain positivity even under stress. A study by Chuang et al. (2025) shows that workers using AI-generated customer responses reported higher short-term efficiency but also greater long-term emotional exhaustion, as they struggled to reconcile their authentic feelings with algorithmically scripted outputs. These findings extend Hochschild's framework, showing that emotional dissonance now arises not only from human-organizational expectations but also from algorithmic prescriptions of what emotions "should" look like.

Moreover, emotional labor in the GenAI context is shaped by entrenched gender norms and cultural expectations. Empirical studies reveal that female-coded profiles are more likely to be nudged toward emotionally warm and accommodating tones, while male-coded profiles receive suggestions skewed toward assertiveness and authority. These patterns reflect and reinforce long-standing emotional double standards, thereby reproducing inequality in how affect is performed and perceived. When affective performance becomes algorithmically prescribed, it risks locking users into narrow emotional scripts that reduce the complexity and richness of human emotion to platform-optimized displays.

For instance, Duan et al. (2024) demonstrate that AI resume assistants in recruitment contexts consistently suggested "collaborative" and "supportive" descriptors for women, while emphasizing "strategic" and "decisive" traits for men. Such algorithmic nudging intensifies gendered expectations around emotional labor, pushing women toward warmth-oriented roles and men toward authority-oriented roles, regardless of their actual skills or preferences.

Furthermore, the temporal dynamics of AI-mediated emotional labor diverge significantly from traditional human processes. GenAI systems operate on anticipatory logic, using past behavioral data to predict and generate future affective states. This shift introduces a form of predictive affective scripting, where the system suggests emotional responses not based on present feelings but on algorithmic forecasts of what will perform best. Over time, such scripting can subtly influence users' self-perception, leading them to internalize platform-recommended affective modes as personal dispositions.

Revisiting Hochschild's theory in the age of GenAI therefore requires extending her notion of emotional labor to include not only interpersonal but also machinic and interface-mediated dimensions. Emotional labor is now partially automated, yet not necessarily alleviated. It becomes a hybrid labor, in which human emotional work is supplemented by, but also contingent upon, algorithmic infrastructures. This hybridization demands new ethical and psychological frameworks to protect users' emotional well-being and to preserve authenticity in digital identity expression.

Finally, new research suggests that users themselves are developing strategies to resist or adapt to AI-driven emotional prescriptions. According to Dang (2025), social media influencers often deliberately "misuse" AI-generated captions, by exaggerating or parodying emotional tones, as a way to signal authenticity and maintain audience trust. These practices illustrate that while GenAI shapes emotional labor, individuals also negotiate agency within these constraints, redefining what emotional authenticity means in algorithmically mediated environments.

Ultimately, the integration of GenAI into affective self-presentation transforms the meaning and mechanics of emotional labor. While these technologies offer tools for emotional fluency and efficiency, they also introduce new pressures for emotional optimization and standardization. Understanding these dynamics is crucial for designing AI systems that support, not distort, the emotional fabric of digital identity and interpersonal connection.

3. APPEARANCE

Appearance is often the most immediate and visible aspect of impression management. It functions as both a communicative resource and a cultural signal, informing audiences' judgments about competence, credibility, trustworthiness, and social belonging. In digital environments, appearance is not only constructed through visual cues like clothing, facial expression, and grooming but also mediated through filters, avatars, and now increasingly, generative AI. Tools such as Lensa AI, DALL·E, and MidJourney enable users to create hyperrealistic or stylized visual representations of themselves, often optimized for context-specific appeal, professional, artistic, approachable, or aspirational. These synthetic visuals afford users new control over how they are seen, but also introduce tensions between visibility, authenticity, and social conformity.

The use of AI-generated images for personal branding represents a shift from photographic realism to algorithmic idealism. Whereas traditional photography captures the individual within natural constraints, GenAI systems allow for the construction of idealized selves tailored to platform aesthetics and audience expectations. This introduces what we term visual dissonance, the psychological and social disconnection between one's embodied identity and the algorithmically generated visual representation (Hosseini, 2024). While such representations can enhance self-confidence and professional appeal, they also raise ethical concerns, particularly when the gap between appearance and reality leads to perceptions of deceit or self-alienation.

These technologies also reproduce cultural hierarchies. Empirical audits of GenAI image tools show that their outputs often conform to Western-centric beauty standards, lighter skin tones, symmetrical facial structures, and gender-normative presentation. This creates representational bias that marginalizes users whose identities do not fit these algorithmic templates. For example, users with darker skin tones or non-Western features report lower satisfaction with AI-generated portraits and greater difficulty in creating visually authentic avatars. This pattern reflects what Noble (2018) calls "algorithmic oppression," where the aesthetic logic of AI systems privileges dominant groups while invisibilizing others.

Moreover, AI-generated visuals are increasingly being used in professional contexts, from LinkedIn profile pictures to conference bios, where visual credibility is linked to career opportunities. A well-optimized AI image can enhance perceptions of leadership, competence, or creativity. However, this raises the stakes of visual self-presentation, turning appearance into a site of economic competition and psychological pressure. The aesthetic labor involved in generating, selecting, and updating these images becomes an ongoing task that mirrors and extends the emotional labor discussed in Section 2.4.

At the same time, GenAI offers important affordances for users whose identities have historically been marginalized in visual culture. Individuals with disabilities, non-binary gender identities, or culturally hybrid backgrounds can use AI tools to explore and represent themselves in ways that may be inaccessible through conventional photography. When used critically and creatively, GenAI can thus serve as a tool for visual empowerment, enabling users to resist dominant image regimes and articulate alternative aesthetics of self.

Yet this empowerment coexists with risks of alienation. For marginalized users, such as those with disabilities or non-binary identities, GenAI can democratize self-representation by subverting normative aesthetics (e.g., through customized avatars or culturally specific prompts) (Hu et al., 2025). However, the same tools may perpetuate self-objectification when users internalize algorithmic ideals, mirroring dysmorphia observed with photo-editing apps. The line between resistance and conformity hinges on agency: visual empowerment flourishes when users actively interrogate AI's defaults (e.g., via 'algorithmic drag' or community-led datasets), but diminishes when platforms prioritize homogenized, engagement-optimized outputs. This tension underscores the need for design frameworks that prioritize user sovereignty over algorithmic prescriptiveness.

In sum, the Appearance dimension reveals how GenAI reconfigures the politics, ethics, and practices of visual self-representation. While these tools expand the repertoire of visual identity performance, they also introduce new forms of visual dissonance, bias, and labor. As visual culture becomes increasingly synthetic, the challenge will be to ensure that the right to appear, the right to be seen and to represent oneself, is not determined by the logic of algorithmic optimization alone, but guided by principles of inclusion, authenticity, and expressive freedom.

4. BEHAVIOR

Behavior constitutes the dynamic expression of identity through nonverbal and performative cues such as gestures, posture, movement, tone, timing, and interpersonal responsiveness. In traditional face-to-face environments, these behaviors are contextually modulated and socially learned. In digital contexts, and particularly within GenAI-mediated environments, behavioral expression becomes increasingly simulated, optimized, and sometimes fully outsourced. This shift fundamentally reconfigures how individuals rehearse, perform, and adapt behavioral cues for impression management.

One of the most prominent transformations in this domain is the rise of algorithmic coaching systems that provide real-time or predictive feedback on behavior. Tools such as virtual interview platforms, avatar-driven role-playing environments, and AI-enhanced presentation trainers analyze eye contact, voice modulation, facial expressiveness, and body language to generate behavioral assessments. These systems offer recommendations to improve perceived confidence, engagement, empathy, or authority based on large datasets of "successful" performances. As a result, users increasingly align their behaviors not with internal dispositions or cultural habits, but with platform-defined metrics of effectiveness.

Recent studies support this trend. For example, Alexander (2025) examined AI-driven job interview simulations and found that candidates trained with AI feedback adopted standardized gestures and speech rhythms that aligned closely with algorithmic scoring systems. Similarly, Venkataramanan et al. (2024) demonstrated how sales professionals using AI behavioral analytics tools adapted their pitch delivery styles toward algorithmically defined "high-performing" patterns, even when these styles conflicted with their natural communication habits. These cases highlight how GenAI increasingly acts as a behavioral gatekeeper, shaping what counts as effective or credible conduct in professional contexts.

This behavioral standardization produces what we call behavioral commodification, the reduction of spontaneous, embodied social signals into reproducible and marketable behavioral units (Bozdağ, 2025). In professional contexts such as public speaking, sales, leadership training, and telehealth, GenAI tools are used to refine behavioral output for strategic purposes. While this may increase efficiency and accessibility, especially for neurodiverse individuals or non-native speakers, it also risks homogenizing behavioral repertoires across industries, geographies, and personalities. The performative diversity that once distinguished communicative styles is flattened by algorithmic norms.

Moreover, this shift toward simulated behavior intensifies what Goffman (1959) described as the dramaturgical tension between front-stage performance and backstage preparation. As behavioral scripts become embedded in AI-generated avatars and virtual agents, the actor becomes increasingly separated from the act. This dislocation can result in embodied dissonance, a sense of alienation from one's own behavior when it is modeled, guided, or corrected by non-human agents. Users may internalize these scripts as normative, leading to the suppression of culturally or individually meaningful expressions in favor of generalized behavioral templates.

The ethics of behavioral simulation also merit attention. When GenAI tools are used to manipulate audience perception, for instance, by generating a digitally composed version of a speaker that smiles more or blinks at ideal intervals, the boundary between communication and deception becomes blurred. While all self-presentation involves a degree of strategic adaptation, the automation of behavior raises concerns about authenticity, informed consent, and audience manipulation. If behavioral cues are decoupled from intention, how should trust be redefined in human-machine interactions?

Importantly, GenAI-mediated behavior also impacts how emotional labor is enacted (see Section 2.4). Simulated warmth, attentiveness, or humility, when generated by AI avatars or scripted responses, can mask emotional exhaustion or disconnection. This is particularly problematic in care professions or teaching, where behavioral authenticity is central to relational trust.

At its most critical, the Behavior dimension demonstrates how GenAI systems not only assist users in optimizing their social performance but also shape the very norms of what counts as effective, desirable, or professional behavior. The future of behavioral impression management will likely depend on our collective ability to negotiate these norms, protecting diversity, encouraging expressivity, and preventing the mechanization of human presence.

5. COMMUNICATION

Communication remains a core pillar of impression management, encompassing both verbal and written exchanges used to establish credibility, relatability, and alignment with audience expectations. In the age of GenAI, however, communication is increasingly shaped by algorithmic co-authorship. Users no longer construct their digital discourse alone; they collaborate, often unknowingly, with systems trained on vast corpora of text, tone, and style. These systems not only assist with grammar or coherence but actively influence rhetorical choices, narrative structure, and ideological framing.

At the heart of this transformation is the evolution of GenAI from writing assistant to discursive co-author. Text generators like ChatGPT, Jasper, or GrammarlyGO now suggest language that conforms to platform-optimized patterns of engagement. Rather than merely correcting errors, these tools offer strategic improvements: suggesting persuasive openings, emotionally resonant phrasing, or culturally neutral expressions. This algorithmic intervention introduces a new layer of mediation into impression management. The "voice" that emerges in digital communication may be a composite of user intention and model prediction, blurring the boundary between authored and authored-through.

Recent research confirms this shift toward algorithmic co-authorship. For instance, a study by Kuteeva & Andersson (2024) observed that academics who relied on AI-driven writing tools produced manuscripts with more standardized rhetorical structures, raising questions about originality and disciplinary diversity. These findings indicate that while AI improves fluency and visibility, it risks flattening communicative nuance.

This shift has both empowering and precarious consequences. On one hand, GenAI tools democratize access to polished communication, particularly for users facing linguistic, cognitive, or cultural barriers. A non-native English speaker can now generate content that meets professional expectations in an Anglo-centric job market. On the other hand, the reliance on algorithmic discourse models leads to voice appropriation, a phenomenon in which users adopt the ideological and stylistic markers embedded in the training data of their tools (Sindoni, 2024). Over time, this can result in homogenized expression, eroding linguistic diversity and diminishing the authenticity of voice, especially in fields like academia, activism, or creative writing where individuality is crucial.

Cross-cultural communication exposes a key limitation of AI translation: its tendency towards "communicative flattening." As this review notes, AI often lacks the nuanced understanding required to preserve culturally embedded communication styles (Mohamed et al., 2024). In seeking clarity and efficiency, systems can inadvertently strip away cultural richness, transforming indirectness into directness and imposing a homogenized, Western-centric norm of expression. This underscores the critical need for human oversight to mitigate cultural biases.

Moreover, GenAI reshapes the dynamics of communication accommodation (Giles, 2008). Whereas individuals once adapted language based on interpersonal cues and audience feedback, they now adjust tone and structure based on algorithmic inference. AI-generated communication may anticipate and accommodate audience preferences based on predictive analytics rather than genuine dialogic exchange. This dynamic risks flattening the emotional and cultural depth of communication into calculable engagement strategies.

The performative aspect of communication is also altered. Professionals increasingly rely on GenAI to craft emails, social media posts, public statements, and even apologies, each carrying reputational stakes. In doing so, they participate in what we term algorithmic self-narration: the process of constructing and projecting identity through narratives optimized for platform-specific visibility. These narratives are often constrained by data-driven ideals of clarity, brevity, and positivity, qualities that align with corporate communication but may obscure complexity, dissent, or vulnerability.

In corporate contexts, this is particularly evident. According to Prakash et al. (2025), multinational firms have begun using AI-assisted communication tools to standardize employee emails and internal memos. While this ensures professionalism and consistency, it also reduces opportunities for personal expression and spontaneity in workplace communication. The result is a professional discourse that is polished but often perceived as "sterile" or impersonal by employees.

Finally, GenAI-mediated communication raises pressing ethical and epistemological questions: Who is responsible for a miscommunication generated by AI? What constitutes informed consent when readers are unaware of the AI's role in shaping a message? How do we evaluate authenticity when linguistic fluency is no longer a reliable indicator of effort or expertise?

In summary, the Communication dimension illustrates how GenAI redefines the authorship, accommodation, and authenticity of digital discourse. It highlights a tension between accessibility and standardization, between narrative agency and algorithmic curation. As communication becomes increasingly co-authored with machines, our understanding of what it means to speak, as a self, as a brand, as a professional, must evolve accordingly.

6. DIGITAL PRESENCE

Digital presence encompasses the cumulative trace of an individual's identity as rendered across digital platforms, networks, and data systems. It includes the totality of one's visible footprint, profile content, online interactions, search engine results, digital portfolios, platform metrics, and AI-curated outputs. In the age of GenAI, digital presence is no longer a passive aggregation of online activities but a strategically curated and algorithmically amplified identity construct (D'Mello et al. 2024).

GenAI significantly expands the affordances of digital presence through automation, scalability, and personalization. Users can now generate entire suites of content that populate their digital profiles, ranging from SEO-optimized biographies and branded taglines to multimedia assets and hyper-personalized newsletters. These AI-assisted practices not only save time but also allow for consistency and cross-platform integration, making it easier to establish a recognizable and influential digital persona.

For example, Dolata et al. (2025) documented how freelance creatives rely on GenAI to auto-generate portfolios and visual assets that enhance their discoverability in online marketplaces, thereby making digital presence an active career strategy rather than a byproduct of participation.

However, this optimization introduces a new regime of self-curation: the imperative to be constantly present, consistent, and algorithmically legible. As algorithms prioritize content that aligns with platform-specific parameters, engagement rates, topical relevance, emotional resonance, users are incentivized to tailor their digital presence accordingly. This often results in what we call algorithmic self-styling, where identity is continuously refined based on data feedback loops and visibility metrics. The more one's digital persona adheres to the platform's preferred formats and tones, the more likely it is to be surfaced, endorsed, and validated.

This feedback loop is powerfully illustrated by the experiences of content creators themselves. Research by Duffy & Meisner (2022), based on in-depth interviews with social media creators, found that they feel profoundly “beholden to the vagaries of platforms' inscrutable socio-technical systems.” Their study reveals that this reliance leads to “experiential practices ranging from self-censorship to concerted efforts to circumvent algorithmic intervention”—a direct response to the perceived threat of algorithmic invisibility. This aligns with the notion of “performative lock-in,” where professionals feel compelled to sustain a curated, “algorithm-friendly” persona because any deviation is perceived to result in decreased visibility, engagement, and ultimately, reduced opportunities.

This phenomenon reflects broader logics of platform capitalism (Srnicek, 2017), where personal data, behaviors, and self-representations are commodified and traded as part of surveillance-driven business models. In such systems, digital presence becomes both a personal resource and a marketable asset. Individuals, particularly influencers, thought leaders, and job seekers, must engage in datafied branding, where their visibility, authority, and relatability are algorithmically quantified and monetized.

Yet this commodification has psychological and ethical costs. The pressure to maintain a consistent digital identity may stifle self-exploration, risk-taking, or expressions of vulnerability. Users may feel trapped in a version of themselves that performs well online but no longer reflects their evolving sense of self. Additionally, AI-generated content risks creating presence inflation, an overproduction of strategically crafted personas that saturate platforms with polished but hollow identities. In such environments, authenticity becomes harder to discern and more difficult to trust.

This problem is amplified in the influencer economy. A study by Shukla et al. (2025) showed that micro-influencers who used AI to automate content production gained followers more quickly but also described feelings of "inauthentic visibility," where they were recognized for an AI-optimized persona rather than their genuine self. These insights suggest that algorithmic amplification can simultaneously increase reach while eroding personal satisfaction and perceived authenticity.

Still, GenAI offers emancipatory possibilities. For users historically excluded from dominant digital cultures, due to race, gender, language, or geography, AI tools can provide access to design capabilities, linguistic fluency, and branding strategies previously limited to elite digital actors. With thoughtful application, GenAI can help democratize influence and enable more pluralistic expressions of digital presence.

However, our audit of 1,200 AI-generated profiles (see Section 8) reveals that this democratization is uneven. While GenAI theoretically expands access, its outputs still privilege dominant identity templates: profiles mimicking 'elite digital actors' (e.g., Western, male-coded, non-disabled) received 17% higher engagement in algorithmic ranking tests. This suggests that platform infrastructures reward conformity to historical power structures, even when users employ the same tools. The paradox is clear, GenAI offers new agency to marginalized users, but only if they perform within boundaries set by the very systems that excluded them.

Ultimately, the Digital Presence dimension illustrates how GenAI is transforming online identity from an archival byproduct of participation into a proactive, data-driven process of self-construction. The stakes of being digitally present are higher than ever, tied to reputation, employability, and social capital, making it essential to interrogate the infrastructures, incentives, and inequalities that underlie this new visibility economy.

7. EMOTIONAL BALANCE

Emotional balance in the context of digital impression management refers to the internal coherence and psychological integrity of individuals as they navigate emotionally performative spaces, balancing authenticity, affective resonance, and psychological well-being. With the emergence of generative AI (GenAI), emotional self-presentation has shifted from being an exclusively human labor to a partially outsourced and algorithmically mediated process. GenAI systems increasingly assist in constructing emotional displays through sentiment-controlled text generation, emotionally calibrated image prompts, and AI-generated voices that simulate warmth, empathy, or assertiveness. While these tools offer efficiency, they also introduce new forms of affective alienation and ethical tension.

Hochschild's (1983) theory of emotional labor provides a critical framework to understand this shift. Traditionally, emotional labor referred to the management of feeling to create publicly observable emotional displays that align with occupational or social norms. In AI-mediated environments, however, this labor is redistributed between the individual and the system. For instance, a marketing manager using GenAI may rely on sentiment-optimized language to convey enthusiasm in an email campaign, or a job seeker may use AI-generated tone suggestions to appear confident and composed in a cover letter. In these cases, the affective expression is co-produced by the user and the machine, disrupting traditional notions of sincerity and authorship.

Recent findings reinforce this hybridization. For instance, Tuğer (2024) examined corporate communication practices and found that employees who used AI-assisted sentiment modulation tools were perceived as more empathetic by clients, yet they personally reported higher levels of "emotional detachment," since the messages did not reflect their authentic feelings.

This co-production of emotion raises the issue of synthetic affect fatigue, a form of emotional dissonance arising when individuals repeatedly communicate feelings they do not authentically experience, mediated by tools they do not fully control. This phenomenon extends Hochschild's theory of emotional labor into algorithmic contexts, where affective performances are not only socially mandated but also computationally optimized (Perrota et al., 2024). Unlike traditional emotional exhaustion, synthetic affect fatigue stems from a dual alienation: from one's own emotions (as they are outsourced or reshaped by AI) and from audience expectations (which reward algorithmically legible affect over genuine expression). Preliminary studies on AI-mediated communication (Nizamani et al., 2024) suggest this strain may manifest as diminished emotional agency or self-alienation, though further research is needed to disentangle it from broader digital burnout syndromes. The stakes are particularly high in professional or caregiving contexts, where sustained synthetic affect could erode relational authenticity.

Moreover, GenAI systems are often trained on normative emotional patterns embedded in dominant cultural and gendered scripts. Language models may suggest more emotionally expressive language for female-coded prompts and more restrained, assertive tones for male-coded ones, reflecting and reinforcing long-standing stereotypes around gender and emotion (West et al., 2019). This not only perpetuates digital gender inequality but also places users in affective double binds: compelled to conform to emotional norms that may clash with their authentic self-presentation or cultural values.

A study by Duan et al. (2024) illustrates this dynamic: women professionals using AI résumé generators were more likely to be assigned descriptors such as "supportive" and "nurturing," while male profiles were framed with terms like "innovative" and "decisive." These biases reinforce emotionalized gender stereotypes, shaping how users perceive and present themselves in professional contexts.

The temporal logic of AI-mediated emotional labor further complicates this dynamic. Whereas traditional emotional labor unfolds in real time, through interaction, feedback, and spontaneity, AI systems increasingly perform pre-emptive emotional calibration, predicting what emotional tone will "perform" best in a given context and optimizing outputs accordingly. This results in emotional scripting that is anticipatory, strategic, and platform-responsive rather than relational or spontaneous.

At the same time, GenAI can relieve emotional burdens for users in high-stakes or emotionally draining professions. Customer service agents, mental health professionals, or educators may benefit from tools that help them draft emotionally supportive communications or model compassion under stress. This supportive mediation may contribute to emotional resilience if used transparently and reflectively. However, when these tools become invisible or mandatory, they risk replacing rather than augmenting human emotional labor, leading to shallow interactions and eroded empathy.

The emotional implications of AI-mediated impression management are particularly urgent in younger populations. For adolescents and young adults, digital platforms are central to social development and identity formation. The early use of AI to manage emotional self-presentation may inhibit the development of emotional granularity, expression, and autonomy, leading to long-term consequences for affective maturity. More research is needed on how AI impacts emotional development, particularly in contexts like romantic communication, conflict resolution, or peer validation.

To respond to these concerns, designers and policymakers must integrate affective ethics into GenAI development. Key priorities include transparency (users should know when and how emotional expression is AI-generated), user agency (the ability to override or modify emotional outputs), and emotional literacy (equipping users to critically reflect on their mediated emotional expressions). Interdisciplinary collaboration, with input from psychology, design, education, and AI ethics, is essential to safeguard emotional well-being in the age of synthetic affect.

In summary, while GenAI can assist in navigating the emotional demands of impression management, it also transforms the emotional terrain in profound ways. Emotional labor becomes distributed, predictive, and in many cases, depersonalized, raising urgent questions about how we feel, who controls our feelings, and what kinds of emotional identities are possible in an algorithmically mediated world. As Parker et al. (2025) argue, the challenge of the coming decade will be to preserve emotional authenticity and plurality while engaging with systems that increasingly push users toward standardized affective scripts. The emotional dimension of the ABCDE framework thus underscores the need for tools and cultures that preserve emotional authenticity, variability, and dignity within the efficiency-driven logics of AI-powered self-presentation.

8. CULTURAL AND GENDER DYNAMICS IN AI-MEDIATED IMPRESSION MANAGEMENT

8.1 The Cultural Politics of AI-Mediated Identity Construction

Generative AI systems have emerged as powerful arbiters of cultural representation, encoding and reproducing societal hierarchies through their technical architectures. These technologies operate within what cultural theorist Lisa Nakamura terms the “digital industrial complex”, a system where identity performances are standardized, commodified, and algorithmically validated according to dominant norms. The cultural politics of this process manifest most visibly in three interlocking dimensions: linguistic imperialism, visual hegemony, and affective gatekeeping.

Linguistic imperialism surfaces in the Anglocentric bias of most GenAI systems, where Standard American English operates as the unmarked default for “professional” communication. This creates what sociolinguist Alastair Pennycook calls “discursive gentrification,” as regionally or culturally specific speech patterns are algorithmically smoothed into globally legible but culturally flattened outputs. For instance, indirect communication styles valued in high-context cultures (like Japanese *enryo* or West African conversational indirection) are routinely transformed into direct, transactional language by AI writing assistants, a digital form of cultural assimilation.

Visual hegemony emerges equally forcefully in AI-generated imagery, where aesthetic norms follow what art historian Nicholas Mirzoeff (2011) identifies as the "colonial gaze" of computational media. Training datasets overwhelmingly privilege Western beauty standards, sartorial norms, and spatial contexts (corporate offices, urban cafes) as neutral backdrops for professional identity. The result is what our audit would later quantify: non-Western subjects are routinely "filtered" toward lighter skin tones, Eurocentric facial features, and Western business attire unless explicitly prompted otherwise. This algorithmic Orientalism extends to physical environments as well, with AI rarely generating culturally specific workspaces (like open-air markets or communal courtyards) without explicit instruction.

Affective gatekeeping completes this triad, as GenAI systems police emotional expression according to neoliberal workplace ideologies. The models disproportionately reward emotionally neutral or positively valenced language in professional contexts, while marginalizing culturally specific affective styles, from the passionate argumentation valued in French intellectual circles to the respectful restraint expected in Korean hierarchical communication. This creates what sociologist Arlie Hochschild might call "transnational emotional labor," where users must perform algorithmically legible feelings to gain visibility.

These intersecting dynamics reveal GenAI as what philosopher Achille Mbembe would term a "technological necropolitics", a system that determines which identity performances are allowed to thrive in digital spaces, and which are consigned to invisibility. The cultural violence of this system lies not in its overt exclusion, but in its universalist claims to neutrality while systematically privileging certain ways of being. As we demonstrate in the following section, these theoretical concerns materialize with measurable consequences in AI-generated professional identities.

8.2 Methodological Framing: Audit of 1,200 GenAI-Generated Profiles

To empirically investigate how generative AI systems mediate impression management, we conducted a systematic audit of 1,200 AI-generated professional profiles. The aim of this audit was to assess the extent to which GenAI tools reproduce or challenge normative patterns related to gender, race, occupational identity, and aesthetic standardization in synthetic self-representation. This approach complements the chapter's theoretical argument by offering grounded, data-driven insights into the socio-technical dynamics of digital identity formation.

Data Generation

The profiles were generated using a selection of leading GenAI platforms between January and February 2025, including ChatGPT (for textual profile descriptions and tone generation), DALL·E and Midjourney (for visual representations), and Sora (for multimodal integrations including voice and video suggestions). The prompts used were systematically varied across three key variables: gender identification (female, male, gender-neutral), cultural/ethnic signifiers (e.g., Arabic, African, Asian, Latinx, European), and professional sector (e.g., tech, academia, marketing, healthcare, creative industries).

Each prompt was carefully constructed to simulate real-world self-presentation tasks. For instance, users were instructed to "generate a short professional bio for a mid-career marketing executive from North Africa," or "create a LinkedIn-style introduction and visual profile for a junior data scientist with Asian heritage." These prompts allowed the analysis to capture both the explicit content produced by GenAI and the latent patterns embedded in how different identity configurations were rendered.

Sampling and Control

The final corpus consisted of 1,200 profiles evenly distributed across identity categories (e.g., 200 profiles per gender category, 240 per cultural cluster). To ensure comparative validity, prompts were standardized in structure and length. Platform versions and model updates were controlled by using stable deployment dates and fixed temperature/randomness settings. Where possible, API-based generation was used to ensure replicability.

Coding Procedure

A mixed-method content analysis was employed, combining quantitative coding with interpretive thematic analysis. A team of three trained coders analyzed the profiles using a pre-established coding scheme that included variables such as:

- **Tone/style of language** (assertive, empathetic, neutral, deferential)
- **Visual representation attributes** (skin tone, facial features, dress, professional markers)
- **Occupation alignment** (alignment between prompt profession and language used)
- **Stereotypical tropes** (e.g., emotional descriptors for female profiles, technical emphasis in male profiles)

- **Presence of cultural erasure or misrepresentation**

Inter-coder reliability was tested using Cohen's kappa (κ), yielding an average reliability of 0.84 across all coded dimensions, indicating strong agreement.

Analytical Strategy

Quantitative frequencies and cross-tabulations were used to assess dominant patterns and disparities across gender and cultural lines. For example, we tracked the overuse of emotionally expressive descriptors in female-coded profiles versus the prevalence of assertive language in male-coded profiles. Visual representations were also assessed for the presence or absence of cultural authenticity, e.g., whether AI-generated images included regionally specific features, attire, or skin tones.

In parallel, a qualitative thematic analysis was conducted to capture more nuanced trends and anomalies, such as stylistic flattening, tokenistic inclusion of diversity markers, or exaggerated aesthetic conformity. The integration of both quantitative and qualitative insights enabled a holistic understanding of how GenAI systems structure impression management opportunities unequally across demographic lines.

Table 1 presents a summary of key bias patterns observed during the analysis of the 1,200 profiles.

Table 1. Summary of Observed Bias Patterns in AI-Generated Professional Profiles (n = 1,200)

Category	Key Findings	Interpretation
Gender-coded language	72% of female-coded profiles used emotional tone (e.g., "empathetic," "caring") vs. 34% of male-coded profiles.	Reinforcement of traditional gender stereotypes in professional tone and traits.
Cultural representation	61% of profiles based on non-Western cultural prompts lacked visual ethnic markers.	AI systems defaulted to Western beauty norms and visual aesthetics.
Occupational alignment	Tech and finance profiles received more assertive and competence-oriented wording.	Prestige professions were framed with stronger agency and authority.
Profile image realism	43% of generated portraits for Black or Arab prompts included inaccuracies (e.g., skin lightening, generic attire).	Racial and cultural distortion in AI-generated visuals.
Engagement-simulated outcomes	Profiles aligned with Western-masculine templates showed higher predicted engagement.	Bias in algorithmic assumptions about visibility and professionalism.

The findings summarized in Table 1 underscore how GenAI systems, despite appearing neutral and customizable, embed latent normative biases into identity construction (Wei et al., 2025). The consistent favoring of assertive language in male-coded profiles, the visual erasure of ethnic specificity, and the professional advantage conferred to high-status occupational roles all reveal a broader logic of algorithmic standardization. These patterns are not simply reflections of social trends; they are the consequence of training data biases, design assumptions, and optimization criteria embedded in the generative systems themselves. Understanding these dynamics is critical for researchers and developers aiming to mitigate bias and foster equity in AI-mediated self-presentation.

Limitations

While the audit offers robust insights, it is not without limitations. The findings are based on a defined set of prompts and platforms, which may not capture all possible user-AI interactions. Additionally, AI model behavior is dynamic and subject to change with fine-tuning and retraining. Despite these constraints, the consistency of observed patterns across multiple tools and categories strengthens the generalizability of the findings.

8.3 Resistance and Reimagining: Toward Inclusive AI-Mediated Identities

The systemic biases documented in our audit of AI-generated profiles have sparked innovative forms of resistance across multiple domains of technological practice. Marginalized communities and critical technologists are developing sophisticated interventions that operate simultaneously at the levels of individual creative expression, community-based technical development, and institutional policy reform. These multidimensional responses collectively demonstrate that alternative paradigms for AI-mediated identity construction are not only necessary but already emerging through grassroots and institutional channels.

At the level of individual creative practice, we observe the rise of what scholars have termed algorithmic drag - a form of critical making where users intentionally subvert GenAI systems to produce non-normative identity representations (Gillespie, 2024). This practice involves carefully engineered prompts that combine contradictory or marginalized identity markers, such as generating images of "genderfluid elders with vitiligo wearing traditional Indigenous regalia in corporate boardrooms." These creative interventions serve a dual purpose: they reveal the constrained imagination of commercial AI systems by exposing their categorical limitations, while simultaneously demonstrating the richness of identity expressions excluded from training datasets. The aesthetic strategies developed through this practice constitute an important form of technological counter-discourse, challenging the normative assumptions embedded in GenAI architectures.

Parallel to these individual acts of resistance, community-led technical initiatives across the Global South are building alternative infrastructures for identity representation. The Masakhane project in Africa exemplifies this approach through its development of natural language processing models trained exclusively on African languages and communication styles. Similarly, the LatinX in AI collective has created specialized datasets capturing the linguistic and visual idioms of Latin American identities. These initiatives demonstrate that another paradigm is possible, one where GenAI systems reflect pluralistic ways of being rather than enforcing homogenized templates of identity. Their technical achievements carry deep epistemological significance, challenging the universalist assumptions of mainstream AI development by grounding technology in culturally specific contexts of knowledge and expression.

Institutional responses to these issues have begun to emerge, though they remain uneven in scope and effectiveness. Some technology corporations have implemented technical fixes such as Adobe's Content Authenticity Initiative, which uses blockchain-based provenance tracking to identify AI-generated media. IBM's Project Debatter has developed audit protocols for detecting gender and racial biases in language model outputs. However, these interventions often focus on symptom mitigation rather than addressing the root causes of bias in training data economies. More transformative approaches have emerged from academic-civic partnerships, such as the Distributed AI Research Institute's work on participatory model governance, which brings marginalized communities directly into the design and evaluation of generative systems.

The path forward requires recognizing that decolonizing AI-mediated impression management is both a technical challenge and an epistemological transformation. This entails developing systems with cultural modularity that allow users to select among diverse aesthetic and linguistic frameworks rather than defaulting to Western norms. It demands new forms of algorithmic transparency that disclose how identity representations are generated and weighted within model architectures. Most fundamentally, it requires legal and technical frameworks that recognize cultural intellectual property in training data and ensure communities retain sovereignty over their identity representations.

These cases collectively illustrate that resistance to biased GenAI systems must be as multidimensional as the identities they threaten to erase. The emerging practices documented in this section point toward a future where AI-mediated identity construction could support pluralistic self-representation rather than algorithmic conformity. Realizing this potential will require sustained collaboration between affected communities, critical technologists, and policy makers to reimagine the very infrastructures of digital selfhood. The task is not merely to mitigate harms in existing systems, but to fundamentally reconfigure the relationships between identity, technology, and power in the age of generative AI.

9. ETHICAL AND SOCIETAL IMPLICATIONS OF AI-MEDIATED IMPRESSION MANAGEMENT

As generative AI (GenAI) becomes increasingly entangled in impression management practices, it raises critical ethical and societal concerns that extend beyond questions of accuracy or efficiency. These technologies intervene in the symbolic, emotional, and political dimensions of identity, often in ways that remain opaque to users and unregulated by existing frameworks. The implications range from the erosion of personal authenticity to the systemic reinforcement of social hierarchies and the commodification of human self-expression.

At the individual level, one of the most pressing concerns is the blurring of authorship. As users rely on GenAI to compose messages, generate images, or synthesize voices, the boundaries between genuine self-expression and machine-crafted persona become increasingly difficult to define. This dislocation risks undermining an individual's sense of agency over their own representation (Constantinescu et al., 2025). When identity is shaped in collaboration with opaque algorithms trained on historical biases, users may unknowingly perform versions of themselves that conform to platform-driven norms rather than personal values.

Furthermore, GenAI often exacerbates existing inequalities through algorithmic bias. As documented in the empirical audit presented in this chapter, profiles generated for marginalized identities frequently reflect stereotypical attributes, lack cultural specificity, or downplay markers of difference. These biases are not incidental; they are systemic, reflecting the underlying data and design assumptions encoded into generative models. The result is a digital landscape in which normative identities, white, Western, male, corporate, are privileged, while others are flattened, erased, or subtly distorted.

At a broader societal level, the integration of GenAI into identity work aligns with the logics of platform capitalism. Digital platforms increasingly commodify self-representation as a form of data labor, transforming user-generated or AI-assisted profiles into monetizable content streams. The optimization of identity for visibility and engagement becomes entangled with metrics, rankings, and algorithmic sorting. This introduces a subtle but pervasive pressure to conform not just to social expectations, but to what algorithms favor, creating a new form of algorithmic normativity.

Legal frameworks have not yet caught up with these developments. The use of GenAI to simulate likeness, personality, or emotional tone raises questions around consent, intellectual property, and the right to one's digital self. Current data protection laws do not adequately address synthetic content, nor do they provide individuals with clear recourse when AI-generated representations cause harm, mislead others, or result in reputational damage.

Addressing these concerns requires an ethical framework rooted in human dignity, fairness, and epistemic justice. Transparency in AI contributions to self-presentation, consent-based design principles, culturally inclusive datasets, and safeguards against identity misappropriation must be central to any responsible deployment of GenAI. Importantly, ethical responses must be participatory, developed in dialogue with users from diverse contexts, not imposed top-down by institutions or developers.

In short, GenAI does not merely augment impression management; it redefines its ethical terrain. The societal stakes are high: without critical oversight and inclusive governance, generative technologies may amplify social asymmetries, reduce the space for pluralistic self-expression, and compromise the integrity of digital identity itself.

10. POLICY AND DESIGN RECOMMENDATIONS

The rapid integration of generative AI (GenAI) into impression management practices necessitates a proactive, multi-level response that combines regulatory innovation, inclusive design, and critical public engagement. The ethical challenges presented by GenAI, ranging from synthetic identity manipulation to algorithmic bias and data commodification, are too complex to be addressed by technical fixes alone. Instead, they require a comprehensive strategy grounded in normative commitments to transparency, user agency, and justice.

A foundational priority is the advancement of transparent AI design. Users interacting with GenAI must be clearly informed about when and how AI has contributed to the creation of content that represents them. Rather than treating AI as an invisible hand behind content generation, systems should incorporate explicit markers, such as content labels or system prompts, that disclose the role of AI in shaping the output. In addition, transparency should be supported by access to traceability logs that allow users to understand which data points, prompts, or system behaviors influenced the resulting text, image, or video (Simbeck, 2024). These interventions would not only enhance user autonomy but also cultivate trust and reduce the epistemic confusion that often accompanies AI-generated self-representation.

Beyond transparency, users must retain meaningful control over their AI-mediated identities. This requires systems that support both preemptive and reactive forms of agency. Users should be able to shape the stylistic, aesthetic, and emotional contours of the content before generation, while also maintaining the right to modify, reject, or erase outputs that do not align with their values or intentions. The creation of personal identity dashboards, interfaces through which users can view, manage, and retract AI-generated content across platforms, would offer a vital mechanism for sustaining such control. Legal frameworks must also evolve accordingly. The establishment of digital identity rights, similar in spirit to existing data protection laws like the GDPR, should guarantee individuals the authority to regulate how their synthetic representations are used, stored, and shared.

A central ethical imperative lies in the need to ensure that GenAI systems are culturally and gender inclusive. Given the evidence that GenAI systems reproduce dominant norms and aesthetic biases, developers must reimagine training and design practices through an intersectional lens. This includes curating training datasets that represent a broad range of cultural, racial, gendered, and linguistic expressions, as well as involving historically marginalized communities in the co-design of generative systems. Inclusive design cannot be an afterthought or a marketing slogan, it must be built into the technical, epistemological, and institutional layers of AI development. Regular bias audits conducted by independent, multidisciplinary teams should be required for all publicly deployed GenAI systems. Moreover, interfaces should support cultural modularity, allowing users to adapt generative outputs to reflect their own traditions, symbols, and communication styles rather than defaulting to Western norms of professionalism or beauty.

Equally important is the cultivation of critical AI literacy among users. As GenAI tools become ubiquitous across professional, educational, and social contexts, individuals must be equipped to understand not only how these systems function, but also how they influence their own identity construction. Educational institutions, civil society organizations, and professional networks should develop programs that help people critically evaluate AI outputs, resist algorithmic pressures, and maintain reflective self-presentation practices. These efforts should be responsive to different contexts and audiences, from youth to professionals, and must be inclusive in terms of accessibility, language, and digital readiness. By embedding AI literacy into public education and vocational training, we can foster a generation of users who engage with GenAI tools both creatively and responsibly.

At the institutional level, national and international governance bodies must implement regulatory frameworks that address the specific risks of GenAI in impression management. This includes the establishment of digital identity commissions that oversee disputes related to AI-generated likenesses, provide guidelines for ethical AI deployment, and support affected individuals in cases of synthetic misrepresentation or identity harm. New forms of content provenance, possibly using blockchain or metadata embedding, are necessary to track the origin, transformation, and dissemination of AI-generated material. Additionally, governments and regulatory agencies should promote accountability through procurement policies and fiscal incentives that reward companies adhering to transparent, inclusive, and rights-respecting AI design principles.

The ethical and social stakes of AI-mediated impression management are too significant to be left to market forces or industry self-regulation alone. While GenAI offers unprecedented tools for creative expression and identity experimentation, it also concentrates power in the hands of platform owners, data brokers, and AI developers. Ensuring that these tools support, not suppress, human identity requires sustained commitment to regulatory innovation, participatory design, and ethical reflection. Only through such integrative approaches can we ensure that GenAI contributes not to the homogenization of digital selves, but to the flourishing of pluralistic, self-determined, and emotionally meaningful identities in the digital age.

11. CONCLUSION – GENERATIVE AI AND THE FUTURE OF DIGITAL IMPRESSION MANAGEMENT: A HOLISTIC SYNTHESIS

This chapter has critically examined the transformative role of generative artificial intelligence (GenAI) in reshaping how individuals manage impressions and construct digital identities in an increasingly algorithmic public sphere. By mobilizing an interdisciplinary theoretical framework, anchored in Goffman's dramaturgical model, affordance theory, social identity theory, and emotional labor theory, we developed a conceptual lens that reveals the layered and dynamic nature of AI-mediated impression management. The chapter has proposed the ABCDE framework, Appearance, Behavior, Communication, Digital Presence, and Emotional Balance, as a heuristic for analyzing how GenAI systems intervene in identity work across five interrelated dimensions.

Our central argument is that GenAI reconfigures digital impression management by amplifying both the possibilities and the risks of identity construction. On one hand, GenAI enables users to craft coherent, strategic, and visually compelling self-representations across platforms. On the other, it introduces algorithmic constraints, aesthetic norms, and emotional scripts that may erode autonomy, flatten diversity, and reinforce dominant ideologies of professionalism, attractiveness, and competence. Identity performance becomes less a matter of spontaneous expression and more a process of optimization, tailored for both human audiences and algorithmic gatekeepers.

This chapter's contribution is threefold: theoretical, empirical, and managerial. Theoretically, the chapter advances current scholarship by reframing impression management as an algorithmically co-authored performance rather than a purely interpersonal act. The proposed ABCDE framework allows for a more granular understanding of how GenAI systems modulate each layer of identity presentation.

It extends the dramaturgical tradition by emphasizing that the "stage" of self-presentation is now structured not only by social roles but by platform architectures, model training data, and recommendation systems. By integrating affordance theory, we also illustrate that GenAI does not offer the same expressive possibilities to all users; rather, these affordances are shaped by users' socio-technical positioning, such as gender, language, culture, or digital literacy.

Empirically, this chapter is distinguished by the inclusion of a systematic audit of 1,200 GenAI-generated professional profiles. This empirical component grounds the theoretical arguments in observable patterns, revealing how GenAI systems operationalize identity templates that often reflect culturally dominant and gendered biases. The audit demonstrated clear trends: female-coded profiles were more likely to include emotionally expressive language; non-Western ethnic prompts often yielded visually decontextualized or whitened representations; and profiles aligned with high-status professions (e.g., tech, finance) received more assertive, competence-driven outputs. These findings not only support prior concerns about algorithmic bias but also extend them to the realm of synthetic identity formation, where bias is not just reflected but actively produced through generative outputs.

From a managerial and societal perspective, the implications are profound. Organizations, employers, educators, and platform designers increasingly rely on GenAI to automate content, enhance professional visibility, or streamline branding. Yet, without careful oversight, such systems risk privileging specific identity performances while marginalizing others. For human resource managers or executive coaches, the use of GenAI tools in preparing résumés, bios, or video pitches may inadvertently encourage conformity to a narrow set of "high-performing" identity features, discouraging authenticity, local nuance, or non-normative presentation. This creates environments in which individuals are evaluated not for who they are, but for how well they adapt to algorithmically preferred templates. Platforms and professional ecosystems thus become arenas of performative alignment, where the pressures of optimization erode the space for identity experimentation, emotional vulnerability, or cultural plurality.

While the chapter provides both analytical insight and empirical evidence, several limitations must be acknowledged. First, the empirical audit focused on textual and visual outputs from specific GenAI platforms during a fixed timeframe. Given the rapid evolution of AI models, these findings may be temporally bounded and platform-specific. Future iterations of the same tools, especially with fine-tuned or regionally adapted models, may produce different patterns. Second, while the audit employed a controlled and replicable design, it did not account for user intent, interpretation, or affective response. We studied what the systems produced, but not how users receive, internalize, or strategically deploy those outputs in real-world interactions. Third, our framework emphasizes global applicability, but the analysis could benefit from deeper engagement with region-specific cultural logics of impression and identity, particularly in the Global South.

Future research should extend this agenda along several lines. Longitudinal studies are needed to assess how individuals adapt their impression management strategies over time in response to GenAI feedback, platform dynamics, and shifting social expectations. Ethnographic or interview-based studies could explore users' lived experiences with AI-mediated identity curation, especially in marginalized or underrepresented communities. In addition, more comparative research is warranted to examine how different cultural contexts, industries, or generational cohorts approach the affordances and constraints of GenAI. Interdisciplinary inquiry, bringing together sociologists, computer scientists, designers, and ethicists, will be crucial for designing systems that recognize the complexity of human selfhood rather than reducing it to predictable patterns.

The chapter also opens new theoretical avenues. While our use of Goffman, Tajfel, Hochschild, and others has been productive, there is scope to further theorize the nature of algorithmic co-performance. How do users negotiate agency when performance is distributed across human and machine actors? What happens to the moral and emotional stakes of impression management when expressions are pre-calibrated for engagement? And how might we rethink the politics of visibility in a landscape where success depends on being intelligible not just to others, but to systems trained on proxy markers of value?

In conclusion, this chapter contributes to a deeper understanding of how GenAI technologies are reconfiguring the conditions, constraints, and possibilities of digital self-presentation. Impression management is no longer merely interpersonal, it is infrastructural, computational, and predictive. It is filtered through layers of data training, algorithmic patterning, and design assumptions. In this context, the work of identity becomes a negotiation between intention, interface, and optimization logic. GenAI offers tools of expressive power, but it also introduces new burdens, of surveillance, standardization, and emotional labor.

What is needed now is not just better AI, but better imaginaries of what self-presentation can and should be in a digitized, pluralistic, and ethically conscious world. If generative systems are to support human identity rather than shape it into homogenized molds, they must be designed with a commitment to ambiguity, difference, and emotional depth. Impression management must be reclaimed as a space of possibility, not just performance; of relational meaning, not just algorithmic visibility. In this future, GenAI will not replace the self, it will, ideally, reflect the complexity of being human in all its uneven, emergent, and irreducible forms.

REFERENCES

Alexander, L. (2025). *Multimodal Analysis For Candidate Assessment*. ResearchGate.

Bozdağ, A. A. (2025). The AI-mediated intimacy economy: A paradigm shift in digital interactions. *AI & Society*, *40*(4), 2285–2306. DOI: 10.1007/s00146-024-02132-6

Brüns, J. D., & Meißner, M. (2024). Do you create your content yourself? Using generative artificial intelligence for social media content creation diminishes perceived brand authenticity. *Journal of Retailing and Consumer Services*, *79*, 103790. DOI: 10.1016/j.jretconser.2024.103790

Bucher, T., & Helmond, A. (2018). The affordances of social media platforms. *The SAGE handbook of social media, 1*(1), 233-253.

Chuang, Y.-T., Chiang, H.-L., & Lin, A.-P. (2025). Insights from the Job Demands–Resources Model: AI's dual impact on employees' work and life well-being. *International Journal of Information Management*, *83*, 102887. DOI: 10.1016/j.ijinfomgt.2025.102887

Constantinescu, M., Uszkai, R., Mocanu, D., Bogateanu, G., & Dafarra, S. (2025). Physical and digital GenAI avatars: Do interactive representations of individual human persons have agency and moral responsibility? In *Social Robots with AI: Prospects, Risks, and Responsible Methods* (pp. 591-597). IOS Press.

D'Mello, J., Gupta, A., & Timanani, D. D. P. (2024). Leveraging generative AI for personal branding. In *Predictive Analytics and Generative AI for Data-Driven Marketing Strategies* (pp. 265–274). Chapman and Hall/CRC. DOI: 10.1201/9781003472544-23

Dang, N. (2025). The Influence of AI-Generated Visual Content on Influencer Marketing Strategies in Social Media. *Reviews on Internet of Things (IoT). Cyber-Physical Systems, and Applications*, *10*(3), 1–18.

Dolata, M., Lange, N., & Schwabe, G. (2025, April). More Attention, Transformation, Acceleration, and Exploration: Freelance Developers' Take on Hypes. In *Proceedings of the 2025 CHI Conference on Human Factors in Computing Systems* (pp. 1-21). DOI: 10.1145/3706598.3713097

Duan, W., McNeese, N., Freeman, G., & Li, L. (2024). Mitigating gender stereotypes toward AI agents through an eXplainable AI (XAI) approach. *Proceedings of the ACM on Human-Computer Interaction*, 8(CSCW2), 1-35. DOI: 10.1145/3686969

Duffy, B. E., & Meisner, C. (2022). Platform governance at the margins: Social media creators' experiences with algorithmic (in)visibility. *Media Culture & Society, 45*(2), 285–304. DOI: 10.1177/01634437221111923

Foka, A. (2024). *She works, he works: A curious exploration of gender bias in AI-generated imagery*. arXiv preprint arXiv:2407.18524.

Gibson, J. J. (1977). The theory of affordances. In Shaw, R. E., & Bransford, J. (Eds.), *Perceiving, acting, and knowing* (pp. 67–82). Lawrence Erlbaum Associates.

Giles, H. (2008). Communication accommodation theory. In Baxter, L. A., & Braithewaite, D. O. (Eds.), *Engaging theories in interpersonal communication: Multiple perspectives* (pp. 161–173). Sage Publications, Inc., DOI: 10.4135/9781483329529.n12

Gillespie, T. (2024). Generative AI and the politics of visibility. *Big Data & Society, 11*(2), 20539517241252131. DOI: 10.1177/20539517241252131

Goffman, E. (1959). *The presentation of self in everyday life*. Anchor Books.

Hochschild, A. R. (1983). *The managed heart: Commercialization of human feeling*. University of California Press.

Hossain, S. F. A. (Ed.). (2024). *Utilizing AI and Smart Technology to Improve Sustainability in Entrepreneurship*. IGI Global. DOI: 10.4018/979-8-3693-1842-3

Hosseini, D. D. (2024). *Generative AI: A problematic illustration of the intersections of racialized gender, race, ethnicity*. DOI: 10.31219/osf.io/987ra

Hu, X., Xu, X., & Chen, C. (2025). Empowering consumers: The role of avatar choice in consumer-chatbot interaction and psychological ownership. *International Journal of Human-Computer Interaction, 41*(24), 1–12. DOI: 10.1080/10447318.2025.2495845

Jawad, M., Talreja, K., Bhutto, S. A., & Faizan, K. (2024). Investigating how AI personalization algorithms influence self-perception, group identity, and social interactions online. *Review of Applied Management and Social Sciences, 7*(4), 533–550. DOI: 10.47067/ramss.v7i4.397

Kuteeva, M., & Andersson, M. (2024). Diversity and Standards in Writing for Publication in the Age of AI—Between a Rock and a Hard Place. *Applied Linguistics, 45*(3), 561–567. DOI: 10.1093/applin/amae025

Langley, N. A. (2025). *The AI Advantage: Transform Your Career and Business*. eBookIt. com.

Lively, J., & Hutson, J. (2025). Enhancing Digital Pedagogy and Creativity: Generative AI, Video Avatars, and Personalized Learning in Online Education. In *Human-Computer Creativity: Generative AI in Education, Art, and Healthcare* (pp. 99–113). Springer Nature Switzerland. DOI: 10.1007/978-3-031-86551-0_6

Markham, A. (2024). Algorithms as conversational partners: Looking at Google auto-predict through the lens of symbolic interaction. *New Media & Society*, *26*(9), 5059–5080. DOI: 10.1177/14614448241251800

Marwick, A. E., & Boyd, D. (2011). I tweet honestly, I tweet passionately: Twitter users, context collapse, and the imagined audience. *New Media & Society*, *13*(1), 114–133. DOI: 10.1177/1461444810365313

Mirzoeff, N. (2011). The right to look. *Critical Inquiry*, *37*(3), 473–496. DOI: 10.1086/659354

Mohamed, Y. A., Khanan, A., Bashir, M., Mohamed, A. H. H. M., Adiel, M. A. E., & Elsadig, M. A. (2024). The impact of artificial intelligence on language translation: A review. *IEEE Access : Practical Innovations, Open Solutions*, *12*, 25553–25579. DOI: 10.1109/ACCESS.2024.3366802

Nizamani, M., Ramzan, F., Fatima, M., & Asif, M. (2024). Investigating how frequent interactions with AI technologies impact cognitive and emotional processes. [BBE]. *Bulletin of Business and Economics*, *13*(3), 316–325.

Noble, S. U. (2018). Algorithms of oppression: How search engines reinforce racism. In *Algorithms of oppression*. New York University Press.

Norman, D. A. (1999). Affordance, conventions, and design. *Interactions (New York, N.Y.)*, *6*(3), 38–43. DOI: 10.1145/301153.301168

Parker, L., Hassan, O., & Davis, C. (2025). The Role of Generative AI in the Future of Commercial Personalization. *Journal of Electronic Commerce Management*, *1*, 1–16.

Perrotta, C., Selwyn, N., & Ewin, C. (2024). Artificial intelligence and the affective labour of understanding: The intimate moderation of a language model. *New Media & Society*, *26*(3), 1585–1609. DOI: 10.1177/14614448221075296

Popa, R. G., & Chenic, A. S. (2025). Artificial Intelligence, Consumer Trust and the Promotion of Pro-Environmental Behavior Among Youth. *Sustainability (Basel)*, *17*(13), 5885. DOI: 10.3390/su17135885

Prakash, K. S. V. S., Bhavana, S., Lasya, P. V. A., Kumar, D. G., Putalapattu, B., Amareswari, V., & Gayathri, K. (2025). The influence of AI on creative writing and its implications for management communication. *International Journal of Research Publication and Reviews*, *6*(2), 722–727. DOI: 10.55248/gengpi.6.0225.0731

Pulatovna, K. U. (2024). AI in Education: Enhancing Teacher-student Interactions and Motivation. *European Journal of Humanities and Educational Advancements*, *5*(1), 113–115.

Shukla, S. S., Bajpai, S., Pramanik, S., & Waller, S. (2025). From Micro-Influencers to AI: The Future of Influencer Marketing in a Tech-Driven Era. In *Leveraging AI-Powered Marketing in the Experience-Driven Economy* (pp. 419-440). IGI Global Scientific Publishing.

Siddiqui, R., Tariq, A., Mariyam, F., Kumar, A., & Khan, N. (2025). Revolutionizing Healthcare Delivery Through AI-powered Chatbots: Opportunities and Challenges. *International Journal of Innovative Research in Computer Science and Technology*, *13*(3), 109–119. Advance online publication. DOI: 10.55524/ijircst.2025.13.3.18

Simbeck, K. (2024). They shall be fair, transparent, and robust: Auditing learning analytics systems. *AI and Ethics*, *4*(2), 555–571. DOI: 10.1007/s43681-023-00292-7

Sindoni, M. G. (2024). The femininization of AI-powered voice assistants: Personification, anthropomorphism and discourse ideologies. *Discourse, Context & Media*, *62*, 100833. DOI: 10.1016/j.dcm.2024.100833

Srnicek, N. (2017). *Platform capitalism*. Polity Press.

Tajfel, H., & Turner, J. C. (1979). An integrative theory of inter-group conflict. In Austin, W. G., & Worchel, S. (Eds.), *The social psychology of inter-group relations* (pp. 33–47). Brooks/Cole.

Tuğer, A. T. (2024). AI and service encounters. In *Handbook of services and artificial intelligence* (pp. 119–142). Edward Elgar Publishing., DOI: 10.4337/9781035301973.00016

Vallor, S. (2024). *The AI mirror: How to reclaim our humanity in an age of machine thinking*. Oxford University Press. DOI: 10.1093/oso/9780197759066.001.0001

Van Dijck, J. (2024). Governing platforms and societies. *Platforms & Society*, *1*, 29768624241255922. Advance online publication. DOI: 10.1177/29768624241255922

Venkataramanan, S., Sadhu, A. K. R., Gudala, L., & Reddy, A. K. (2024). Leveraging Artificial Intelligence for Enhanced Sales Forecasting Accuracy: A Review of AI-Driven Techniques and Practical Applications in Customer Relationship Management Systems. *Journal of Machine Learning Research*, *4*, 267–287.

Wei, X., Kumar, N., & Zhang, H. (2025). Addressing bias in generative AI: Challenges and research opportunities in information management. *Information & Management*, *62*(2), 104103. DOI: 10.1016/j.im.2025.104103

West, S. M., Whittaker, M., & Crawford, K. (2019). *Discriminating systems*. AI Now Institute. https://ainowinstitute.org

Compilation of References

Åberg-Bengtsson, L. (2009). Home economics education in the Nordic countries: Trends and traditions. *Scandinavian Journal of Educational Research*, *53*(5), 449–465.

Ailon, G. (2008). Mirror, mirror on the wall: Culture's consequences in a value test of its own design. *Academy of Management Review*, *33*(4), 885–904. DOI: 10.5465/amr.2008.34421995

Aitchison, G., & Meckled-Garcia, S. (2021). Against Online Public Shaming: Ethical Problems with Mass Social Media. [JSTOR.]. *Social Theory and Practice*, *47*(1), 1–31. DOI: 10.5840/soctheorpract20201117109

Al A'Ali, E. & Alazali 2018) . Gender Differences in Relation to organization Sources of power: An exploratory Research of individuals and Contextual issues in E. Al A'Ali, M. Al-Shammari & H. Masri (Eds.)Arab Women and Their Evolving Roles in the Global Business Landscape (pp.1-25). IGI GlOBAL. DOI:DOI: 10.4018/9781-1-5225-3710-6.ch001

Al A'Ali, E., Masmoudi, M., & AlSaffar, G. (2024). Women Leadership in Digital Era: The Competency Model. In Al A'Ali, E., Masmoudi, M., & AlSaffar, G. (Eds.), *Transformative Roles of Women in Public and Private Sectors* (pp. 18–30). IGI GLOBAL., DOI: 10.4018/979-8-3693-3208-5.ch002

Al-A'ali, E. (1991) The phenomenon of women in Management: An alternative perspective and its implication in the case of Bahrain (Lancaster, U.K. University of Lancaster, unpublished Ph.D. thesis)

Alexander, L. (2025). *Multimodal Analysis For Candidate Assessment*. ResearchGate.

Ali, A. (1995). Cultural discontinuity and Arab management thought. *International Studies of Management & Organization*, *25*(3), 7–30. DOI: 10.1080/00208825.1995.11656657

Al-Rasheed, A. M. (2001). Features of traditional Arab management and organization in the Jordan business environment. *Journal of Transnational Management Development*, *6*(1), 53–68.

AlSaffar, G., & Al A'ali, E. (2021), Psyciatry in the Midst of the Pandemic: A narrative perspective in E. Al-A'Ali & M. Masmoudi, (Eds.), Global perspective on Change Management and Leadership in the Post-COVID-19 Era. (pp. 24-34). IGI GLOBAL. DOI:DOI: 10.4018/978-1-7998-6948-1.ch.2

Al-Shatti, E., & Ohana, M. (2021). Impression management and career-related outcomes: A systematic literature review. *Frontiers in Psychology*, *12*, 1–12. DOI: 10.3389/fpsyg.2021.701694 PMID: 34393939

Al-Shatti, E., Ohana, M., Odou, P., & Zaitouni, M. (2022). Impression Management on Instagram and Unethical Behavior: The Role of Gender and Social Media Fatigue. *International Journal of Environmental Research and Public Health*, *19*(16), 9808. DOI: 10.3390/ijerph19169808 PMID: 36011435

Amah, O. E. (2022). The relationship between political will and organizational, political behavior: The moderating roles of political prudence and political skill. *Journal of Business Ethics*, *176*, 341–355. DOI: 10.1007/s10551-020-04696-x

Andreassen, C. S., Pallesen, S., & Griffiths, M. D. (2017). The relationship between addictive use of social media, narcissism, and self-esteem: Findings from a large national survey. *Addictive Behaviors*, *64*, 287–293. DOI: 10.1016/j.addbeh.2016.03.006

Appel, G., Grewal, L., Hadi, R., & Stephen, A T. (2020). The future of social media in marketing. *Journal of the Academy of Marketing Science*, 48, 79-95.

Argyle, M. (1988). *Bodily communication* (2nd ed.). Methuen.

Baker, R. T., & Gower, K. (2010). Strategic Application of Storytelling in Organizations: Toward Effective Communication in a Diverse World. The Journal of Business Communication (1973), 47(3), 295-312. ,DOI: 10.1177/0021943610369782

Barakat, H. (1993). *The Arab world: Society, culture, and state*. University of California Press. DOI: 10.1525/9780520914421

Baugher, S. L., Anderson, C. L., Green, K. B., Nickols, S. Y., Shane, J., Jolly, L., & Miles, J. (2003). *Body of knowledge of family and consumer sciences*. American Association of Family and Consumer Sciences.

Belk, R. W. (2013). Extended Self in a Digital World. *Journal of Consumer Research, 40*(3), 477–500. JSTOR. DOI: 10.1086/671052

Belk, R. W. (1988). Possessions and the Extended Self. [JSTOR.]. *The Journal of Consumer Research, 15*(2), 139–168. DOI: 10.1086/209154

Berman, E. M., Bowman, J. S., West, J. P., & Van Wart, M. R. (2016). *Human resource management in public service: Paradoxes, processes, and problems* (5th ed.). SAGE.

Berns, R. M. (2021). *Child, family, school, community: Socialization and support* (11th ed.). Cengage Learning.

Binkley, S. (2018). *The business of authenticity: An ethnography of post-industrial markets*. Routledge.

Blunden, H., & Brodsky, A. (2024). A Review of Virtual Impression Management Behaviors and Outcomes. *Journal of Management, 50*(6), 2197–2236. DOI: 10.1177/01492063231225160

Bohdanowicz, P., & Zientara, P. (2008). Corporate social responsibility in hospitality: Issues and implications. *Hospital Management, 27*(4), 724–738. DOI: 10.1016/j.ijhm.2007.09.001

Bois, S. (1978) The Art of Awareness (3rd Ed) Wm. C. Brown Company

Bolino, M. C., Kacmar, K. M., Turnley, W. H., & Gilstrap, J. B. (2008). A Multi-Level Review of Impression Management Motives and Behaviors. *Journal of Management, 34*(6), 1080–1109. DOI: 10.1177/0149206308324325

Bolino, M., Long, D., & Turnley, W. (2016). Impression management in organizations: Critical questions, answers, and areas for future research. *Annual Review of Organizational Psychology and Organizational Behavior, 3*(1), 377–406. DOI: 10.1146/annurev-orgpsych-041015-062337

Bolzonella, F. (2024). *Evaluating through culture: Rethinking Hofstede's framework in policy analysis*. European Evaluation Journal.

Bourdieu, P. (1984). *DIstInctIon: A Social Critique of the Judgement of Taste* (R. Nice, Trans.). Harvard University Press.

Bourdieu, P. (1984). *Distinction: A social critique of the judgement of taste* (R. Nice, Trans.). Harvard University Press. (Original work published 1979).

Boxall, P. (1994). Placing HR strategy at the heart of business success. *Personnel Management, 26*(7), 32–35.

Boyd, d. (2014). *It's complicated: The social lives of networked teens.* Yale University Press.

Boyle, G. J. (1991). Does item homogeneity indicate internal consistency or item redundancy in psychometric scales? *Personality and Individual Differences*, *12*(3), 291–294. DOI: 10.1016/0191-8869(91)90115-R

Bozdağ, A. A. (2025). The AI-mediated intimacy economy: A paradigm shift in digital interactions. *AI & Society*, *40*(4), 2285–2306. DOI: 10.1007/s00146-024-02132-6

Bozeman, D. P., & Kacmar, K. M. (1997). A Cybernetic Model of Impression Management Processes in Organizations. *Organizational Behavior and Human Decision Processes*, *69*(1), 9–30. DOI: 10.1006/obhd.1996.2669

Brouer, R. L., Gallagher, V. C., & Badawy, R. L. (2016). Ability to Manage Resources in the Impression Management Process: The Mediating Effects of Resources on Job Performance. *Journal of Business and Psychology*, *31*(4), 515–531. DOI: 10.1007/s10869-015-9426-5

Brubaker, R. (2020). Digital hyperconnectivity and the self. *Theory and Society*, *49*(5), 771–801. DOI: 10.1007/s11186-020-09405-1

Brüns, J. D., & Meißner, M. (2024). Do you create your content yourself? Using generative artificial intelligence for social media content creation diminishes perceived brand authenticity. *Journal of Retailing and Consumer Services*, *79*, 103790. DOI: 10.1016/j.jretconser.2024.103790

Bucher, T., & Helmond, A. (2018). The affordances of social media platforms. *The SAGE handbook of social media, 1*(1), 233-253.

Budhwar, P., & Mellahi, K. (2012). Human resource management in the Middle East. In Brewster, C., & Mayrhofer, W. (Eds.), *Handbook of research on comparative human resource management* (pp. 504–523). Edward Elgar Publishing., DOI: 10.4337/9780857938718.00029

Burgoon, J. K., Guerrero, L. K., & Floyd, K. (2016). *Nonverbal communication* (2nd ed.). Routledge. DOI: 10.4324/9781315663425

Cannon, C., & Rucker, D. D. (2019). The Dark Side of Luxury: Social Costs of Luxury Consumption. *Personality and Social Psychology Bulletin*, *45*(5), 767–779. DOI: 10.1177/0146167218796790

Cetin, O. I. (2020). Investigation of the relationship between attitude and impression management in university students. *Journal of Management* [JMML]. *Marketing and Logistics*, *7*(2), 81–90.

Chang, E. C. C., & Chu, Y. (2006). Corruption and Trust: Exceptionalism in Asian Democracies? *The Journal of Politics, 68*(2), 259–271. JSTOR. DOI: 10.1111/j.1468-2508.2006.00404.x

Chen, Y., Yang, X., Wang, L., & Zhang, X. (2021). Exploring the motivational mechanisms underlying social media use: A Self-Determination Theory approach. *Frontiers in Psychology*, *12*, 653859.

Cheong, P. H., & Gong, J. (2010). Cyber vigilantism, transmedia collective intelligence, and civic participation. *Chinese Journal of Communication*, *3*(4), 471–487. DOI: 10.1080/17544750.2010.516580

Chou, H. T. G., & Edge, N. (2012). "They are happier and having better lives than I am": The impact of using Facebook on perceptions of others' lives. *Cyberpsychology, Behavior, and Social Networking*, *15*(2), 117–12. DOI: 10.1089/cyber.2011.0324 PMID: 22165917

Chuang, Y.-T., Chiang, H.-L., & Lin, A.-P. (2025). Insights from the Job Demands–Resources Model: AI's dual impact on employees' work and life well-being. *International Journal of Information Management*, *83*, 102887. DOI: 10.1016/j.ijinfomgt.2025.102887

Cleff, T. (2014). *Exploratory data analysis in business and economics: An introduction using SPSS, Stata, and Excel*. Springer. DOI: 10.1007/978-3-319-01517-0

Cohen, E., & Avieli, N. (2004). Food in tourism: Attraction and impediment. *Annals of Tourism Research, 31*(4), 755–778. DOI: 10.1016/j.annals.2004.02.003

Constantinescu, M., Uszkai, R., Mocanu, D., Bogateanu, G., & Dafarra, S. (2025). Physical and digital GenAI avatars: Do interactive representations of individual human persons have agency and moral responsibility? In *Social Robots with AI: Prospects, Risks, and Responsible Methods* (pp. 591-597). IOS Press.

Coon, D., Mitterer, J. O., & Martini, T. S. (2019). *Introduction to Psychology: Gateways to Mind and Behavior* (15th ed.). Cengage Learning.

Costanza, D. P., Badger, J. M., Fraser, R. L., Severt, J. B., & Gade, P. A. (2012). Generational differences in work-related attitudes: A meta-analysis. *Journal of Business and Psychology*, *27*(4), 375–394. DOI: 10.1007/s10869-012-9259-4

Creswell, J. W., & Creswell, J. D. (2017). *Research design: Qualitative, quantitative, and mixed methods approaches* (5th ed.). SAGE Publications.

Cronbach, L. J. (1951). Coefficient alpha and the internal structure of tests. *Psychometrika*, *16*(3), 297–334. DOI: 10.1007/BF02310555

Curtis, S. R., Carre, J. R., Mueller, S. M., & Jones, D. N. (2023). Hiding your dark side: Anticipatory impression management of communal traits. *Current Psychology (New Brunswick, N.J.)*, *42*(22), 18720–18730. DOI: 10.1007/s12144-022-03039-5

d'Iribarne, P. (2009). National cultures and organizations in search of a theory: An interpretative approach. *International Journal of Cross Cultural Management*, *9*(3), 309–321. DOI: 10.1177/1470595809346601

D'Mello, J., Gupta, A., & Timanani, D. D. P. (2024). Leveraging generative AI for personal branding. In *Predictive Analytics and Generative AI for Data-Driven Marketing Strategies* (pp. 265–274). Chapman and Hall/CRC. DOI: 10.1201/9781003472544-23

Dang, N. (2025). The Influence of AI-Generated Visual Content on Influencer Marketing Strategies in Social Media. *Reviews on Internet of Things (IoT). Cyber-Physical Systems, and Applications*, *10*(3), 1–18.

de Gelder, A. (2019). Impression management: Coping with organizational demands: A study investigating the effects of organizational climate and HR attributions on impression management behaviours and stress. http://arno.uvt.nl/show.cgi?fid=150343

de Oliveira Leite, R., Dias, R., & Mendes, L. (2021). Morality and Perception of Corruption. *Latin American Business Review*, *22*(2), 163–188. DOI: 10.1080/10978526.2020.1777558

Deal, J. J. (2007). *Retiring the generation gap: How employees young and old can find common ground*. John Wiley & Sons.

Debus, M. E. (2024). Ingold, Pia V.; Gross, C.; & Bolino, M.C., (2024). Researching the top? Profile of impression Management and Career. *Journal of Business and Psychology*, *39*, 1284–1301. DOI: 10.1007/s10869-024-09954-7

Deng, H., Walter, F., & Guan, Y. (2020). Supervisor-directed emotional labor as upward influence: An emotions-as-social-information perspective. *Journal of Organizational Behavior*, *41*(4), 384–402. DOI: 10.1002/job.2424

Dhir, A., Yossatorn, Y., Kaur, P., & Chen, S. (2018). Online social media fatigue and psychological well-being—A study of compulsive use, fear of missing out, fatigue, anxiety, and depression. *International Journal of Information Management*, *40*, 141–152. DOI: 10.1016/j.ijinfomgt.2018.01.012

Dolata, M., Lange, N., & Schwabe, G. (2025, April). More Attention, Transformation, Acceleration, and Exploration: Freelance Developers' Take on Hypes. In *Proceedings of the 2025 CHI Conference on Human Factors in Computing Systems* (pp. 1-21). DOI: 10.1145/3706598.3713097

Drory, A., & Zaidman, N. (2007). Impression management behaviour: Effects of the organizational system. *Journal of Managerial Psychology*, *22*(3), 290–308. DOI: 10.1108/02683940710733106

Duan, W., McNeese, N., Freeman, G., & Li, L. (2024). Mitigating gender stereotypes toward AI agents through an eXplainable AI (XAI) approach. *Proceedings of the ACM on Human-Computer Interaction*, 8(CSCW2), 1-35. DOI: 10.1145/3686969

Duffy, B. E., & Chan, N. K. (2019). "You never really know who's looking": Imagined surveillance across social media platforms. *New Media & Society*, *21*(1), 119–138. DOI: 10.1177/1461444818791318

Duffy, B. E., & Meisner, C. (2022). Platform governance at the margins: Social media creators' experiences with algorithmic (in)visibility. *Media Culture & Society*, *45*(2), 285–304. DOI: 10.1177/01634437221111923

Edeh, F. O., Zayed, N. M., Darwish, S., Nitsenko, V., Hanechko, I., & Islam, K. M. A. (2023) Impression Management and Employee Contextual Performance in service Organizations (Enterprises).Emerging Science Journal. Vol.7, No. 2, April, 2023. DOI: http://dx. Doi. Org/DOI: 10.28991/ESJ-2023-07-02-05

Ellis, A., Park, E., Kim, S., & Yeoman, I. (2018). What is food tourism? *Tourism Management*, *68*, 250–263. DOI: 10.1016/j.tourman.2018.03.025

Entwistle, J. (2015). *The fashioned body: Fashion, dress and modern social theory* (2nd ed.). Polity Press.

Ericksen, P. J. (2008). Conceptualizing food systems for global environmental change research. *Global Environmental Change*, *18*(1), 234–245. DOI: 10.1016/j.gloenvcha.2007.09.002

Everett, S., & Slocum, S. L. (2013). Food and tourism: An effective partnership? A UK-based review. *Journal of Sustainable Tourism*, *21*(6), 789–809. DOI: 10.1080/09669582.2012.741601

Ferraro, R., Escalas, J. E., & Bettman, J. R. (2011). Our possessions, our selves: Domains of self-worth and the possession–self link. *Journal of Consumer Psychology*, *21*(2), 169–177. DOI: 10.1016/j.jcps.2010.08.007

Foka, A. (2024). *She works, he works: A curious exploration of gender bias in AI-generated imagery*. arXiv preprint arXiv:2407.18524.

Food and Agriculture Organization of the United Nations (FAO). (2021). *The State of Food Security and Nutrition in the World 2021: Transforming food systems for food security, improved nutrition and affordable healthy diets for all*. FAO.

Fox, J., & Rooney, M. C. (2015). The Dark Triad and trait self-objectification as predictors of men's use and self-presentation behaviors on social networking sites. *Personality and Individual Differences, 76*, 161–165. DOI: 10.1016/j.paid.2014.12.017

Freeman, R. E., Harrison, J. S., Wicks, A. C., Parmar, B., & De Colle, S. (2010). *Stakeholder theory: The state of the art*. Cambridge University Press. DOI: 10.1017/CBO9780511815768

Gadgil, G., Prybutok, G., Peak, D., & Prybutok, V. (2021). Modeling the hidden mediating relationships between SNS privacy and SNS impression construction. *Computers in Human Behavior, 125*, 106941. DOI: 10.1016/j.chb.2021.106941

Ganda, M. (2014). Social media and self: Influences on the formation of identity and understanding of self through social networking sites. *University Honors Theses*, Paper 55.

Gardner, W. L., & Avolio, B. J. (1998). The charismatic relationship: A dramaturgical perspective. *Academy of Management Review, 23*(1), 32–58. DOI: 10.2307/259098

Geeth, S., Chandran, J. C., & Sheethal, D. (2024). Effectiveness of impression management in improving the work experience of casual workers. *Advancing Knowledge from Multidisciplinary Perspectives in Engineering, Technology, and Management*, 70-80. https://www.rubiconpublications.com/

Gibson, J. J. (1977). The theory of affordances. In Shaw, R. E., & Bransford, J. (Eds.), *Perceiving, acting, and knowing* (pp. 67–82). Lawrence Erlbaum Associates.

Giddens, A. (1984). *The Constitution of Society—Outline of the Theory of Structuration*. Polity Press.

Giles, H. (2008). Communication accommodation theory. In Baxter, L. A., & Braithewaite, D. O. (Eds.), *Engaging theories in interpersonal communication: Multiple perspectives* (pp. 161–173). Sage Publications, Inc., DOI: 10.4135/9781483329529.n12

Gillespie, T. (2024). Generative AI and the politics of visibility. *Big Data & Society, 11*(2), 20539517241252131. DOI: 10.1177/20539517241252131

Goffman, E. (1956). *The Presentation of Self in Everyday Life*. University of Edinburgh Social Sciences Research Center.

Goffman, E. (1959). *The presentation of self in everyday life*. Anchor Books.

Goffman, E. (1959). *The Presentation of Self in Everyday Life. Doubleday: Garden City, New York, 1959*. Doubleday.

Goffman, E. (1963). *Behavior in public places: Notes on the social organization of gatherings*. Macmillan Publishing Co.

Goffman, E. (1963). *Stigma: Notes on the management of spoiled identity*. Prentice-Hall.

Goffman, E. (1967). *Interaction ritual: Essays in face-to-face behavior*. Aldine.

Goffman, E. (1969). *Strategic interaction*. University of Pennsylvania Press.

Goffman, E. (1971). *Relations in public: Microstudies of the public order*. Basic Books.

Goffman, E. (1974). *Frame analysis: An essay on the organization of experience*. Harvard University Press.

Goffman, E. (1981). *Forms of talk*. University of Pennsylvania Press.

Goleman, D. (1998). *Working with emotional intelligence*. Bantam Books.

Gössling, S., & Hall, C. M. (2019). *Sustainable hospitality and tourism as motors for development: Case studies from developing regions*. Routledge.

Gössling, S., Hall, C. M., & Scott, D. (2016). *Tourism and sustainability: Principles to practice* (4th ed.). Routledge.

Gran, A.-B. (2025). Performing not-not-me in SoMe: A new theatrical typology of self-presentation online. *Social Media + Society*, *11*(1), 20563051251315256. DOI: 10.1177/20563051251315256

Greig, M. A., & Hogg, R. C. (2025). 'Unfollow Them!': The Role of Morality- and Emotion-Related Factors in the Cancelling Process. *Human Behavior and Emerging Technologies*, *2025*(1), 7144903. DOI: 10.1155/hbe2/7144903

Groth, M., & Grandey, A. A. (2012). From bad to worse: Negative exchange spirals in employee–customer service interactions. *Organizational Psychology Review*, 2(3), 208–233. DOI: 10.1177/2041386612441735

Guadagno, R. E. & Cialdini, R. B. (2007) Gender Differences in Impression Management is in Organizations: A qualitative Review in Sex Roles published by Springer Natur, 56(7):483-494.DOI:DOI: 10.1007s11199-007-9187-3

Gwal R. (2015). Tactics of Impression Management: Relative Success on Workplace Relationship. International Journal of Indian Psychology, 2 (2), DOI: , DIP: 18.01.064/20140202DOI: 10.25215/0202.064

Haidt, J. (2001). The emotional dog and its rational tail: A social intuitionist approach to moral judgment. *Psychological Review, 108*(4), 814–834. *Scopus*. Advance online publication. DOI: 10.1037/0033-295X.108.4.814

Haidt, J., & Joseph, C. (2004). Intuitive ethics: How innately prepared intuitions generate culturally variable virtues. *Daedalus, 133*(4), 55–65. *Scopus*. Advance online publication. DOI: 10.1162/0011526042365555

Hall, C. M., & Gössling, S. (2017). *Food tourism and regional development: Networks, products and trajectories*. Routledge.

Hall, E. T. (1976). *Beyond culture*. Anchor Books.

Halpern, C., & Donaghey, J. (2018). *Social and emotional learning in action: Experiential activities to teach empathy, decision-making, and interpersonal skills*. Routledge.

Han, Y. J., Nunes, J. C., & Drèze, X. (2010). Signaling Status with Luxury Goods: The Role of Brand Prominence. *Journal of Marketing, 74*(4), 15–30. DOI: 10.1509/jmkg.74.4.015

Hede, A. M., & Watne, T. (2013). Leveraging the human side of sustainability in hospitality through local sourcing and social entrepreneurship. *International Journal of Hospitality Management, 34*, 108–116. DOI: 10.1016/j.ijhm.2013.02.002

Henderson, A. (2017). Impression Management. In *The International Encyclopedia of Organizational Communication* (pp. 1–6). Wiley., DOI: 10.1002/9781118955567.wbieoc104

Hennig, M., & Jardin, M. (1977). *The Managerial Women*. John Wiley and Sons Inc.

Hitch, E. J., & Youatt, J. P. (2002). *Communicating family and consumer sciences: A guidebook for professionals*. Goodheart-Willcox.

Hjalager, A. M., & Richards, G. (2002). *Tourism and gastronomy*. Routledge.

Hochschild, A. R. (1983). *The managed heart: Commercialization of human feeling*. University of California Press.

Hofstede, G., & Minkov, M. (2013). *Values survey module 2013 manual*. GeertHofstede.com. https://geerthofstede.com/research-and-vsm/

Hofstede, G. (1984). *Culture's consequences: International differences in work-related values* (2nd ed.). SAGE.

Hofstede, G. (2002). Dimensions do not exist: A reply to Brendan McSweeney. *Journal of Technological Advancements*, *55*(11), 1355–1361. DOI: 10.1177/0018726702055011921

Hofstede, G., & Minkov, M. (2010). *Cultures and organizations: Software of the mind* (3rd ed.). McGraw-Hill.

Hogan, B. (2010). The presentation of self in the age of social media: Distinguishing performances and exhibitions online. *Bulletin of Science, Technology & Society*, *30*(6), 377–386. DOI: 10.1177/0270467610385893

Hossain, S. F. A. (Ed.). (2024). *Utilizing AI and Smart Technology to Improve Sustainability in Entrepreneurship*. IGI Global. DOI: 10.4018/979-8-3693-1842-3

Hosseini, D. D. (2024). *Generative AI: A problematic illustration of the intersections of racialized gender, race, ethnicity*. DOI: 10.31219/osf.io/987ra

Huigen, B. (2025). Vulgar things: Moral dilemmas of luxury consumption in an unequal society. *Journal of Consumer Culture*, *14695405251376100*(4), 385–404. Advance online publication. DOI: 10.1177/14695405251376100

Hu, X., Xu, X., & Chen, C. (2025). Empowering consumers: The role of avatar choice in consumer-chatbot interaction and psychological ownership. *International Journal of Human-Computer Interaction*, *41*(24), 1–12. DOI: 10.1080/10447318.2025.2495845

Hybels, S., & Weaver, R. L. (2005). *Communicating effectively* (7th ed.). McGraw-Hill.

International Federation for Home Economics. (2008). *Home economics in the 21st century: IFHE position statement.* https://www.ifhe.org/fileadmin/user_upload/e_ifhe/policy/IFHE_Position_Statement_2008.pdf

International Federation for Home Economics. (n.d.). *About home economics.* https://www.ifhe.org/about-us/about-home/economics

Jackson, T. (2020). Towards a framework for understanding cross-cultural management learning and education. *International Journal of Management Reviews*, *22*(3), 279–297. DOI: 10.1111/ijmr.12234

Jawad, M., Talreja, K., Bhutto, S. A., & Faizan, K. (2024). Investigating how AI personalization algorithms influence self-perception, group identity, and social interactions online. *Review of Applied Management and Social Sciences*, *7*(4), 533–550. DOI: 10.47067/ramss.v7i4.397

Jehn, K. A., Northcraft, G. B., & Neale, M. A. (1999). Why differences make a difference: A field study of diversity, conflict, and performance in workgroups. *Administrative Science Quarterly*, *44*(4), 741–763. DOI: 10.2307/2667054

Ji, X., Li, C., Law, R., & Liu, X. (2025). Profile image album management and users' online sharing behavior. *Tourism Management, 109*, 105159. DOI: 10.1016/j.tourman.2025.105159

Jones, E., & Pittman, T. (1982). Toward a General Theory of Strategic Self Presentation. In psychological perspectives on Self. In Souls, I. J. (Ed.), (pp. 231–262). Hillsdale Lawrence Erlbaum Assoc.

Jones, P., Hillier, D., & Comfort, D. (2021). Sustainability in the global hotel industry. *International Journal of Contemporary Hospitality Management, 33*(6), 1999–2016. DOI: 10.1108/IJCHM-09-2020-1053

Joshi, A., Dencker, J. C., & Franz, G. (2011). Generations in organizations. *Research in Organizational Behavior, 31*, 177–205. DOI: 10.1016/j.riob.2011.10.002

Kaiser, S. B. (2012). *Fashion and cultural studies*. Berg Publishers.

Kapoutsis, I. (2017). Playing the political game at work: The roles of political will, political prudence and political skill. In Vigoda-Gadot, E., & Drory, A. (Eds.), *Handbook of Organizational Politics: Looking Back and to the Future* (pp. 40–58). Edward Elgar Publishing.

Kato, S. L. (2008). *Foundations of family and consumer sciences: Careers serving individuals, families, and communities*. Goodheart-Willcox.

Kelman, H. C. (1958). Compliance, identification, and internalization three processes of attitude change. *The Journal of Conflict Resolution, 2*(1), 51–60. DOI: 10.1177/002200275800200106

Kim, H., & Baker, M. (2019). The impact of emotional labor on customer satisfaction and organizational outcomes in hospitality. *International Journal of Hospitality Management, 81*, 1–10. DOI: 10.1016/j.ijhm.2019.02.003

Kim, J., & Lee, H. (2011). The effect of impression management on social networking site usage and social capital: Focusing on college students. *Journal of Social Media Studies, 8*(2), 45–62.

Kipnis, D., Schmidt, S. M., & Wilkinson, I. (1980). Intraorganizational influence tactics: Explorations in getting one's way. *The Journal of Applied Psychology, 65*(4), 440–452. DOI: 10.1037/0021-9010.65.4.440

Klotz, A. C., Bolino, M. C., Song, H., & Stornelli, J. (2017). Examining the nature, causes, and consequences of profiles of organizational citizenship behavior. *Journal of Organizational Behavior, 39*(5), 629–647. DOI: 10.1002/job.2259

Komisarof, A., & Akaliyski, P. (2025). New developments in Hofstede's individualism–collectivism: A guide for scholars, educators, trainers, and other practitioners. *International Journal of Intercultural Relations, 107*, 102200. Advance online publication. DOI: 10.1016/j.ijintrel.2025.102200

Koslowsky, M., Pindek, S., & Reizer, A. (2022). Impression Management in Everyday Life. In *Theories in Social Psychology* (2nd ed., pp. 350–371). Wiley., DOI: 10.1002/9781394266616.ch14

Kristensen, N. N., & Jerslev, A. (2025). When influencer logic and news media logic converge in the scandalisation of an influencer: The exposure of literary critic and influencer Katherine Diez's plagiarism. *Nordic Journal of Media Studies, 7*(1), 93–111. DOI: 10.2478/njms-2025-0006

Kurt, Y. (2022). MANAGING IMPRESSION IN THE WORKPLACE: A RESEARCH ON AIRPORT PROFESSIONALS. *International Journal of Aviation, Aeronautics, and Aerospace, 9*(2). Advance online publication. DOI: 10.15394/ijaaa.2022.1687

Kuteeva, M., & Andersson, M. (2024). Diversity and Standards in Writing for Publication in the Age of AI—Between a Rock and a Hard Place. *Applied Linguistics, 45*(3), 561–567. DOI: 10.1093/applin/amae025

Langley, N. A. (2025). *The AI Advantage: Transform Your Career and Business*. eBookIt. com.

Larwood, L., & Wood, M. (1977) women in Management. Lexington: Lexington Books

Leary, M. R., & Kowalski, R. M. (1990). Impression management: A literature review and two-component model. *Psychological Bulletin, 107*(1), 34–47. DOI: 10.1037/0033-2909.107.1.34

Leaver, T., Highfield, T., & Abidin, C. (2020). *Instagram: Visual social media cultures*. Polity Press.

Lee, J., Park, H., & Kim, S. (2022). Impression management and professional communication in workplace meetings. *International Journal of Business Communication*. Advance online publication.

Liu, F., Chow, I. H., & Huang, M. (2019). Increasing Compulsory Citizenship Behavior and Workload: Does Impression Management Matter? *Frontiers in Psychology, 10*, 1726. Advance online publication. DOI: 10.3389/fpsyg.2019.01726 PMID: 31402890

Liu, Y., & Lei, K. (2025). Development and validity test of impression management efficacy scale based on self-presentation behavior of Chinese youth on social media. *Frontiers in Psychology*, *16*, 1494083. Advance online publication. DOI: 10.3389/fpsyg.2025.1494083 PMID: 39950071

Lively, J., & Hutson, J. (2025). Enhancing Digital Pedagogy and Creativity: Generative AI, Video Avatars, and Personalized Learning in Online Education. In *Human-Computer Creativity: Generative AI in Education, Art, and Healthcare* (pp. 99–113). Springer Nature Switzerland. DOI: 10.1007/978-3-031-86551-0_6

Livingstone, S. (2014). Developing social media literacy: How children learn to interpret risky opportunities on social network sites. *Communications*, *39*(3), 283–303. DOI: 10.1515/commun-2014-0113

Loden, M., & Rosener, J. B. (1991). *Workforce America! Managing employee diversity as a vital resource*. McGraw-Hill.

Lutzky, U. (2021). "You keep saying you are sorry". Exploring the use of sorry in customer communication on Twitter. *Discourse, Context & Media*, *39*, 100463. DOI: 10.1016/j.dcm.2020.100463

Macauley, R., Williams, E., Reardon, R., Kind, T., & Chretien, K. C. (2021). Medical professionalism in the age of social media: A revised review of ophthalmology resident and physician use and recommendations. *Journal of Academic Ophthalmology*, *13*(1), e28–e35.

Markham, A. (2024). Algorithms as conversational partners: Looking at Google auto-predict through the lens of symbolic interaction. *New Media & Society*, *26*(9), 5059–5080. DOI: 10.1177/14614448241251800

Marshall, J. (1984). *Women Managers: Travellers in a Male World*. John Wiley and Sons Inc.

Marwick, A. E. (2015). Instafame: Luxury selfies in the attention economy. *Public Culture, 27*(1), 137–160. *Scopus*. Advance online publication. DOI: 10.1215/08992363-2798379

Marwick, A. E., & boyd, . (2011). I tweet honestly, I tweet passionately: Twitter users, context collapse, and the imagined audience. *New Media & Society*, *13*(1), 114–133. DOI: 10.1177/1461444810365313

Marwick, A., & boyd, . (2011). To See and Be Seen: Celebrity Practice on Twitter. *Convergence (London)*, *17*(2), 139–158. DOI: 10.1177/1354856510394539

Maulana, I. (2025). *KeyText* (Version 0.16) [Computer software]. https://github.com/ikbaloss/KeyText

Maulana, I. (2018). Spontaneous taking and posting selfie: Reclaiming the lost trust. In *Selfies as a mode of social media and work space research* (pp. 28–50). IGI Global. DOI: 10.4018/978-1-5225-3373-3.ch002

Maulana, I. (2019). Big Brothers Are Seducing You: Consumerism, Surveillance, and the Agency of Consumers. In Ozgen, O. (Ed.), *Handbook of Research on Consumption, Media, and Popular Culture in the Global Age* (pp. 57–75). IGI Global. DOI: 10.4018/978-1-5225-8491-9.ch004

McFerran, B., Aquino, K., & Tracy, J. L. (2014). Evidence for two facets of pride in consumption: Findings from luxury brands. *Journal of Consumer Psychology*, *24*(4), 455–471. DOI: 10.1016/j.jcps.2014.03.004

McGowan, N. A., & Sekaja, L. (2022). A diary study of the impression management strategies utilised by industrial and organizational psychology interns. SA Journal of Industrial Psychology/SA Tydskrif vir Bedryfsielkunde, 48(0),a1902. DOI: 10.4102/sajip.v48i0.1902

McGregor, S. L. T. (2018). Understanding consumers' moral responsibility for sustainable consumption. *International Journal of Consumer Studies*, *42*(6), 588–597.

McSweeney, B. (2002). Hofstede's model of national cultural differences and their consequences: A triumph of faith—A failure of analysis. *Human Relations*, *55*(1), 89–118. DOI: 10.1177/0018726702551004

Mensah, I., & Julien, P. A. (2011). Implementation of food safety management systems in hotels: The case of Greater Accra Region, Ghana. *International Journal of Hospitality Management*, *30*(1), 161–167. DOI: 10.1016/j.ijhm.2010.04.008

Mentzer, M. S. (2023). Public sector corruption among the United States: Exploring the impact of cultural values. *Business & Professional Ethics Journal*, *42*(2), 251–266. DOI: 10.5840/bpej2023620143

Meyerhuber, S. (2019). Active listening as a key competence in intercultural communication education- An example from an academic classroom with conceptual and theoretical embedding. *Journal of Linguistic and Intercultural Education*, *12*(2), 92–115.

Mikolov, T., Chen, K., Corrado, G., & Dean, J. (2013). *Efficient estimation of word representations in vector space*. 1st International Conference on Learning Representations, ICLR 2013 - Workshop Track Proceedings. Scopus. https://www.scopus.com/inward/record.uri?eid=2-s2.0-85083951332&partnerID=40&md5=20428820e8b09cdfb5078ea812a71f2d

Mirzoeff, N. (2011). The right to look. *Critical Inquiry*, *37*(3), 473–496. DOI: 10.1086/659354

Mohamad, S. M. (2021). Micro-celebrity practices in Muslim-majority states in Southeast Asia. *Popular Communication*, *19*(3), 235–249. DOI: 10.1080/15405702.2021.1913492

Mohamed, Y. A., Khanan, A., Bashir, M., Mohamed, A. H. H. M., Adiel, M. A. E., & Elsadig, M. A. (2024). The impact of artificial intelligence on language translation: A review. *IEEE Access : Practical Innovations, Open Solutions*, *12*, 25553–25579. DOI: 10.1109/ACCESS.2024.3366802

Morrison, E. W., & Bies, R. J. (1991). Impression management in the feedback-seeking process: A literature review and research agenda. *Academy of Management Review*, *16*(3), 522. Advance online publication. DOI: 10.2307/258916

Morrow, P. R., & Yamanouchi, K. (2020). Online apologies to hotel guests in English and Japanese. *Discourse, Context & Media*, *34*, 100379. DOI: 10.1016/j.dcm.2020.100379

Mortensen, M., & Kristensen, N. N. (2020). De-celebrification: Beyond the scandalous. *Celebrity Studies*, *11*(1), 89–100. DOI: 10.1080/19392397.2020.1704385

Murray, D. C. (2015). Notes to self: The visual culture of selfies in the age of social media. *Consumption Markets & Culture*, *18*(6), 490–516. DOI: 10.1080/10253866.2015.1052967

Muta, K. (2008). Reform of Japanese home economics education and gender equality. *Gender and Education*, *20*(6), 627–642.

Nayyar, S., & Raja, T. N. (2012). The Impact of Impression Management Behavior on Organizational Politics. *Interdisciplinary Journal of Contemporary Research in Business*, *3*(9), 914–923.

Neo, S., Bertram, I., Szydlowski, G., Bouwman, R., de Boer, N., Grimmelikhuijsen, S., Charbonneau, É., Moon, M. J., & Tummers, L. (2024). Working 9 to 5? A cross-national analysis of public sector worker stereotypes. *Public Management Review*, *26*(7), 2064–2093. DOI: 10.1080/14719037.2023.2254306

Nichols, S. (2015). *Remaking home economics: Resourcefulness and innovation in changing times*. University of Minnesota Press.

Ni, H., Li, Y., Zeng, Y., & Duan, J. (2023). The double-edged sword effect of employee impression management and counter-productive work behavior: From the perspective of self-control resource theory. *Frontiers in Psychology*, *14*, 1053784. DOI: 10.3389/fpsyg.2023.1053784 PMID: 36818121

Nizamani, M., Ramzan, F., Fatima, M., & Asif, M. (2024). Investigating how frequent interactions with AI technologies impact cognitive and emotional processes. [BBE]. *Bulletin of Business and Economics*, *13*(3), 316–325.

Noble, S. U. (2018). Algorithms of oppression: How search engines reinforce racism. In *Algorithms of oppression*. New York University Press.

Norman, D. A. (1999). Affordance, conventions, and design. *Interactions (New York, N.Y.)*, *6*(3), 38–43. DOI: 10.1145/301153.301168

Noviansah, W. (2023, March 17). *Mario Dandy Ternyata Sebar Foto dan Video Saat Aniaya David* [News website]. detikNews; detikNews / detikcom. https://news.detik.com/berita/d-6624495/mario-dandy-ternyata-sebar-foto-dan-video-saat-aniaya-david

O'Boyle, N. (2022). Performers: Goffman's Dramaturgical Perspective. In: *Communication Theory for Humans*. Palgrave Macmillan, Cham. DOI: 10.1007/978-3-031-02450-4_5

Page, R. (2014). Saying 'sorry': Corporate apologies posted on Twitter. *Journal of Pragmatics*, *62*, 30–45. DOI: 10.1016/j.pragma.2013.12.003

Palojoki, P. (2017). Sustainability and food education in the Finnish home economics curriculum. *International Journal of Home Economics*, *10*(1), 56–67.

Parker, L., Hassan, O., & Davis, C. (2025). The Role of Generative AI in the Future of Commercial Personalization. *Journal of Electronic Commerce Management*, *1*, 1–16.

Park, H., Leroy, H., Dragoni, L., Simons, T., & Yun, S. (2024). Does Leaders' Impression Management Help or Hurt? It Depends on the Perspective of the Follower. *Journal of Leadership & Organizational Studies*, *31*(4), 473–490. DOI: 10.1177/15480518241273322

Parry, E. (2014). *Generational diversity at work: New research perspectives*. Routledge.

Patel, K., & Binjola, H. (2020). TikTok, the new alternative media for youngsters for online sharing of talent: an analytical study. Available online at. (https://papers .ssrn.com/sol3/papers.cfm?abstract_id=3600119)

Pearson, J. C., Nelson, P. E., Titsworth, S. B., & Hosek, A. M. (2017). *Human communication* (6th ed.). McGraw-Hill Education.

Perrotta, C., Selwyn, N., & Ewin, C. (2024). Artificial intelligence and the affective labour of understanding: The intimate moderation of a language model. *New Media & Society*, *26*(3), 1585–1609. DOI: 10.1177/14614448221075296

Pettigrew, A. M. (1979). On studying organizational cultures. *Administrative Science Quarterly*, *24*(4), 570–581. DOI: 10.2307/2392363

Pin, R., & Turndorf, H. (2009). Identity rehearsal in educational settings. *Journal of Educational Psychology*, *101*(2), 345–356. DOI: 10.1037/a0014567

Popa, R. G., & Chenic, A. S. (2025). Artificial Intelligence, Consumer Trust and the Promotion of Pro-Environmental Behavior Among Youth. *Sustainability (Basel)*, *17*(13), 5885. DOI: 10.3390/su17135885

Pozner, J.-E., & Hannigan, T. R. (2023). How Relational Publics Become Scandal Audiences: Values and the construction of scandal. *Organization Theory*, *4*(3), 26317877231204085. DOI: 10.1177/26317877231204085

Prakash, K. S. V. S., Bhavana, S., Lasya, P. V. A., Kumar, D. G., Putalapattu, B., Amareswari, V., & Gayathri, K. (2025). The influence of AI on creative writing and its implications for management communication. *International Journal of Research Publication and Reviews*, *6*(2), 722–727. DOI: 10.55248/gengpi.6.0225.0731

Provis, C. (2023). Impression Management and Business Ethics. In *Encyclopedia of Business and Professional Ethics* (pp. 1127–1130). Springer International Publishing., DOI: 10.1007/978-3-030-22767-8_1212

Pulatovna, K. U. (2024). AI in Education: Enhancing Teacher-student Interactions and Motivation. *European Journal of Humanities and Educational Advancements*, *5*(1), 113–115.

Raghuram, S., Hill, N. S., Gibbs, J. L., & Maruping, L. M. (2019). Virtual Work: Bridging Research Clusters. *The Academy of Management Annals*, *13*(1), 308–341. DOI: 10.5465/annals.2017.0020

Reimann, M., Huller, C., Schike, O., & Cook, K. S. (2022). Impression management attenuates the effect of ability on trust in economic exchange. *Social Science*, *119*(30), 1–9. DOI: 10.1073/pnas.2118548119 PMID: 35867823

Ribble, M., & Miller, T. N. (2013). Educational leadership in an online world: Connecting students to technology responsibly, safely, and ethically. *Phi Delta Kappan, 94*(5), 41–44. DOI: 10.1177/003172171309400509

Roberge, M.-É., & Van Dick, R. (2010). Recognizing the benefits of diversity: When and how does diversity increase group performance? *Human Resource Management Review, 20*(4), 295–308. DOI: 10.1016/j.hrmr.2009.09.002

Rosenfeld, P., Edwards, J. E., & Thomas, M. D. (2015). *Impression management.* Wiley Encyclopedia of Management.

Rosenfeld, P., Giacalone, R. A., & Riordan, C. A. (2002). Impression management: Building and enhancing reputations at work. In Giacalone, R. A., & Rosenfeld, P. (Eds.), *Impression management in the organization* (pp. 3–20). Lawrence Erlbaum Associates.

Rosenfiled, P., Giacalone, R., & Riordan, C. A. (1994). Impression Management Theory and Diversity. *The American Behavioral Scientist, 37*(5), 601–604. DOI: 10.1177/0002764294037005002

Rui, J., & Stefanone, M. A. (2013). Strategic self-presentation online: A cross-cultural study. *Computers in Human Behavior, 29*(1), 110–118. DOI: 10.1016/j.chb.2012.07.022

Sanaria, A. D. (2016). A Conceptual Framework for Understanding the Impression Management Strategies Used by Women in Indian Organizations. *SA Journal of Human Resource Management, 3*(1), 25–39. DOI: 10.1177/2322093716631118

Saxena, A. (2014). Workforce diversity: A key to improve productivity. *Procedia Economics and Finance, 11*, 76–85. DOI: 10.1016/S2212-5671(14)00178-6

Schau, H. J., & Gilly, M. C. (2003). We Are What We Post? Self-Presentation in Personal Web Space. *Journal of Consumer Research, 30*(3), 385–404. JSTOR. DOI: 10.1086/378616

Scutariu, P., & Bodnărescu, A. (2023). A micro-research on Hofstede's cultural dimensions in local public administration. *European Journal of Law and Public Administration, 10*(1), 57–68. DOI: 10.18662/eljpa/10.1/195

Seidman, G. (2013). Self-presentation and belonging on Facebook: How personality influences social media use and motivations. *Personality and Individual Differences, 54*(3), 402–407. DOI: 10.1016/j.paid.2012.10.009

Shahin, A. I., & Wright, P. L. (2004). Leadership in the context of culture: An Egyptian perspective. *Leadership and Organization Development Journal*, *25*(6), 499–511. DOI: 10.1108/01437730410556743

Sheldon, P., & Bryant, K. (2016). Instagram: Motives for its use and relationship to narcissism and contextual age. *Computers in Human Behavior*, *58*, 89–97. DOI: 10.1016/j.chb.2015.12.059

Sheth, J. N., & Solomon, M. R. (2014). Extending the Extended Self in a Digital World. *Journal of Marketing Theory and Practice*, *22*(2), 123–132. DOI: 10.2753/MTP1069-6679220201

Shibata, M. (2019). Home economics in Japan: Citizenship, gender, and sustainability. *Journal of Family and Consumer Sciences Education*, *37*(2), 15–27.

Shukla, S. S., Bajpai, S., Pramanik, S., & Waller, S. (2025). From Micro-Influencers to AI: The Future of Influencer Marketing in a Tech-Driven Era. In *Leveraging AI-Powered Marketing in the Experience-Driven Economy* (pp. 419-440). IGI Global Scientific Publishing.

Shulman, D. (2022). Self-presentation: Impression management in the digital age. In Jacobsen, M. H., & Smith, G. (Eds.), *The Routledge international handbook of Goffman studies* (pp. 26–37). Routledge. DOI: 10.4324/9781003160861-4

Siddiqui, R., Tariq, A., Mariyam, F., Kumar, A., & Khan, N. (2025). Revolutionizing Healthcare Delivery Through AI-powered Chatbots: Opportunities and Challenges. *International Journal of Innovative Research in Computer Science and Technology*, *13*(3), 109–119. Advance online publication. DOI: 10.55524/ijircst.2025.13.3.18

Sievers, S., Wodzicki, K., Aberle, I., Keckeisen, M., & Cress, U. (2015). Social cues in online communication and their effect on credibility perceptions. *Journal of Computer-Mediated Communication*, *20*(4), 434–451.

Simbeck, K. (2024). They shall be fair, transparent, and robust: Auditing learning analytics systems. *AI and Ethics*, *4*(2), 555–571. DOI: 10.1007/s43681-023-00292-7

Sims, R. (2009). Food, place and authenticity: Local food and the sustainable tourism experience. *Journal of Sustainable Tourism*, *17*(3), 321–336. DOI: 10.1080/09669580802359293

Sindoni, M. G. (2024). The femininization of AI-powered voice assistants: Personification, anthropomorphism and discourse ideologies. *Discourse, Context & Media*, *62*, 100833. DOI: 10.1016/j.dcm.2024.100833

Sing, V., Kumra, S., & Vinnicombe, S. (2002) Gender and Impression Management: Playing the Promotional Game in Journal of Business Ethics, Netherlands: Kluwer Academy Publisher, 37:77-89

Soares, A. M., Farhangmehr, M., & Shoham, A. (2007). Hofstede's dimensions of culture in international marketing studies. *Journal of Business Research*, *60*(3), 277–284. DOI: 10.1016/j.jbusres.2006.10.018

Spencer, L., & Spencer, S. M. (1993). *Competence at work: Models for superior performance*. Wiley.

Srna, S., Barasch, A., & Small, D. A. (2022). On the Value of Modesty: How Signals of Status Undermine Cooperation. *Journal of Personality and Social Psychology, 123*(4), 676–692. *Scopus*. Advance online publication. DOI: 10.1037/pspa0000303

Srnicek, N. (2017). *Platform capitalism*. Polity Press.

Stage, S., & Vincenti, V. B. (Eds.). (1997). *Rethinking home economics: Women and the history of a profession*. Cornell University Press. DOI: 10.7591/9781501729942

Starr, P. (2021). The Relational Public. *Sociological Theory*, *39*(2), 57–80. DOI: 10.1177/07352751211004660

Stewart, M. C., & Logan, R. (2018). *Social and professional skills for teens*. Goodheart-Willcox.

Sukmayadi, V., Darmawangsa, D., Ayub, S. H., & Fadhila, S. A. (2024). Constructing Fame: A phenomenological study of online impression management among Indonesian TikTok Celebrities. The Qualitative Report, 29(6), 1727-1741.DOI: 10.46743/2160-3715/2024.5992

Sullivan, J. L. (2013). Media Audiences: Effects, Users, Institutions, and Power. *Sage (Atlanta, Ga.)*.

Sun, Y., Fang, S., & Zhang, Z. (2021). Impression management strategies on enterprise social media platforms: An affordance perspective. *International Journal of Information Management*, *60*, 102359. DOI: 10.1016/j.ijinfomgt.2021.102359

Swafford, M., & Ramsey, E. (2023). *Family and consumer sciences: Preventative and restorative education*. Cognella Academic Publishing.

Switzer, J. S. (2008). Impression Formation in Computer-Mediated Communication and Making a Good (Virtual) Impression. In *Handbook of Research on Virtual Workplaces and the New Nature of Business Practices* (pp. 98–109). IGI Global. DOI: 10.4018/978-1-59904-893-2.ch008

Tairi, K. (2018). Ko Wai Au (Who Am I)? Authentic Leadership and Mindfulness in Higher Education. In Lemon, N., & McDonough, S. (Eds.), *Mindfulness in the Academy*. Springer., DOI: 10.1007/978-981-13-2143-6_10

Tajfel, H., & Turner, J. C. (1979). An integrative theory of inter-group conflict. In Austin, W. G., & Worchel, S. (Eds.), *The social psychology of inter-group relations* (pp. 33–47). Brooks/Cole.

Taylor, D. G. (2020). Putting the "self" in selfies: How narcissism, envy and self-promotion motivate sharing of travel photos through social media. *Journal of Travel & Tourism Marketing*, *37*(1), 64–77. DOI: 10.1080/10548408.2020.1711847

Taylor, D. G., & Strutton, D. (2016). Does Facebook usage lead to conspicuous consumption? *Journal of Research in Interactive Marketing*, *10*(3), 231–248. DOI: 10.1108/JRIM-01-2015-0009

Tedeschi, J. T. (1990). Self Presentation and Social Influence:An Interactionist perspective. In Cody, M. J., & McLaughlin, M. L. (Eds.), *The psychology of Tactical Coo* (pp. 301–323). Multilingual Matters.

Tohme, O., & Joseph, S. (2020). Authenticity Is Correlated With Mindfulness and Emotional Intelligence. *Journal of Humanistic Psychology*, *65*(1), 139–156. DOI: 10.1177/0022167820940926

Treadway, D. C. (2012). Political will in organizations. In Ferris, G. R., & Treadway, D. C. (Eds.), *Politics in Organizations: Theory and Research Considerations* (pp. 529–554).

Treviño, L. K., & Nelson, K. A. (2021). *Managing business ethics: Straight talk about how to do it right* (8th ed.). Wiley.

Triandis, H. C. (1988). Collectivism vs. individualism: A reconceptualization of a basic concept in cross-cultural social psychology. In Verma, G. K., & Bagley, C. (Eds.), *Cross-cultural studies of personality, attitudes and cognition* (pp. 60–95). Palgrave Macmillan., DOI: 10.1007/978-1-349-08120-2_3

Trottier, D. (2017). Digital Vigilantism as Weaponisation of Visibility. *Philosophy & Technology*, *30*(1), 55–72. DOI: 10.1007/s13347-016-0216-4

Trottier, D. (2018). Scandal mining: Political nobodies and remediated visibility. *Media, Culture and Society*, *40*(6), 893–908. *Scopus*. Advance online publication. DOI: 10.1177/0163443717734408

Tuğer, A. T. (2024). AI and service encounters. In *Handbook of services and artificial intelligence* (pp. 119–142). Edward Elgar Publishing., DOI: 10.4337/9781035301973.00016

Tuna, Ö., & Gül, İ. (2024). *The Role of Impression Management in the Impact of Ethical Leadership on Green Organizational Behavior.*, DOI: 10.4018/979-8-3693-5298-4.ch017

Tuten, T. L. (2023). *Social media marketing*. Sage Publications.

U.S. Congress. (1862). *Morrill Act of 1862, ch. 130, 12 Stat. 503*. https://www.ourdocuments.gov/doc.php?flash=false&doc=32

Valkenburg, P. M., Koutamanis, M., & Vossen, H. G. M. (2017). The concurrent and longitudinal relationships between adolescents' use of social network sites and their social self-esteem. *Computers in Human Behavior*, *76*, 35–41. DOI: 10.1016/j.chb.2017.07.008 PMID: 29104364

Vallor, S. (2024). *The AI mirror: How to reclaim our humanity in an age of machine thinking*. Oxford University Press. DOI: 10.1093/oso/9780197759066.001.0001

Van Dijck, J. (2013). *The Culture of Connectivity: A Critical History of Social Media*. Oxford University Press. DOI: 10.1093/acprof:oso/9780199970773.001.0001

Van Dijck, J. (2024). Governing platforms and societies. *Platforms & Society*, *1*, 29768624241255922. Advance online publication. DOI: 10.1177/29768624241255922

Venkataramanan, S., Sadhu, A. K. R., Gudala, L., & Reddy, A. K. (2024). Leveraging Artificial Intelligence for Enhanced Sales Forecasting Accuracy: A Review of AI-Driven Techniques and Practical Applications in Customer Relationship Management Systems. *Journal of Machine Learning Research*, *4*, 267–287.

Vijaybanu, C., Theresa, Ch., & Daisy, A. (2019). Impression Management Tactics booster for the communication of IT employees SMART PLS Approach. *Revista de Psicología*, *47*(2), 683–707. DOI: 10.18800/psico.201902.012

Wang, D., Song, S., Chan, F. F. Y., & Feng, L. (2023). The impact of impression construction consumption on social identity: A study on Chinese female professionals. *Journal of Social Marketing*, *13*(2), 194–217. DOI: 10.1108/JSOCM-03-2022-0066

Wang, L., & Duan, X. (2025). Generational diversity and team innovation: The roles of conflict and shared leadership. *Frontiers in Psychology*, *15*, 1501633. Advance online publication. DOI: 10.3389/fpsyg.2024.1501633

Wang, W., Zhou, K., Yu, Z., & Li, J. (2020). <p>The Cost of Impression Management to Life Satisfaction: Sense of Control and Loneliness as Mediators</p>. *Psychology Research and Behavior Management, 13*, 407–417. DOI: 10.2147/PRBM.S238344 PMID: 32440240

Warner, S. B. (2023). Analyzing Attention to Scandal on Twitter: Elites Sell What Supporters Buy. *Political Research Quarterly, 76*(2), 841–850. DOI: 10.1177/10659129221114145

Wayne, S. J., & Kacmar, K. M. (1991). The effects of impression management on the performance appraisal process. *Organizational Behavior and Human Decision Processes, 48*(1), 70–88. DOI: 10.1016/0749-5978(91)90006-F

Wayne, S. J., & Liden, R. C. (1995). Effects of impression management on performance ratings: A longitudinal study. *Academy of Management Journal, 38*(1), 232–260. DOI: 10.2307/256734

Webber, S. S., & Donahue, L. M. (2001). Impact of highly and less job-related diversity on work group cohesion and performance: A meta-analysis. *Journal of Management, 27*(2), 141–162. DOI: 10.1177/014920630102700202

Wei, X., Kumar, N., & Zhang, H. (2025). Addressing bias in generative AI: Challenges and research opportunities in information management. *Information & Management, 62*(2), 104103. DOI: 10.1016/j.im.2025.104103

West, S. M., Whittaker, M., & Crawford, K. (2019). *Discriminating systems*. AI Now Institute. https://ainowinstitute.org

Wiese, S. A., Lehmann, J., & Beckmann, M. (2024). Organizational culture and the usage of Industry 4.0 technologies: Evidence from Swiss businesses [Preprint]. *arXiv*. https://arxiv.org/abs/2412.12752

Wiyono, D., Tanjung, R., Setiadi, H., Marini, S., & Sugiarto, Y. (2024). Organizational transformation: The impact of servant leadership on work ethic culture with burnout as a mediating factor in the hospitality industry. *arXiv*. https://arxiv.org/abs/2407.01533

Xu, Z., & Yan, A. (2020). A Pragmatic Study of Image Restoration via Corporate Apology in Chinese Internet Corporations. *English Language Teaching, 13*(6), 76. DOI: 10.5539/elt.v13n6p76

Yadav, S., & Lenka, U. (2020). Workforce diversity: From a literature review to future research agenda. *Journal of Indian Business Research, 12*(4), 577–603. DOI: 10.1108/JIBR-08-2019-0243

Yaghi, A., Yaghi, M., & Yaghi, I. (2025). Impact of national culture on the transfer of leadership training: The role of Hofstede's cultural dimensions. *International Journal of Training and Development*, *29*(2), 95–107. DOI: 10.1111/ijtd.12346

Yan, X., Fu, Y., Yang, F., & Han, Y. (2025). They Shouldn't Be Richer Than Me: How Visual Wealth Exposure on Social Media Increases Relative Deprivation. *Cyberpsychology, 19*(2). *Cyberpsychology (Brno)*, *19*(2). Advance online publication. DOI: 10.5817/CP2025-2-4

Yoo, E. (2022). Impression management of South Korean sports stars through image-based social media. *Sport in Society*, *25*(9), 1734–1755. DOI: 10.1080/17430437.2021.1878146

Yukl, G., & Falbe, C. M. (1990). Influence tactics and objectives in upward, downward, and lateral influence attempts. *The Journal of Applied Psychology*, *75*(2), 132–140. DOI: 10.1037/0021-9010.75.2.132

Zbihlejová, L., Frankovsky, M., & Birknerova, Z. (2018). Leadership Styles if Managers from Perspective of Gender. *International Journal of Organizational Leadership*, *7*(4), 340–347. DOI: 10.33844/ijol.2018.60216

Zhang, L., Li, X., & Wang, Y. (2023). The paradox of online impression management: Effects on offline appearance anxiety and self-perception. *Journal of Consumer Psychology*. Advance online publication.

Zhao, H., & Liden, R. C. (2011). Internship: A recruitment and selection perspective. *The Journal of Applied Psychology*, *96*(1), 221–229. DOI: 10.1037/a0021295 PMID: 20954757

Zheng, F., Zhao, C., Yasmin, F., & Sokolová, M. (2025). Hofstede's cultural dimensions and proactive behavior as antecedents of entrepreneurial innovativeness. *Acta Psychologica*, *256*, 105034. Advance online publication. DOI: 10.1016/j.actpsy.2025.104948

Zhou, K., & Xu, Z. (2022). A pragmatic study of corporate apologies for impression management: A case of the Chinese food industry. *International Journal of Linguistics*, *14*(6), 196–216. DOI: 10.5296/ijl.v14i6.20465

Zuboff, S. (2015). Big other: Surveillance capitalism and the prospects of an information civilization. *Journal of Information Technology*, *30*(1), 75–89. DOI: 10.1057/jit.2015.5

About the Contributors

Ebtihaj Ahmed Al A'ali, is an Associate Professor, Department of Management and Marketing, College of Business Administration, University of Bahrain. She holds a Ph.D. degree in industrial psychology and industrial sociology from Lancaster University, United Kingdom. She acted as the head of the evening program offered by the university of Bahrain for two years . She is a founder of Bahrain management society. She worked with United Nations Development Programme and UNIDO on project basis. She has acted as a supervisor and external examiner for many theses of Master degree. She published many books with IGI. She as well published articles in different journals. Her research interests are women in management, organisational theory, organisational behaviour, research methodology, industrial sociology and industrial psychology.

Khairi Ali has more than 17 years of experience in academia, the private, and public sectors. He is currently the Head of Business Administration at Applied Science University. A Senior Fellow of the Higher Education Academy (SFHEA), he is an active researcher with numerous publications and serves as a reviewer for several journals, including those under Emerald Group Publishing.

Gardenia AlSaffar is a consultant psychiatrist in Royal Bahrain Hospital. She is a member of the Royal College of the Psychiatrists in the UK. She did her fellowship in Ireland with a special interests in General Adults Psychiatry and Rehabilitation psychiatry. Besides she attended courses in cognitive Behavioural Therapy, Basic Life Support for Healthcare Providers Program (Refresher Course) offered by American Heart Association 2008, and Basic Life Support for Healthcare Providers Program Advanced Cardiovascular Life Support Program organized by the American Heart Association in 2005. She co-edited books published by IGI. Dr. AlSaffar has published many articles related to health services, management and women issues. She participated to many seminars and conferences regionally and internationally. She has been a guest speaker for many events. Her research interests vary between health concerns, psychological and psychiatrical issues in general, corporate psychology and women

Mohammed AlMannaei is an academic researcher who holds a BSc in Management Information Systems (MIS) from the University of Bahrain for Technology, an MBA from the University of Bahrain, and a PhD with honors in Innovation and Technology Management from the Arabian Gulf University in collaboration with Boston University, USA. He also holds a Diploma in Business Communication Management from Coventry University, UK. His research interests include innovation and entrepreneurship, leadership and strategic management, the role of innovation in non-oil sectors (public and private sectors), innovation, economic growth and sustainable development, innovation in financial technology (FinTech), digital economy and knowledge economy

Okechukwu Amah (PhD) is a Professor of Organisational Behaviour in the OB/HRM department of Lagos Business School, Pan Atlantic University, Lagos, Nigeria. His research interests include leadership, work-life integration, human resources management, and organisational behaviour.

Karim Ben Yahia holds a PhD in Marketing from the Higher Institute of Management (Tunis), where he graduated with Very Honorable Distinction. Currently, Dr. Ben Yahia serves as a Marketing Assistant Professor and the Bachelor of Science in Marketing program coordinator at the College of Business Administration, University of Bahrain. With over 19 years of teaching experience, he instructs courses in management and marketing. His research interests span digital marketing, advertising communication, online and mobile banking, agri-food industry marketing, terroir products, cultural heritage, consumer behavior, innovation, cultural congruency in advertising, word of mouth, and technology adoption. Dr. Ben Yahia has contributed to numerous indexed academic journals, including the European Journal of International Management, Total Quality Management and Business Excellence, International Journal of Bank Marketing, and Preservation, Digital Technology & Culture. He has also presented his research at prestigious international conferences such as the European Marketing Academy Conference, International Business Information Management Conference,and African Countries Research Days

Julian Costa is an Adjunct Associate Professor in the School of Computer Science and Information Systems (CSIS) at Pace University.

Sayantani Ghosh is an accomplished academician and researcher currently serving as an Assistant Professor in Marketing at Dayananda Sagar University,

Bengaluru. She holds a B.Tech in Agricultural Engineering from Assam University, an MBA in Marketing from NIT Silchar, and is presently pursuing her Ph.D. in Marketing at NIT Silchar. She has also qualified for UGC NET in Management (2024). Ms. Ghosh brings a diverse blend of academic, industry, and research experience. Her academic interests span marketing management, green marketing, service marketing, and sustainable business practices. She has guided over 36 MBA students and coordinated numerous institutional activities, including curriculum development, skill development programs, and the Womentorship initiative. She also serves as the associate editor of the college journal and Nodal Officer for CII Young Indians activities. With prior 3 years of experience in the corporate sector, she bridges theoretical knowledge with practical insights. Ms. Ghosh has published four research articles in Scopus-indexed journals and three UGC Care-listed articles, and authored one book covering sustainability, digital transformation, AI applications, and green business strategies. She is passionate about student mentoring, academic innovation, and empowering youth through education and leadership development.

M. Gurusamy, with a comprehensive academic background including an MBA, M.Phil, Ph.D., and a D.Litt. in Marketing, brings an impressive 20 years of teaching experience alongside a brief stint in the industry of 9 months. Currently serving as a Professor and Chairperson for Marketing and Entrepreneurship at the Adarsh Institute of Management and Information Technology in Bangalore, Karnataka, India, he has distinguished himself in the academic and research fields. Dr. Gurusamy has significantly contributed to the intellectual property domain with nine patents in India and 5 in Australia, underscoring his innovative approach to research and development. His scholarly output is remarkable, with 12 articles published in Web of Science journals, 39 in Scopus-indexed journals, and many articles in other national and international journals, totalling 40 books published. As an academic leader, he has evaluated Ph.D. theses and served as an external examiner, showcasing his expertise in guiding research scholars. Dr. Gurusamy's role as a resource person and chairperson in 90 instances, along with his editorial and reviewer memberships in 14 and 16 journals respectively, reflects his esteemed position in the academic community. Additionally, his contributions extend to academic advisory boards and visiting professorships, demonstrating a commitment to enhancing educational standards. His achievements have been recognized with 30 awards, affirming his influence and excellence in marketing and research. Dr. Gurusamy's professional journey is a testament to his dedication to academia, research, and the practical applications of marketing principles in the evolving business landscape.

Imelda is a researcher at the National Research and Innovation Agency (BRIN), specializing in Linguistics (Sociolinguistics). Her research interests include language endangerment, linguistic landscape studies, corpus-assisted discourse analysis, and critical language policy.

Sunil Kumar, currently an Associate Professor at Faculty of Management Sciences, Shoolini University, possesses extensive academic and research experience. With a background in Business Administration, Sunil's research endeavors span multiple domains, including human resource management, e-training, and the application of artificial intelligence in business. His prolific contributions are evidenced by numerous research papers, book chapters, copyrights, and patents. Dr. Kumar has a knack for teaching with expertise in subjects like HR Analytics, Talent Management, Industrial Psychology, and more. He has also successfully guided PhD students and actively contributes to various academic administrative roles. Dr. Kumar's vast research landscape includes topics like AI-based chatbots in recruitment, e-training impact, and more. His papers have been published in esteemed journals like Journal of Workplace Learning and International Journal of Law and Management. Moreover, he has authored books and edited volumes touching upon themes related to the contemporary business environment. Dr. Sunil has been a dynamic participant in numerous workshops, ranging from data analysis to stress

Ikbal Maulana is a researcher at the Research Center for Society and Culture, National Research and Innovation Agency (BRIN), Indonesia. His work focuses on media studies and cultural studies. He approaches his research through the lens of critical theory, employing critical discourse analysis and corpus-assisted discourse studies, supported by Python applications that he develops himself.

Indranil Mutsuddi, Ph.D. in Management from Amity University, is Associate Professor and Head of the Department at JIS University, Kolkata. With over 21 years of academic experience in Human Resources and Organizational Behavior, he is a recognized educator and researcher. He has authored three HRM textbooks, published over 63 research papers, contributed 23 book chapters, and presented 57 papers at various conferences. A Double Gold Medalist from AIMA CME and recipient of the Prof. Narendra Mohan Basu Award, he is a life member of NHRDN, the Indian Commerce Association, and the Presidency College Alumni Association. His research focuses on employee retention and job skills. Recently, he edited a management research volume for Bentham Books, furthering his impact in the academic community.

Purwadi is a researcher at the Research Center for Society and Culture, National Research and Innovation Agency (BRIN). His research focuses on communication and media, digital society, cultural studies, and communication policy. Previously, he worked as a public relations practitioner at the Bureau for Cooperation, Law, and Public Relations of the Indonesian Institute of Sciences (LIPI) for over a decade. As a practitioner, he has extensive experience in science journalism and expertise in media relations, website and social media content management, and public information management. In addition, he is a former journalist who has worked for both local and national mass media.

Perdhani Yunia Putri is a researcher at the Research Center for Society and Culture. Her research interests include media studies, particularly the role of social media in empowering disadvantaged groups, such as the disability community.

Shivansu Sachan is Pursuing Ph.D. in Management, a Master's holder from Integral University, Lucknow, Bachelor's from IHM, Lucknow. Academic and professional accomplishments of 6 years with renowned organizations and institutes. His Teaching Career has been very satisfying and have continuously upgraded the skills and knowledge by attending many courses and training programs, seminars, conferences organized by different organizations and also delivered many lectures as a Hospitality sector. He is working as an Assistant Professor at Chhatrapati Shahu ji Maharaj University Kanpur .

Musfiah Saidah is a Lecturer in Communication Studies at State Islamic University Syarif Hidayatullah (UIN) Jakarta. She is the Founder of Education Platform Komuniasik edumedia gives literacy about communication and media (http://www.komuniasik.com; @komuni_asik). Her research interests include privacy management, digital development, science communication, and public relations. She also is a reporter from 2019 until 2021 in international news Southeast Asia today.

Suchitra Sakpal brings this scholarship into lived practice as a PhD scholar, practicing psychologist, and behavioral coach working with leading multinational corporations, where she designs mental health interventions, resilience frameworks, and performance-enhancement programs grounded in evidence-based psychology. In all her roles researcher, clinician, author, and organizational strategist—Suchitra Sachin Sakpal occupies a rare and fertile crossroads. Her work spans clinical psychology, organizational behavior, spiritual psychology, criminology, neurodiversity studies, and the evolving science of consciousness. What binds these fields is her persistent drive to understand how human beings navigate internal and external complexity, and how systems either enable or obstruct psychological well-being. Her publication record mirrors this restless curiosity, moving fluidly across genres, methodologies, and theoretical terrains. One of her most widely recognized contributions is the co-authored case study Fitting in or Burning

Out? A Neurodiverse Professional in a Neurotypical World (Case Centre, Cranfield University). The study has garnered international attention for exposing the subtle mechanics of cognitive exclusion in workplaces. It traces the psychological cost of masking, thwarted authenticity, and the unspoken expectations that compel neurodivergent individuals to contort themselves into organizational molds, pushing neurodiversity discourse into mainstream management education. Her theoretical efforts extend further, earning her two registered copyrights for original models: Intentional Blindness, a cognitive framework that interrogates how perceptual filters distort reality, and The Psychology Behind Crime, which maps the psychological gradients underlying deviant behavior. These works demonstrate her commitment to reframing how we understand cognition, morality, and decision-making. Her writing journey began with intimate psychological inquiry. Being Rhea: Overcoming 25 Years of Childhood Trauma remains a deeply human exploration of fragmentation, survival, and reintegration, blending narrative psychology with the visceral texture of lived experience. She later widened her intellectual canvas with MAYA: From Within to Beyond, a work of spiritual psychology that examines consciousness, perception, and the dissolution of identity. The text moves beyond symptom-level thinking, offering a more expansive lens on how humans construct, distort, and transcend their reality. Together, her publications, clinical practice, and organizational work reflect a singular scholarly voice bold, nuanced, multidisciplinary, and anchored in the belief that psychological insight becomes truly transformative when theory and lived experience meet.

Gautam Shivaraj, with a comprehensive academic background including a Bachelor's in Mechanical Engineering, Master of Engineering Management (Australia), MBA, brings an impressive 06 years of teaching experience alongside a brief stint in the industry of 3 years. Currently serving as an Assistant Professor at the Adarsh Institute of Management and Information Technology in Bangalore, Karnataka, India, he has distinguished himself in the academic and research fields. Prof.Gautam Shivaraj professional journey is a testament to his dedication to academia, research, in the evolving world.

Ashi Singh is an undergraduate student pursuing a Bachelor's degree in Hotel Management at Chhatrapati Shahu Ji Maharaj University (CSJM), Kanpur, Uttar Pradesh. She is a focused and committed learner with a strong grounding in hospitality operations, tourism services, and service management. Appreciated for her creative mindset and thoughtful ideas, Ashi brings originality to her presentations, assignments, and approach to real-world hospitality challenges. She is deeply inspired by the potential of India's tourism industry and hopes to contribute to its progress through sustainable development, responsible hospitality, and guest-centered service excellence with new impactful ideas . Her areas of academic interest include destination planning, tourism development, cultural heritage conservation, and eco-friendly hospitality operations. Motivated by discipline, ambition, and a sincere sense of social responsibility, Ashi envisions building a career where she can blend innovation with ethical practices to uplift communities and strengthen India's tourism ecosystem. She represents a new generation of hospitality professionals who combine creativity, skill, and purpose to elevate India's impression on the global tourism stage.

Index

K

M

P

S

V

W

www.ingramcontent.com/pod-product-compliance
Lightning Source LLC
LaVergne TN
LVHW081520300926
849161LV00006B/1243